2ⁿᵈ Corinthians
Preaching Verse-by-Verse

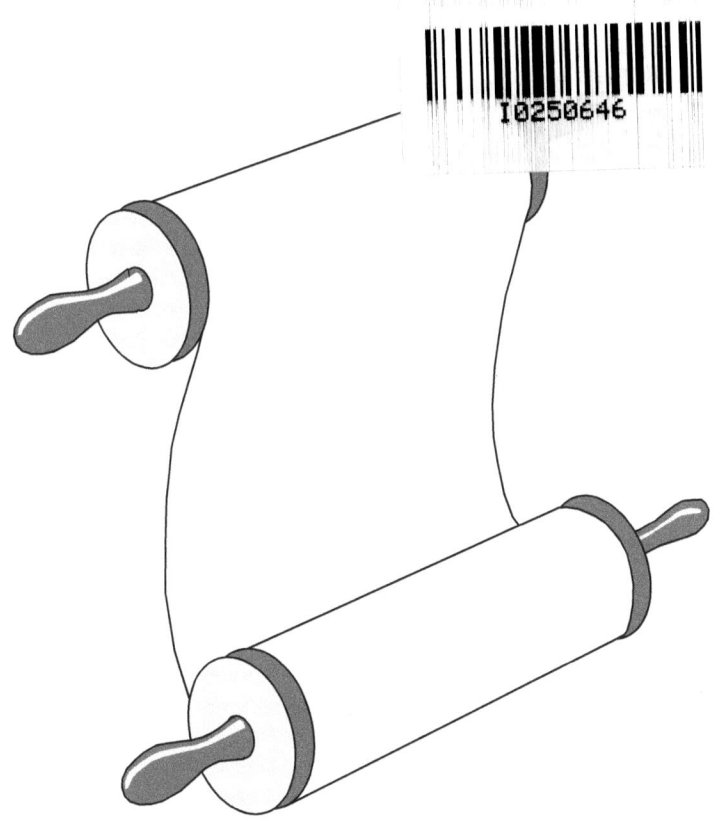

Pastor D. A. Waite, Th.D., Ph.D.

Published by

THE BIBLE FOR TODAY PRESS
900 Park Avenue
Collingswood, New Jersey 08108 U.S.A.
Pastor D. A. Waite, Th.D., Ph.D.

Bible For Today Baptist Church
Church Phone: 856-854-4747
BFT Phone: 856-854-4452
Orders: 1-800-John 10:9
e-mail: BFT@BibleForToday.org
Website: www.BibleForToday.org

FAX: 856-854-2464

We Use and Defend
the King James Bible

Publishing Assisted by:
The Old Paths Publications, Inc
www.theoldpathspublications.com
TOP@theoldpathspublications.com

Copyright, 2019

All Rights Reserved
July, 2019
BFT #4194
ISBN #978-1-56848-120-3

Acknowledgments

I wish to thank and to acknowledge the assistance of the following people:

- **The Congregation of the Bible For Today Baptist Church**–for whom these messages were prepared, to whom they were delivered, and by whom they were published. They listened attentively and encouraged their Pastor.
- **Yvonne Sanborn Waite**–my wife, who encouraged the publication of these sermons, read the manuscript, developed the various boxes, and gave other helpful suggestions and comments. The boxes help the reader to see some of the more important topics that are covered in the various chapters.
- **Pastor Daniel Waite**–our church's Assistant Pastor for helping to keep our computers up-to-date and working properly day by day so that this book could be written and published.
- **Patricia Canter**–a friend of mine and Mrs. Waite who volunteered to take the cassette tapes of the verse-by-verse exposition of the book of 2 Corinthians and put these words into the computer in digital format to be used for this book. She also volunteered to help with the final step of proofreading the entire book once the first draft was completed. Without her assistance, this book, and many other books she has worked on, could not have been completed for publication.
- **Dr. Kirk DiVietro**–a friend for many years, one of our Dean Burgon Society faithful Vice Presidents, who is an expert on the use of computers. He has helped in many ways to make the computer work easier and in the proper manner when performing the tasks needed to complete this book. He took Patricia Canter's words of the sermon and formatted them to make them much easier for me to edit.

Foreword

- **The Beginning.** This book is the **seventeenth** in a series of verse-by-verse preaching from various New Testament books of the Bible. It is an attempt to bring to the minds of the readers two things: (1) the **meaning** of the words in the verses, and (2) some practical **applications** of those words to the lives of both genuine Christians and non-Christians.
- **Preached Sermons.** These were messages that I preached to our **Bible For Today Baptist Church** in Collingswood, New Jersey. They were broadcast over the Internet by computer-streaming around the world. I preached verse-by-verse on half a chapter of the book each Sunday as the messages were preached. All verses quoted are from the King James Bible.
- **Other Verses.** In connection with both the **meaning** and **application** of the verses in this book, there are many verses from other places in the Bible that have been quoted for further elaboration on the teachings in this book. All the verses of Scripture that were used to illustrate further truth are written out in full for easy reference.
- **A Transcription.** This entire book was typed into computer format by Patricia Canter from the tape recordings of the messages as they were preached. In addition to the words used as I preached these sermons, I have added other words for clarification as needed.
- **The Audience.** The intended audience for this book is the same as the audience that listened to the messages in the first place. These studies are not meant to be overly scholarly, though there are many references to various Greek or Hebrew Words used. My aim and burden was to try to help genuine Christians to understand and follow the Words of God. It is also my hope that my children, grandchildren, great grandchildren, and others might profit from this study. There is a **10-page INDEX of words and phrases** to help the reader easily find the various topics they are looking for.

Yours For God's Words,

D. A. Waite
Pastor D. A. Waite, Th.D., Ph.D.
Bible For Today Baptist Church

Table of Contents

Publisher's Data i
Acknowledgments ii
Foreword iii
Table of Contents iv
2 Corinthians Chapter One 1
2 Corinthians Chapter Two 15
2 Corinthians Chapter Three 41
2 Corinthians Chapter Four 61
2 Corinthians Chapter Five 87
2 Corinthians Chapter Six 117
2 Corinthians Chapter Seven 149
2 Corinthians Chapter Eight 169
2 Corinthians Chapter Nine 197
2 Corinthians Chapter Ten 219
2 Corinthians Chapter Eleven 239
2 Corinthians Chapter Twelve 263
2 Corinthians Chapter Thirteen 283
Index of Words and Phrases 305
About the Author 315
Order Blank Pages 317
Defined King James Bible Orders 323

2 Corinthians Chapter One

2 Corinthians 1:1

"Paul, an apostle of Jesus Christ by the will of God, and Timothy *our* brother, unto the church of God which is at Corinth, with all the saints which are in all Achaia:"

Paul is the apostle of Jesus Christ by God's will. Before this, he imprisoned and agreed to the killing of Christians. The Lord Jesus Christ met him as he was going to Damascus to imprison Christians. On his way there, the Lord Jesus Christ saved him and called him to be an apostle. I believe Paul, not Mathias, was chosen by the Lord Jesus Christ to take the place of Judas Iscariot who betrayed the Saviour. Timothy was with Paul when he wrote 2 Corinthians and he was right there in the church of Corinth with all the genuine Christians in Achaia or northern Greece. This was Paul's second letter to them. In his first letter, he excoriated them because one of the men had committed incest with his father's wife. Paul is trying to encourage them in the things of the Lord Jesus Christ.

2 Corinthians 1:2

"Grace *be* to you and peace from God our Father, and *from* the Lord Jesus Christ."

Notice grace and peace. Grace (***charis***) is the Greek greeting for those who are Greeks. Peace (***shalom***) is the Hebrew greeting for those who are Hebrews. Both of these greetings come from God the Father and the Lord Jesus Christ. This shows clearly that the Lord Jesus Christ is one of the Members of the Bible's Triune God. All three Members of the Trinity are joined together, yet are separate Persons of the Godhead, **united together**. It is very important to understand that both grace and peace come from both of these Persons in the Godhead.

2 Corinthians 1:3

"Blessed *be* God, even the Father of our Lord Jesus Christ, <u>the Father of mercies</u>, and <u>the God of all comfort;</u>"

The Lord Jesus Christ was sent from Heaven by God the Father. God is called the Father of mercies. Grace has been properly defined as *"getting something we **do not deserve**."* Mercy has been properly defined as "Not getting something that we ***do deserve***." God is the Father of these mercies. He is a merciful God. If He were not merciful, He would have wiped out the United States of America and the entire world decades ago. He is both a gracious and a merciful God.

Verses On Mercy

- **Genesis 32:10**

"<u>I am not worthy of the least of all the mercies</u>, and of all the truth, which thou hast shewed unto thy servant; for with my staff I passed over this Jordan; and now I am become two bands."

Jacob was honest about this. Not many people are as honest as Jacob. They say that they are worthy.

- **2 Samuel 24:14**

"And David said unto Gad, I am in a great strait: let us fall now into the hand of the LORD; for <u>his mercies *are* great</u>: and let me not fall into the hand of man."

There were three choices that David had because he numbered the people. One was to fall into the hands of the LORD; *"for his mercies are great: and let me not fall into the hand of man."*

- **Nehemiah 9:19**

"<u>Yet thou in thy manifold mercies forsookest them not in the wilderness</u>: the pillar of the cloud departed not from them by day, to lead them in the way; neither the pillar of fire by night, to shew them light, and the way wherein they should go."

The Lord did not forsake His people, Israel, because of His mercies.

- **Psalms 25:6**

"<u>Remember, O LORD, thy tender mercies</u> and thy lovingkindnesses; for <u>they *have been* ever of old</u>."

The Lord did not just begin his mercies in David's time. They were from ancient times.

- **Psalms 51:1**
  "<u>Have mercy upon me, O God</u>, according to thy lovingkindness: according unto the multitude of thy tender mercies blot out my transgressions."

David was guilty, not only of adultery, but also murder. He murdered Bathsheba's husband Uriah and yet prayed to the Lord prayed for His tender mercies rather than what he deserved.

- **Lamentations 3:22**
  "<u>*It is of* the L<small>ORD</small>'s mercies</u> that we are not consumed, because his compassions fail not."

All of us could be consumed if it were not for God's mercies found by sincerely trusting His Son for salvation.

- **Romans 12:1**
  "<u>I beseech you therefore, brethren, by the mercies of God</u>, that ye present your bodies a living sacrifice, holy, acceptable unto God, *which is* your reasonable service."

These Christians at Rome needed God's mercies. Because of His mercies, they were to present to Him their bodies as living sacrifices. This included their two eyes, two ears, two hands, two feet, their hearts, and their minds.

- **Colossians 3:12**
  "<u>Put on</u> therefore, as the elect of God, holy and beloved, <u>bowels of mercies</u>, kindness, humbleness of mind, meekness, longsuffering;"

Genuine Christians are to be merciful to other people.

Verses On Comfort

- **Psalms 23:4**
  "Yea, though I walk through the valley of the shadow of death, I will fear no evil: for thou *art* with me; <u>thy rod and thy staff they comfort me</u>."

The rod is for the discipline of genuine Christians when they are out of line. The crook of God's staff is to pick these Christians up when they fall into the ditches of sin.

- **Isaiah 61:2**
  "To proclaim the acceptable year of the L<small>ORD</small>, and the day of vengeance of our God; <u>to comfort all that mourn;</u>"

When true Christians are sad and in mourning, God has His comfort available for them.

- **Romans 15:4**
  "For whatsoever things were written aforetime were written for our learning, that <u>we through patience and comfort of the scriptures might have hope</u>."

This is why I encourage all genuine Christians to read the Old Testament as well as the New Testament which gives them God's comfort.

- **Ephesians 6:22**
  "Whom I have sent unto you for the same purpose, that ye might know our affairs, and *that* <u>he might comfort your hearts</u>."

Paul knew that Tychicus was able to comfort the hearts of these true Christians at Ephesus.

- **1 Thessalonians 3:2**
  "And <u>sent Timotheus</u>, our brother, and minister of God, and our fellowlabourer in the Gospel of Christ, to establish you, and <u>to comfort you concerning your faith</u>:"

Paul wanted Timothy to comfort the genuine Christians at Thessalonica.

- **1 Thessalonians 4:16-18**
  "For <u>the Lord himself shall descend from</u> heaven with a shout, with the voice of the archangel, and with the trump of God: and the dead in Christ shall rise first:<u> Then we which are alive *and* remain shall be caught up together with them in the clouds, to meet the Lord in the air</u>: and so shall we ever be with the Lord. Wherefore <u>comfort one another with these words</u>."

The Biblical pre-tribulation rapture by the Lord Jesus Christ of every true Christian is a great comfort to all of them.

2 Corinthians 1:4

"Who comforteth us in all our tribulation, that we may be able to comfort them which are in any trouble, by the comfort wherewith we ourselves are comforted of God."

God has promised to give His comfort to genuine Christians.

Verses On Tribulation

- **Romans 5:3**
  "And not only *so*, but we glory in tribulations also: knowing that <u>tribulation worketh patience</u>;"

True Christians should glory in tribulations because it leads to patience.

- **Romans 12:12**
"Rejoicing in hope; <u>patient in tribulation</u>; continuing instant in prayer;"
That is not easy. Genuine Christians have God the Holy Spirit indwelling them. He can give them <u>patience in tribulation</u>.
- **2 Corinthians 7:4**
"Great is my boldness of speech toward you, great is my glorying of you: I am filled with comfort, <u>I am exceeding joyful in all our tribulation</u>."
Paul had plenty of tribulation but he was joyful in the tribulation. Part of the fruit of the Spirit is love, **<u>joy</u>**, in tribulation, no matter where it is, in trouble, in prison or trials, sickness, true Christians can be joyful in all their tribulation.
- **1 Thessalonians 3:4**
"For verily, when we were with you, we told you before that <u>we should suffer tribulation</u>; even as it came to pass, and ye know."
He warned genuine Christians that they should suffer tribulation

2 Corinthians 1:5

"For as the sufferings of Christ abound in us, so our consolation also aboundeth by Christ."

True Christians in Paul's day abounded in the sufferings of the Lord Jesus Christ.

Verses On Suffering
- **Romans 8:18**
"For I reckon that <u>the sufferings of this present time</u> *are* not <u>worthy *to be compared* with the glory</u> which shall be revealed in us."
Glory for genuine Christians will be greater than their sufferings.
- **Philippians 3:10**
"<u>That I may know him</u>, and the power of his resurrection, <u>and the fellowship of his sufferings</u>, being made conformable unto his death;"
Paul wanted to have fellowship of Christ's sufferings and be a part of them, regardless of the cost.
- **Hebrews 2:9**
"But we see <u>Jesus, who was made a little lower than the angels for the suffering of death</u>, crowned with glory and honour; that he by the grace of God should taste death for every man."
The Lord Jesus Christ came into this world for the purpose of suffering death for the sins of the world, tasting death for every

person.
- **James 5:10**
"Take, my brethren, the prophets, who have spoken in the name of the Lord, for an example of suffering affliction, and patience."

The Old Testament prophets were examples of suffering.

2 Corinthians 1:6

"And **whether we be afflicted**, *it is* for your consolation and salvation, which is effectual in the **enduring of the same sufferings which we also suffer:** or whether we be **comforted**, *it is* for your **consolation and salvation.**"

Paul endured the same suffering that the genuine Christians at Corinth were enduring.

Verses On Consolation
- **Romans 15:5**
"Now the God of patience and consolation grant you to be likeminded one toward another according to Christ Jesus:"

True Christians should partake in God's consolation as those in Rome did.

- **2 Corinthians 7:6-7**
"Nevertheless God, that comforteth those that are cast down, comforted us by the coming of Titus; And not by his coming only, but by the consolation wherewith he was comforted in you, when he told us your earnest desire, your mourning, your fervent mind toward me; so that I rejoiced the more."

Consolation and comfort work together.

- **2 Thessalonians 2:16**
"Now our Lord Jesus Christ himself, and God, even our Father, which hath loved us, and hath given *us* everlasting consolation and good hope through grace,"

God gives everlasting consolation and good hope to genuine Christians.

- **Hebrews 6:18**
"That by two immutable things, in which *it was* impossible for God to lie, we might have a strong consolation, who have fled for refuge to lay hold upon the hope set before us:"

True Christians have been promised strong consolation.

Verses On Sufferings And Afflictions
- **Psalms 34:19**

"Many are the afflictions of the righteous: but the LORD delivereth him out of them all."
Though genuine Christians have many afflictions, He is able to deliver them.
- **Psalms 119:50**

"This is my comfort in my affliction: for thy word hath quickened me."
God's Words comfort true Christians in their afflictions.
- **Isaiah 63:9**

"In all their affliction he was afflicted, and the angel of his presence saved them: in his love and in his pity he redeemed them; and he bare them, and carried them all the days of old."
God shares the afflictions of His people.
- **Jeremiah 16:19**

"O LORD, my strength, and my fortress, and my refuge in the day of affliction, the Gentiles shall come unto thee from the ends of the earth, and shall say, Surely our fathers have inherited lies, vanity, and *things* wherein *there is* no profit."
God is the strength, fortress and refuge in the afflictions of genuine Christians.
- **2 Corinthians 4:17**

"For our light affliction, which is but for a moment, worketh for us a far more exceeding *and* eternal weight of glory;"
The affliction for true Christians is only for a moment compared to the glory that will follow in Heaven.
- **2 Corinthians 6:4**

"But in all *things* approving ourselves as the ministers of God, in much patience, in afflictions, in necessities, in distresses,"
Genuine Christians should approve themselves in God's patience despite their afflictions.
- **1 Thessalonians 3:3**

"That no man should be moved by these afflictions: for yourselves know that we are appointed thereunto."
True Christians are appointed to afflictions, so they should expect them.

- **2 Timothy 1:8**
  "Be not thou therefore ashamed of the testimony of our Lord, nor of me his prisoner: but be thou partaker of the afflictions of the Gospel according to the power of God;"

Pastor Timothy was to be partaker of the afflictions of the Gospel according to God's power.

- **2 Timothy 3:11**
  "Persecutions, afflictions, which came unto me at Antioch, at Iconium, at Lystra; what persecutions I endured: but out of them all the Lord delivered me."

At Lystra, they stoned Paul and he died, but the Lord raised him up again. He took Paul to Heaven, and then raised him up again. The Lord is a delivering God who delivers from all afflictions.

- **2 Timothy 4:5**
  "But watch thou in all things, endure afflictions, do the work of an evangelist, make full proof of thy ministry."

Do not just pass through afflictions, but endure them. Preach the Word even in affliction.

Verses On Stedfast And Enduring

- **Acts 2:42**
  "And they continued stedfastly in the apostles' doctrine and fellowship, and in breaking of bread, and in prayers."

Stedfastly, continue. That is what we have to do in our doctrines of our church and in our Bible.

- **1 Corinthians 15:58**
  "Therefore, my beloved brethren, be ye stedfast, unmoveable, always abounding in the work of the Lord, forasmuch as ye know that your labour is not in vain in the Lord."

Stedfast means unmoving and firm in the truth.

- **Colossians 2:5**
  "For though I be absent in the flesh, yet am I with you in the spirit, joying and beholding your order, and the stedfastness of your faith in Christ."

Paul was stedfast in his faith, even in jail.

- **Hebrews 6:19**
  "Which hope we have as an anchor of the soul, both sure and stedfast, and which entereth into that within the veil;"

Genuine Christians have a **stedfast** anchor in Christ.

- **1 Peter 5:8-9**
"Be sober, be vigilant; because your adversary the devil, as a roaring lion, walketh about, seeking whom he may devour: Whom <u>resist stedfast in the faith</u>, knowing that the same afflictions are accomplished in your brethren that are in the world."

True Christians must be stedfast in the faith because of their adversary the devil.

2 Corinthians 1:8

"For we would not, brethren, have you ignorant of our trouble which came to us in Asia, that we were pressed out of measure, above strength, insomuch that we despaired even of life:

Asia is the area of land we now call Asia Minor or Turkey. In Asia, Paul and his group were pressed down so hard, above their strength, until they had no strength to resist. Notice, they despaired even of life. That was a death wish of the apostle Paul. Other people have death wishes. Elijah had a death wish. Other people in scripture did also.

It happens to people now as well. For instance, twenty-five to thirty years ago, I had cancer in the lymph glands, Hodgkin's disease. The Lord spared me. A lot of people want to die. Doctors give them drugs to help them die. In some states, that's the law. It's going to get worse and worse. Some social engineers want to de-populate the world by killing off a lot of old people. If you are too old, Obamacare won't let you get certain medical treatments and drugs. "Kill them off!" Paul was pressed out of measure beyond distress.

2 Corinthians 1:9

"But we had the sentence of death in ourselves, that we should not trust in ourselves, but in God which raiseth the dead:"

Paul learned from this stress. The sentence of death taught him "that we should not trust in ourselves." And we should not trust in ourselves, "but in God." He's the one we can trust in all of our afflictions and in all of our troubles. He knows the answers. We can trust Him in the wilderness. We can trust him when affliction came. Trust in the Lord.

God, who raises the dead. If he can raise the dead, he can certainly take care of our petty problems, difficulties and tribulations. Trust in Him and not ourselves.

2 Corinthians 1:10

Who delivered us from so great a death, and doth deliver: in whom we trust that he will yet deliver us;"

God delivered Paul from three deaths--past, present and future.

Verses On Deliverance

- **Psalms 18:17**

"He delivered me from my strong enemy, and from them which hated me: for they were too strong for me."

God delivered David from his enemies.

- **Psalms 22:5**

"They cried unto thee, and were delivered: they trusted in thee, and were not confounded."

Genuine Christians must cry unto the Lord for deliverances as well.

- **Psalms 34:4**

"I sought the LORD, and he heard me, and delivered me from all my fears."

Deliverance from all fears is a great deliverance.

- **Psalms 56:13**

"For thou hast delivered my soul from death: *wilt* not *thou deliver* my feet from falling, that I may walk before God in the light of the living?"

God can deliver from death and feet from falling.

- **Psalms 86:13**

"For great is thy mercy toward me: and thou hast delivered my soul from the lowest hell."

Deliverance is possible by the Lord.

- **Psalms 116:8**

"For thou hast delivered my soul from death, mine eyes from tears, *and* my feet from falling."

These are three different kinds of deliverances.

- **Daniel 6:16**
"Then the king commanded, and they brought Daniel, and cast *him* into the den of lions. *Now* the king spake and said unto Daniel, Thy God whom thou servest continually, he will deliver thee."

Even a heathen king believed in God's deliverance of Daniel from the den of lions.

- **Acts 12:11**
"And when Peter was come to himself, he said, Now I know of a surety, that the Lord hath sent his angel, and hath delivered me out of the hand of Herod, and *from* all the expectation of the people of the Jews."

Peter doubted, but God delivered him from that prison.

- **Colossians 1:13**
"Who hath delivered us from the power of darkness, and hath translated *us* into the kingdom of his dear Son:"

Genuine Christians have been delivered from Satan's power of darkness.

- **2 Timothy 3:11**
"Persecutions, afflictions, which came unto me at Antioch, at Iconium, at Lystra; what persecutions I endured: but out of *them* all the Lord delivered me."

The Lord delivered Paul out of all these afflictions.

- **2 Timothy 4:17**
"Notwithstanding the Lord stood with me, and strengthened me; that by me the preaching might be fully known, and *that* all the Gentiles might hear: and I was delivered out of the mouth of the lion."

God delivered Paul either out of lions in the arena or from Satan as a roaring lion.

- **2 Peter 2:7**
"And delivered just Lot, vexed with the filthy conversation of the wicked:"

God delivered even Lot who He called "just" though he was very carnal.

2 Corinthians 1:11

"Ye also helping together by prayer for us, that for the gift *bestowed* upon us by the means of many persons thanks may be given by many on our behalf."

So, Paul wanted these true Christians to help him by their prayers. Someone gave him a special offering. He thanked them for *"the gift bestowed upon"* him by the Corinthians. Many people gave this gift, not just to Paul but also to poor saints in Jerusalem. He was thanking those that gave to the gift in the name of the people who would receive it.

2 Corinthians 1:12

"For our rejoicing is this, the testimony of our conscience, that in simplicity and godly sincerity, not with fleshly wisdom, but by the grace of God, we have had our conversation in the world, and more abundantly to you-ward."

Notice what Paul said: *"Our rejoicing is this."* Paul was rejoicing in this thing. The testimony of his conscience was his knowledge inside of himself. No other human can see our conscience. But God can see our conscience. Notice what Paul's conscience told him to do. It was to give him simplicity. He also wanted to have godly sincerity. He did not want to lie, cheat, or cover up things. He wanted true sincerity. Also, Paul did not want fleshly wisdom. He had a lot of wisdom, but he did not want to trust in his fleshly wisdom that he had attained through his schools, the law of Moses, or all of the different Jewish traditions that he had been taught. He wanted the wisdom that came by God's grace. That is where Paul stood firm.

Verses On Sincerity

- **Joshua 24:14**

"Now therefore fear the LORD, and serve him in sincerity and in truth: and put away the gods which your fathers served on the other side of the flood, and in Egypt; and serve ye the LORD."

Genuine Christians must serve the Lord in sincerity and genuineness. They must put away the gods which their fathers served on the other side of the flood. They were to "serve the LORD."

- **1 Corinthians 5:8**
"Therefore let us keep the feast, not with old leaven, neither with the leaven of malice and wickedness; but with <u>the unleavened *bread* of sincerity and truth</u>."

This probably refers to the Lord's supper. True Christians must participate the Lord's supper being sincere, honest, just, and truthful.

- **2 Corinthians 2:17**
"For we are not as many, which corrupt the word of God: but <u>as of sincerity</u>, but as of God, in the sight of God speak we in Christ."

All these new modern Bible versions, whether they are in English or in other languages of the world, corrupt the Words of God because of the false Hebrew, and Aramaic Old Testament text and the false Gnostic, Critical New Testament Greek Text they use for their Bibles. Paul was not one of those "*corruptness*." Our church uses the English King James Bible which has been accurately translated from the inspired and preserved Hebrew, Aramaic, and Greek Words. "*We are not as many, which corrupt the word of God: but as of sincerity, but as of God, in the sight of God speak we in Christ.*" That is what every genuine Christian must do so as not to corrupt God's Words.

- **Ephesians 6:24**
"Grace *be* with all them that <u>love our Lord Jesus Christ in sincerity</u>. Amen."

True Christians must love their Saviour in sincerity.

- **Titus 2:7**
"In all things shewing thyself a pattern of good works: in doctrine <u>*shewing* uncorruptness, gravity, sincerity</u>,"

Titus was a pastor on the island of Crete. Every true pastor must show himself a pattern of good works. He must do the work of the Lord Jesus Christ showing a pattern of good works, in doctrine, in teaching, and in all other areas of life.

2 Corinthians Chapter Two

2 Corinthians 2:1

"But I determined this with myself, that I would not come again to you in heaviness."

Paul had written 1 Corinthians. The epistle caused a great deal of grief because of the unrebuked sin of the man that was involved in incest. Paul determined not to physically come again at that time. Instead of returning to Corinth with heaviness, sorrow, or grief, he chose to come by letter. The Greek word for heaviness is LUPA. This grief/sorrow is something that is harmful. He did not want to cause heaviness.

There are various verses that have to do with heaviness:

- **Psalms 69:20**

"Reproach hath broken my heart; and I am full of heaviness: and I looked *for some* to take pity, but *there was* none; and for comforters, but I found none."

And so, Paul did not want this heaviness that the psalmist talked about to come on the Corinthians. He did not his presence, even in a letter, to bring heaviness, grief and sorrow to the people.

- **Psalms 119:28**

"My soul melteth for heaviness: strengthen thou me according unto thy word."

God is able to strengthen us, even when there is heaviness, grief and sorrow. He can strengthen us in heaviness . The Word of God is the thing that will do that for us. We have to trust in his Word. We have to accept it, not only read and study it, but follow it as God gives us the grace to do so.

- **Proverbs 12:25**
    "Heaviness in the heart of man maketh it stoop: but a good word maketh it glad."

We know about stooping shoulders, with our hearts stooping. A stooping heart means there is sadness in heart "but a good word maketh it glad." Good words make hearts glad. Bad things and heaviness makes hearts to stoop, go down, and be discouraged. So, there is **heaviness** in the Scriptures in many places and there are many different things about it.

- **Romans 9:2**
    "That I have great heaviness and continual sorrow in my heart."

He was concerned about his people, the Israelites, the Jews. Paul was a Jew. He came to Christ and now he was a Christian. The unbelieving Jewish people did not go along with Paul. Now he was sort of an outcast and he wanted them to be saved and born again. just like himself. So, he had great heaviness and sorrow, continual sorrow, in his heart. Sorrow of heart is a very serious disease, as you know. We can be sorry in our minds but when it reaches the heart, it really grips us even stronger than ever and Paul had heart sorrow.

The apostle Peter used this term, heaviness, as well,

- **1 Peter 1:5-6**
    "Who are kept by the power of God through faith unto salvation ready to be revealed in the last time."

That is final salvation. God is taking us to heaven and we are kept forever. God promises to keep us who are genuinely trusting Christ as Saviour safe and saved until we meet him in glory. He says, we are "kept by the power of God through faith unto salvation"– unto heaven, all the way until we get to the glorious land. Then he says this, "Wherein ye greatly rejoice, though now for a season, if need be, ye are in heaviness through manifold temptations:"

Those who are genuinely saved, who are going to heaven, should greatly rejoice because that is our destiny. We are kept by the power of God until that time. That is true even "though now for a season," now, for a short length of time, "if need be, ye are in heaviness." Now, everyone does not have the same heaviness, sorrow, and grief that others have. Each one has his own heaviness, your manifold temptations, and testings. So Paul was concerned for his believers, as was Peter for his, that they would not have too many difficulties.

2 Corinthians 2:2

"For if I make you sorry, who is he then that maketh me glad, but the same which is made sorry by me?"

When you bring sorrow to some person, does that make them happy? No. That word is LUPO. It means *to make sorrowful, to afflict with sadness, to cause grief*. When you make someone sorry, are they very happy with you? No. That is what Paul is saying. He could write this letter to the Corinthian church like the first letter in which he confronted them with the situation in 1 Corinthians 5, but if he did, that would make a number of them sorry because he really laid down the law. They were wrong in what they did to this gentleman, this man, who was a sinner. But, Paul said, If I make you sorry, "who is he then that maketh me glad, but the same which is made sorry by me?"

People can be glad when other people are glad and rejoicing with them. In the same way if you bring sorrow to someone, do not expect them to make you happy and glad. See, that is what he is saying here. He did not want to make them sorry. He wanted to make them glad, so they could make him glad. As far as being sorry,

- **Nehemiah 8:10**

"Then he said unto them, Go your way, eat the fat, and drink the sweet, and send portions unto them for whom nothing is prepared: for *this* day is holy unto our Lord: neither be ye sorry; for the joy of the LORD is your strength."

Now Nehemiah was a post-exilic prophet. God sent the Israelites to exile in Babylon for seventy long years. Ezra and Nehemiah were prophets after they came back to the land. Nehemiah said, God has given you all that you need, "neither be ye sorry". Do not be sorry. And then he says this. ". . . [F]or the joy of the LORD is your strength." The joy of the LORD is your strength. We cannot have sorrow when the joy of the LORD is there. Joy is the opposite of sorrow. The Lord can give us joy, His joy, in the midst of our sorrow.

- **2 Corinthians 7:8**

"For though I made you sorry with a letter, I do not repent, though I did repent: for I perceive that the same epistle hath made you sorry, though *it were* but for a season."

I am glad we can take away the sorrow and replace it with the joy of the Lord.

- **2 Corinthians 7:9**

"Now I rejoice, not that ye were made sorry, but that ye sorrowed to repentance: for ye were made sorry after a godly manner, that ye might receive damage by us in nothing."

Paul's letter had caused them to have a change of mind. They straightened themselves out. That is the definition of *repent*. They repented for the wrong they had been doing. There is a godly purpose for sorrow, "that ye might receive damage by us in nothing." And so, Paul was glad that they were no longer sorry.

2 Corinthians 2:3

"And I wrote this same unto you, lest, when I came, I should have sorrow from them of whom I ought to rejoice; having confidence in you all, that my joy is *the joy* of you all."

Paul says, That is what I intended to happen I wrote to you. He wrote in 1 Corinthians about problems they had in the church "lest, when I came, I should have sorrow." He did not want to return to the church till things were corrected.

He said, "lest when I came." He wrote the second epistle of Corinthians rather than the coming to the church at that time. He did not want to come until they were was ready for him to come, until they were ready to receive him. So he wrote this second letter, "lest, when I came, I should have sorrow from them of whom I ought to rejoice;" He said, I do not want to come back to Corinth too soon. He came back once again by writing this 2 Corinthians letter in order to encourage them. He wanted to rejoice in these people that he made sorrowful. Then he said "having confidence in you all, that my joy is the joy of you all." Paul wanted his joy to be their joy and rejoicing, not sorrow, not tears, not afflictions.

2 Corinthians 2:4

"For out of much affliction and anguish of heart I wrote unto you with many tears; not that ye should be grieved, but that ye might know the love which I have more abundantly unto you."

Paul wrote this out of affliction and anguish. The Greek Word for affliction means "tribulation, persecution, oppression, and distress." Paul was in all sorts of distress when he wrote that first letter. He was in affliction and distress. Notice also, not only affliction, outward affliction but anguish of heart. The Greek Word for "*anguish*" means "*holding together and narrowing, constricting, pushing together, pushing in upon.*" He was in anguish with pressure in his heart. "I wrote unto you with many tears;" Paul did not write First Corinthians just with his head. He had tears but he had to do it. When people are wrong, when you love them, you want to correct them and we write and tell them about it, even if they are angry about it, they are sorry about it, maybe mad at us and angry but Paul had to do it. The case in Corinth that was wrong was straightened out by them because he wrote the letter First Corinthians. Straightened out. He said I wrote out of affliction and anguish with many tears. Notice, why he did not write them in First Corinthians. Not that you should be grieved or sorry. That was not the purpose of his writing the First Corinthians letter. "that you might know the love which I have more abundantly unto you" "For whom the Lord loveth he chasteneth," That is what it says. He corrects. Paul said, I love you, Corinthians. You were going astray, you had different problems. I wrote this letter to you so you could see the love that I have to you. I wrote in love. I did not want to grieve you. As far as anguish, he wrote out of anguish of heart.

- **John 16:21**

"A woman when she is in travail hath sorrow, because her hour is come: but as soon as she is delivered of the child, she remembereth no more the anguish, for joy that a man is born into the world."

In this verse the Lord Jesus is talking about a woman, when she has had her baby. My wife has had five of them. You wives know what the Lord Jesus was talking about.

I remember when they let me into the labor room, in Dallas, Texas, with our first child, D. A. Waite Jr.. They put my wife under lots of sedation. She did not even know she was having a baby. But I did! I was there. I had no sedation. I saw the pain. I knew the suffering. I saw it.

They would not let me go in for the second, third, fourth and fifth child. But that first child, they let me go in. I needed to know. It is a great sorrow but after the child is born, she remembers "no more the anguish." I am sure they remember some of it but the scriptures say she "remembereth no more the anguish, for joy that a man is born into the world."

Paul says, to those who do evil,
- **Romans 2:9**
"Tribulation and anguish, upon every soul of man that doeth evil, of the Jew first, and also of the Gentile;"

I wish there would be more feeling of anguish by those who do evil. They seem to do evil and love it. "It is wonderful, let us keep it going. Its fun to do evil." But God says there is anguish upon every soul. There is anguish, trouble, great sorrow, and burden to evil workers. That should cause them to straighten up but it does not seem to work. In many cases, they keep right on doing what they are doing, wrong as it may be.

2 Corinthians 2:5

"But if any have caused grief, he hath not grieved me, but in part: that I may not overcharge you all."

Some people in this church of Corinth were grieved. Paul was not grieved because those people were grieved. They were guilty of sin. They should grieve. But Paul was sorry that they were sorrowful. That word for grieve again is LUPEO. He says I do not want to overcharge you or burden you. That Greek word is EPIBARO. I do not want to over burden you, put a burden upon you, to be burdensome unto you. He was sorry that he had caused them any grief when he wrote the letter because he loved them. He wanted to correct what was in that church. There was something very wrong in that church and he wanted to straighten it out if possible. He did not want to cause any unnecessary grief.

- **Job 2:13**
"So they sat down with him upon the ground seven days and seven nights, and none spake a word unto him: for they saw that *his* grief was very great."

If there is anybody that had grief, it was Job. In one day all his possessions, his cattle and his workers. His children were killed. Then his health was taken away, from the top of his head to the souls of his feet. He had great grief. His friends came and sat down with him for seven day and seven nights without speaking a word.

I am glad they joined him. Sometimes when someone is in grief the best thing to say is nothing. Once they started to speak they just added to his grief. Instead of comforting him they accused him of causing his own grief because his hidden sin. He knew he had done nothing wrong. God knew he had done nothing wrong. But the accusations of his friends forced him to defend his life. They argued with him and that is the thing. When a person is in sorrow and grief and pain, please, do not argue with them. These people just talked back and forth and made Job had to defend his cause.

When someone is in grief, and you go to be a comfort and you do not know what to say, say nothing. They know you are there. They see you. They sense you are concerned. And they are comforted. This is true if you meet them in their home, in the hospital, funeral home, or wherever they are.

That is what these people did for seven days and seven nights. Then they opened their mouths. And it was not helpful. Job said of them, "miserable comforters are ye all" because they did things that were wrong for comfort.

- **Isaiah 53:3**

"He is despised and rejected of men; a man of sorrows, and acquainted with grief: and we hid as it were *our* faces from him; he was despised, and we esteemed him not."

The Lord Jesus, was a man of sorrows and acquainted with grief, at the cross of Calvary. But he had been rejected before the cross. The Bible tells us how the Jewish religious leaders rejected Him. (Matthew 26:4) The crowds abandoned him. (John 6:66). In Pilate's judgement hall he was rejected (We have no king but Caesar). (John 19:15) He was not esteemed. They hated him. And then they crucified him and they esteemed him not. Surely He was despised, rejected, and a man of sorrows acquainted with grief.

- **Hebrews 13:17**

"Obey them that have the rule over you, and submit yourselves: for they watch for your souls, as they that must give account, that they may do it with joy, and not with grief: for that *is* unprofitable for you."

Pastors or Sunday school teachers or missionaries, they watch for your souls, as they that must give an account. Every preacher, every pastor, that preaches the Word, must give an account before his Lord, one day, for you. Are you causing him grief or joy? What are you doing?

Those people that are lost, are the devil's children. They will give an account to the Lord. They will give an account for their attitude toward God's servants. They will give an account for the way they treat them. And, ultimately if they do not get saved they will go to hell, the Lake of Fire for eternity.

Pastors that are saved pastors, born again Christian pastors, are going to have to give an account to the Lord for what they say from the pulpit and in counseling. They must ask themselves: is it right? Is it scriptural? Is it Biblical? Is there a heresy? They have to give an account to the Lord Jesus Christ. "[A]s they that must give account, that they may do it with joy, and not with grief: for that *is* unprofitable for you." Help them to give an account with joy, a joyous account not a grievous account. That preacher must be faithful to the Word of God.

2 Corinthians 2:6

"Sufficient to such a man *is* this punishment, which *was inflicted* of many."

Now Paul goes after what was happening in the church at Corinth. It was bad enough that they followed people. I am of Paul, I am of Peter, I am of Cephas, I am of Christ but then they had this man that committed sin with his father's wife and they were not properly in tune to that. They said, oh, that is fine, no problem. Before Paul's rebuke, they were wonderful and joyful. The people in the church thought there was nothing wrong with that sin! The Corinthians thought that they were being kind and gracious allowing this man who was sleeping with his father's wife to go without rebuke or consequence. They thought tolerating his sin was a virtue. That is the trouble. When the pastor and members of a church allow sin, wickedness, or doctrinal impurity in the church, the church becomes corruptible. Eventually the whole church will become corrupt. Soon, Bible believing people that are sound, sane and spiritual have to leave that church because it is a corrupt church.

What should the church have done? What should be the punishment for open sin? What should be the rebuke for those who tolerate it? That was the real sin. In 1 Corinthians 5:1-7, Paul outlines the problem that is in that church,

- **1 Corinthians 5:1-7**
"It is reported commonly *that there is* fornication among you, and such fornication as is not so much as named among the Gentiles, that one should have his father's wife."
Paul writes to them and says, now, everybody knows there is sin in your church. What is the matter with you people? There is sexual impurity among you. This type of fornication is not even named among the heathen. Incest, wicked incest-- gentiles did not even have that particular situation. So, did Paul mince words with them? No, he did not. He told everything straight to them. "And ye are puffed up, and have not rather mourned, that he that hath done this deed might be taken away from among you."

Because of the sin, they were proud of this wicked sin. Just like people today are proud of all kinds of different sins, whether it is adultery or fornication, homosexuality, lesbianism, whatever it is, they are proud as anything. In fact, there was a note I got today, letter on the internet, that in California, they are punishing a Christian college, the lesbians, the LGBTQ, they are punishing them because the Christian college takes a position that marriage is one man and one woman for life, not two men and two women, so this lesbian crowd is punishing this Christian college in California. "And ye are puffed up, and have not rather mourned," They should have mourned for this sin, of incest, "that he that hath done this deed might be taken away from among you."

Church discipline is a part of the New Testament and those that have committed this sin should be taken away and removed from the church at Corinth. They did not remove him at that time, later they did but not then. Then Paul says, "For I verily, as absent in body, but present in spirit, have judged already, as though I were present, *concerning* him that hath so done this deed," Paul said, I am not there but I have already judged it that it was wrong, it is sinful, it is wicked, it is the scriptures, and I have judged it. "In the name of our Lord Jesus Christ, when ye are gathered together, and my spirit, with the power of our Lord Jesus Christ, To deliver such an one unto Satan for the destruction of the flesh, that the spirit may be saved in the day of the Lord Jesus. Your glorying is not good. Know ye not that a little leaven leaveneth the whole lump?"

To glorify sin or wickedness and corruption, is not good at all. Not good. I am not a baker, but I understand. You put a little leaven in bread it just goes throughout the whole bread. A little poison. A lot of people think that leaven is good. Leaven in scripture is always poison, it is always bad, it is always dangerous. A little leaven. This incestuous man, if he remains in that church, the whole church will be leavened with poison and sin and wickedness and corruption. That is the scripture he uses here.

A little leaven leaveneth the whole lump. When unbelief and godlessness and doctrinal fallacies are in a church, or sexual impurity, whatever it may be, that goes through the whole church. That is where churches begin to go corrupt. As Pastor Dan has mentioned in his History of Fundamentalism, churches of the past have followed this pattern. Many Presbyterian churches started out one way and now are completely gone. Many Baptist churches started one way and now are completely gone. Many Methodist churches started one way and now are completely gone. Many other churches, denominational or non-denominational started out one way but now are completely gone. Not every church goes bad, but many do. A little leaven leaveneth the whole lump. What is Paul's remedy for this wickedness and this sin?

- **1 Corinthians 5:7**
"Purge out therefore the old leaven, that ye may be a new lump, as ye are unleavened. For even Christ our passover is sacrificed for us:"

Clean it out, get rid of this incestuous man, get him out of the church. You are not to have poison among you if you are genuinely saved. One of the things they have to do away with at the Passover feast, there is no leaven. That bread had to be unleavened bread. We remember the Lord's death until he comes. We use unleavened bread in our Communion services as well. Unleavened bread.

2 Corinthians 2:7

"So that contrariwise ye *ought* rather to forgive him, and comfort *him*, lest perhaps such a one should be swallowed up with overmuch sorrow."

Notice, that is the title of our message, *Forgiveness and Comfort*. The Greek word for Forgiveness is XARIZOMAI. We are to forgive and also to comfort. You should not have this man swallowed up with much sorrow. It is interesting, forgiveness. In 1 John 1:9, it talks about Christian forgiveness.

- **1 John 1:9**
"If we confess our sins, he is faithful and just to forgive us *our* sins, and to cleanse us from all unrighteousness." Notice, confess HOMOLOGEO means to say the same thing about that sin that God says. To agree with God that it is sin. People who are lost and unsaved, God forgives their sins when they trust the Lord Jesus Christ, who died for their sins. There must be an acknowledgment of sin, or there can be no forgiveness. Acknowledgment of sin. You cannot forgive sinners who do not think there is sin. They think that there is nothing to forgive. As far as they are concerned, they are fine. Same in 1 John 1:9. God says if we agree with Him, confess our sins, then and only then, does He forgive the sin. He forgives the sins, past, present and future. Having fellowship with him, he does not forgive us unless we agree with him that it is sin. That is what confession means in 1 John 1:9. It is very important to see the basis of forgiveness. It says in one of the Gospels, if a man comes to you and says I have sinned, I am wrong, forgive him. If seven times or seventy times seven, he comes and says I am wrong, forgive him. That is the basis of forgiveness. God does not forgive sinners that do not acknowledge they are sinful. That is the Gospel message. We must realize, number one, I have sinned and I am a sinner in God's eyes. I agree with God. Number two, I trust the Lord Jesus Christ as my Saviour and Redeemer and accept Him and receive Him. We have to realize He died for my sins. I realize He died for my sins. Forgiveness is based on an acknowledgment of sin.

- **Genesis 50:17**
"So shall ye say unto Joseph, Forgive, I pray thee now, the trespass of thy brethren, and their sin; for they did unto thee evil: and now, we pray thee, forgive the trespass of the servants of the God of thy father. And Joseph wept when they spake unto him."
The brethren that sold Joseph into Egypt into slavery acknowledged their sin. They acknowledged their sins. We have done wrong. We acknowledge that and Joseph forgave them because they acknowledged their sin.

Forgiveness. This man acknowledged his sin in 1 Corinthians. He knew he was wrong. They dismissed him out of the church, he acknowledged his sin, they brought him back in and they forgave him because he realized he had sinned.

- **1 Kings 8:36**
"Then hear thou in heaven, and forgive the sin of thy servants, and of thy people Israel, that thou teach them the good way wherein they should walk, and give rain upon thy land, which thou hast given to thy people for an inheritance."
It is after they have acknowledged their sins, then hear from heaven and forgive the sin of thy servants.
- **Psalms 25:18**
"Look upon mine affliction and my pain; and forgive all my sins."
David acknowledged he had sins. He did not say that he did not have any sins. Forgive my sins. You and I must confess, if we have done sin against our fellow believers, our husband, our wife, whatever, we acknowledge it, then they can be forgiven. That is what we should do. Once acknowledgment is given, we forgive. Forgive all my sins, David prayed.
- **Jeremiah 31:34**
"And they shall teach no more every man his neighbour, and every man his brother, saying, Know the LORD: for they shall all know me, from the least of them unto the greatest of them, saith the LORD: for I will forgive their iniquity, and I will remember their sin no more."
God's forgiveness comes when they acknowledge they are sinners and he forgives them.
- **Luke 17:3-4**
"Take heed to yourselves: If thy brother trespass against thee, rebuke him; and if he repent, forgive him. And if he trespass against thee seven times in a day, and seven times in a day turn again to thee, saying, I repent; thou shalt forgive him."
We have to rebuke trespasses. That is what Paul did in the church of Corinth. "If he repent," if he changes his mind, *"re"* is *"change,"* and *"pent"* is *"mind."* It is a *"change of mind."*

The Greek word used in 1 John 1:9 is HOMOLOGEO. HOMO is *"same"* and LOGEO is *"to say."* The meaning of this Greek Word used in 1 John 1:9 is *"To say the same thing about our sin as God does and agree with God that it is sin."*

What if a person does not repent? You cannot forgive what he has not repented of, if he still thinks he is all right, what is there to forgive? He says I have done nothing wrong. Only after they have realized that they have done wrong, can we forgive anything. Acknowledge our wrongness, if he repents, forgive him. If he trespasses against you seven times in a day and seven times a day he turns again to you saying, I repent, I am sorry, I have changed my mind, I have sinned, "thou shalt forgive him." Seventy times. Seven times in a day. In other words, forgiveness should have no end, supply unlimited, forgiveness. First, acknowledgment of sin or trespass then forgiveness. That is God's Word and God's will.

The Lord Jesus at the cross said:
- **Luke 23:34**

"Then said Jesus, Father, forgive them; for they know not what they do. And they parted his raiment, and cast lots." They did not know the terrible, terrible travesty and sin, according to the Saviour, upon the cross of Calvary and he had forgiveness. That verse is taken out of some of our modern versions, by the way, "*Father, forgive them; for they know not what they do.*"

We have said this before,
- **1 John 1:9**

"If we confess our sins, he is faithful and just to forgive us our sins, and to cleanse us from all unrighteousness." This confession of sin should not wait for a week, or a month or a year. When we sin, that is when the confession unto Him should take place. Then he is faithful and just in forgiving us. He is faithful, he will do it if we agree with him that is sin. He is not only faithful, he is just in forgiveness. Christ paid for the sins on the cross at Calvary, all sins, past, present and future. He is just in forgiveness and cleansing. He will cleanse us from all unrighteousness. If that is seven times a day, whatever it is, it should be instantaneous. Then as far as Paul says, I write, contrariwise, this man, forgive him and also you have to comfort him. You Corinthian Christians, you sin a lot in your church, you will receive him back eventually but you have to not only forgive him. You must comfort him, lest he be swallowed up with overmuch sorrow. There are some scriptures on comfort. Here are a few of them,

- **Psalms 23:4**
  "Yea, though I walk through the valley of the shadow of death, I will fear no evil: for thou *art* with me; thy rod and thy staff they comfort me."

The rod, to discipline, staff with a crook, pulls us out of a ditch. The rod and the staff, comfort. This man, this incestuous, sinful man, this leaven that leaveneth the whole lump, needed to be comforted as well as forgiven.

This next verse is at the raising of Lazarus. He had died but had not been raised yet,
- **John 11:19**
  "And many of the Jews came to Martha and Mary, to comfort them concerning their brother."

There is need for comfort when death comes. They were there and we know the story. They did not believe the Lord Jesus was going to raise him but they just said he will be with you in the last days. He said, "I am the resurrection and the life: he that believeth in me, though he were dead, yet shall he live:" He raised Lazarus from the dead. They came to comfort the sisters who had lost their brother, Lazarus, a good man. God raised him up.

This verse speaks about the coming of the Lord,
- **1 Thessalonians 5:11**
  "Wherefore comfort yourselves together, and edify one another, even as also ye do."

Fellow believers are to comfort one another. As they were coming together to Thessalonica, the church of Thessalonica, comfort yourselves together. We are to comfort each other, one another, because all of us need it at one time, comfort.
- **1 Thessalonians 5:14**
  "Now we exhort you, brethren, warn them that are unruly, comfort the feebleminded, support the weak, be patient toward all *men*."

People that do not have all their brains, we are to especially help them and comfort them. So, comfort is that which is given out that helps people to get over the sorrows. We cannot take away their pain but you can certainly be with them in the comfort. You can comfort, try it, the best you can to help them, comfort them. But this man that committed incest with his father's wife, had to have the power of forgiveness but also comfort so he is not overcome with over much sorrow and grief.

2 Corinthians 2:8

"Wherefore I beseech you that ye would confirm your love toward him."

He besought them. This a present tense in Greek. It means he continually asked them to *"confirm your love toward him."* Apparently, he came back. He repented, he changed his mind. He said I have sinned. It was wrong of me to do that. I want to come back to the church. They accepted him back and not only when he comes back in the church, do not put him in the corner and sit him on some stool, separate him, but confirm your love. Show him that you love him, you have forgiven him, you are to comfort him now, confirm your love. Let him know you love him or her, whatever the case might be. Confirm your love toward him, this man that sinned grievously.

This is the lesson that Paul gives us in these first eight verses. He said I wrote this first letter because you had a lot of problems. You have said I am of Paul, I am of Apollos, I am of Cephas and I am of Christ and you are dividing with all the different leaders. There were other problems in the church of Corinth--fighting and bickering and carrying on. Then you had this incestuous man but I determined, I am not going to come to you again to make you sorry about that. I am going to write you this letter. Paul wanted to make them glad. He wanted to make them rejoice in that which they knew and so He came, in this second letter, and told them what they should do about this man. He was very glad they rejoiced in putting him back into the church. Paul chastised them for having this wickedness remain in the church. He said you should not have been glad and rejoicing over this sin. You should have taken care of it, but you did not. Now he has repented and is back in the church, and you have accepted him. He has acknowledged his sin. You are to forgive him, comfort him, and love him, without any question.

So, this should be our guide in our church and our lives today. We should be able to restore things that are wrong.

2 Corinthians 2:9

"For to this end also did I write, that I might know the proof of you, whether ye be obedient in all things."

Paul asked them to do three things in this early letter; (1) to forgive the incestuous man who had repented of his sin; (2) and (3) to comfort him. We must be obedient once we promise things.

Verses On Obedience

- **1 Samuel 15:18-24**

"And the LORD sent thee on a journey, and said, Go and utterly destroy the sinners the Amalekites, and fight against them until they be consumed. <u>Wherefore then didst thou not obey the voice of the LORD</u>, but didst fly upon the spoil, and didst evil in the sight of the LORD? And Saul said unto Samuel, Yea, I have obeyed the voice of the LORD, and have gone the way which the LORD sent me, and have brought Agag the king of Amalek, and have utterly destroyed the Amalekites. But the people took of the spoil, sheep and oxen, the chief of the things which should have been utterly destroyed, to sacrifice unto the LORD thy God in Gilgal. And Samuel said, Hath the LORD *as great* delight in burnt offerings and sacrifices, as in <u>obeying the voice of the LORD? For rebellion *is as* the sin of witchcraft, and stubbornness *is as* iniquity and idolatry</u>. Because thou hast rejected the word of the LORD, he hath also rejected thee from *being* king. And Saul said unto Samuel, I have sinned: for I have transgressed the commandment of the LORD, and thy words: because I feared the people, and obeyed their voice."

If genuine Christians obey people rather than the Lord they will be in serious trouble. They must obey His voice despite what people think or do not think.

- **Proverbs 25:12**

"*As* an earring of gold, and an ornament of fine gold, *so is* <u>a wise reprover upon an obedient ear</u>."

No one likes to be reproved, but it is like an earring of gold on an obedient ear.

- **Ephesians 6:5**
"Servants, be obedient to them that are <u>your</u> <u>masters</u> <u>according to the flesh</u>, with fear and trembling, in singleness of your heart, as unto Christ;"

Some masters are good, some masters are bad. If true Christians are serving someone, they should obey whatever their wishes are, so long as it is not against the Words of God.

- **Philippians 2:8**
"And being found in fashion as a man, he humbled himself, and <u>became obedient unto death, even the death of the cross</u>."

The Lord Jesus was obedient even unto His death on the cross.

- **Matthew 26:39b**
"O my Father, if it be possible, let this cup pass from me: nevertheless <u>not as I will, but as thou *wilt*</u>."

The Father's will was for the Lord Jesus Christ to die for the sins of the world. He was obedient unto death, even the cruel death of the cross.

- **Titus 2:5**
"*To be* discreet, chaste, keepers at home, good, <u>obedient to their own husbands</u>, that the word of God be not blasphemed."

God wanted the older women to teach the younger genuine Christian women to be obedient to their own husbands.

- **1 Peter 1:14**
"<u>As obedient children</u>, not fashioning yourselves according to the former lusts in your ignorance:"

True children of God should be obedient to the Lord and His Words.

2 Corinthians 2:10

"**To whom ye forgive any thing, I *forgive* also: for if I forgave any thing, to whom I forgave *it*, for your sakes *forgave I it* in the person of Christ;**"

Paul was talking about forgiving this incestuous man in the church of Corinth.

Verses On Forgiveness

- **Psalms 130:4**
"But <u>*there* is forgiveness with thee</u>, that thou mayest be feared."

With the Lord, there is forgiveness.

- **Acts 5:31**
"Him hath God exalted with his right hand *to be* a Prince and a Saviour, for to give repentance to Israel, and forgiveness of sins."

The only the way for people to receive forgiveness is for them to receive the Lord Jesus Christ as their Saviour.

- **Acts 13:38**
"Be it known unto you therefore, men *and* brethren, that through this man is preached unto you the forgiveness of sins:"

Forgiveness is only through genuine faith in the Lord Jesus Christ.

- **Acts 26:18**
"To open their eyes, *and* to turn *them* from darkness to light, and *from* the power of Satan unto God, that they may receive forgiveness of sins, and inheritance among them which are sanctified by faith that is in me."

Only by genuine faith in the Lord Jesus Christ can this forgiveness take place.

- **Ephesians 1:7**
"In whom we have redemption through his blood, the forgiveness of sins, according to the riches of his grace;"

The shed blood of the Lord Jesus Christ is the only basis of true forgiveness.

- **1 John 1:9**
"If we confess our sins, he is faithful and just to forgive us *our* sins, and to cleanse us from all unrighteousness."

True Christians must agree with God that they have sinned in order to receive God's forgiveness. This is what "*confess*" means.

2 Corinthians 2:11

"Lest Satan should get an advantage of us: for we are not ignorant of his devices."

Satan wants to get an advantage over genuine Christians.

Verses On Satan

- **Job 1:6-7**
"Now there was a day when the sons of God came to present themselves before the LORD, and Satan came also among them. And the LORD said unto Satan, Whence comest thou? Then Satan answered the LORD, and said, From going to and fro in the earth, and from walking up and down in it."

Satan was an angel of God, with access to Heaven before he sinned.

- **Matthew 4:10**
"Then saith <u>Jesus unto him, Get thee hence, Satan</u>: for it is written, Thou shalt worship the Lord thy God, and him only shalt thou serve."
Satan was tempting the Lord, testing him out in the wilderness for forty days and forty nights.

- **Matthew 16:23a**
"But <u>he turned, and said unto Peter, Get thee behind me, Satan</u>:"
Satan was so influencing Peter's life, the Lord Jesus Christ addressed Satan personally.

- **Matthew 16:23b**
"thou art an offence unto me: for thou savourest not the things that be of God, but those that be of men."
Peter had to be rebuked. Christians that are following Satan in any way, have to be rebuked as well. I do not believe Satan can indwell genuine Christians. He can influence us when we are not guarded against him.

- **Luke 22:3**
"<u>Then entered Satan into Judas surnamed Iscariot</u>, being of the number of the twelve."
Judas was not a true Christian, but was a phony apostle and a servant of Satan.

- **Luke 22:31**
"And the Lord said, <u>Simon, Simon, behold, Satan hath desired to *have* you</u>, that he may sift *you* as wheat:"
Satan wanted to get a hold on Peter, just as he wants to get a hold of genuine Christians today.

- **Acts 5:3**
"But Peter said, <u>Ananias, why hath Satan filled thine heart to lie to the Holy Ghost</u>, and to keep back *part* of the price of the land?"
Ananias and Saphira lied to the Holy Spirit. They did not have to give the whole price of the land that they sold to the Lord, but they lied about it.

- **Acts 26:18**
"To open their eyes, *and* <u>to turn *them* from darkness to light, and *from* the power of Satan unto God</u>, that they may receive forgiveness of sins, and inheritance among them which are sanctified by faith that is in me."
God wants to turn non-Christians from the power of Satan unto God.

- **Romans 16:20**
 "And the God of peace shall bruise Satan under your feet shortly. The grace of our Lord Jesus Christ be with you. Amen."

God was going to bruise Satan.

- **1 Corinthians 7:5**
 "Defraud ye not one the other, except *it be* with consent for a time, that ye may give yourselves to fasting and prayer; and come together again, that Satan tempt you not for your incontinency."

Satan can tempt husbands and wives for not having proper husband and wife sexual love together.

- **2 Corinthians 11:13-15**
 "For such *are* false apostles, deceitful workers, transforming themselves into the apostles of Christ. And no marvel; for Satan himself is transformed into an angel of light. Therefore *it is* no great thing if his ministers also be transformed as the ministers of righteousness; whose end shall be according to their works."

Satan is dark and wicked, but he can transform himself into an angel of light to fool people. He has ministers today who transform themselves into instruments of righteousness when they are Satan's apostates. They are children of Satan.

- **2 Corinthians 12:7**
 "And lest I should be exalted above measure through the abundance of the revelations, there was given to me a thorn in the flesh, the messenger of Satan to buffet me, lest I should be exalted above measure."

We do not know what that was in Paul's life.

- **1 Thessalonians 2:18**
 "Wherefore we would have come unto you, even I Paul, once and again; but Satan hindered us."

Satan was a hindering person to hinder Paul in his ministry.

- **2 Thessalonians 2:6-10**
"And now ye know what withholdeth that he might be revealed in his time. For the mystery of iniquity doth already work: only he who now letteth *will let*, until he be taken out of the way. And then shall that Wicked be revealed, whom the Lord shall consume with the spirit of his mouth, and shall destroy with the brightness of his coming: <u>Even him, whose coming is after the working of Satan with all power and signs and lying wonders, And with all deceivableness of unrighteousness</u> in them that perish; because they received not the love of the truth, that they might be saved."

The Satanic antichrist will be revealed when the true Christians are raptured to Heaven. The first three and a half years of the seven-year tribulation, he will act like a wonderful leader. He will promise many lying things.

- **1 Timothy 5:14-15**
"I will therefore that the younger women marry, bear children, guide the house, give none occasion to the adversary to speak reproachfully. For <u>some are already turned aside after Satan</u>."

Some wives turn aside after Satan.

- **Revelation 12:9**
"And <u>the great dragon was cast out, that old serpent, called the Devil, and Satan, which deceiveth the whole world</u>: he was cast out into the earth, and his angels were cast out with him."

Notice Satan's four names in the above verse.

- **Revelation 20:2**
"And he laid hold on the dragon, that old serpent, which is the Devil, and Satan, and bound him a thousand years,"

Satan will be bound during the millennial reign of the Lord Jesus Christ.

- **Revelation 20:7-8**
"And <u>when the thousand years are expired, Satan shall be loosed out of his prison</u>, And shall go out to deceive the nations which are in the four quarters of the earth, Gog and Magog, to gather them together to battle: the number of whom *is* as the sand of the sea."

Satan will be loosed after the thousand year reign of the Saviour upon this earth.

2 Corinthians 2:12

"Furthermore, when I came to Troas to preach Christ's Gospel, and a door was opened unto me of the Lord,"

The Gospel is good news about the Lord Jesus Christ.

Verses On Gospel

- **Romans 1:16**

"For <u>I am not ashamed of the Gospel of Christ</u>: for it is the power of God unto salvation to every one that believeth; to the Jew first, and also to the Greek."

Paul was not ashamed of the Gospel of the Lord Jesus Christ.

- **John 3:16**

"For God so loved the world, that he gave his only begotten Son, that whosoever believeth in him should not perish, but have everlasting life."

This is a clear presentation of the Gospel.

Verses On Doors

- **John 10:9**

"<u>I am the door</u>: by me if any man enter in, he shall be saved, and shall go in and out, and find pasture."

The only door to Heaven is by exercising genuine faith in the Lord Jesus Christ.

- **Acts 14:27**

"And when they were come, and had gathered the church together, they rehearsed all that God had done with them, and <u>how he had opened the door of faith unto the Gentiles</u>."

God opened the door of faith unto the heaven Gentiles.

- **1 Corinthians 16:9**

"For <u>a great door and effectual is opened unto me</u>, and *there are* many adversaries."

God opened a door for Paul, but the adversaries were still giving him trouble.

- **Colossians 4:3**

"Withal praying also for us, <u>that God would open unto us a door of utterance</u>, to speak the mystery of Christ, for which I am also in bonds:"

Even in prison, Paul wanted a door opened to preach about the Lord Jesus Christ.

- **Revelation 3:8**
"I know thy works: behold, I have set before thee an open door, and no man can shut it: for thou hast a little strength, and hast kept my word, and hast not denied my name."
Here is a mention of God's open door.
- **Revelation 3:20**
"Behold, I stand at the door, and knock: if any man hear my voice, and open the door, I will come in to him, and will sup with him, and he with me."
In this verse, the Lord Jesus Christ was standing at the door of this church at Laodicea wanting them to open it.

2 Corinthians 2:13

"I had no rest in my spirit, because I found not Titus my brother: but taking my leave of them, I went from thence into Macedonia."

Paul wanted Titus to be with him, but he could not be found. So Paul went to Macedonia.

2 Corinthians 2:14

"Now thanks *be* unto God, which always causeth us to triumph in Christ, and maketh manifest the savour of his knowledge by us in every place."

Paul was thanking God Who always caused him to triumph in Christ.

Verses On Triumph
- **Psalms 25:2**
"O my God, I trust in thee: let me not be ashamed, let not mine enemies triumph over me."
Enemies many times do triumph over genuine Christians.
- **Psalms 41:11**
"By this I know that thou favourest me, because mine enemy doth not triumph over me."
God did not allow David's enemies to triumph over him.
- **Psalms 94:3**
"LORD, how long shall the wicked, how long shall the wicked triumph?"
Thousands and thousands and even tens of thousands are being slaughtered by the terrible Islamic terrorists who are triumphing in many countries.

2 Corinthians 2:15

"**For we are unto God a sweet savour of Christ, in them that are saved, and in them that perish:**"

Genuine Christians are a sweet savour pr fragrance of Christ to both the saved and the lost.
- Ephesians 5:2

"And walk in love, as Christ also hath loved us, and hath given himself for us an offering and a sacrifice to God for a sweetsmelling savour."

The offering of the Lord Jesus Christ was, to God, a sweet smelling savour.

2 Corinthians 2:16

"**To the one *we are* the savour of death unto death; and to the other the savour of life unto life. And who *is* sufficient for these things?**"

To those that are not genuine Christians, true Christians are a fragrance of death unto death, but to genuine Christians, they are a savour of life unto live.
- 2 Corinthians 3:5

"Not that we are sufficient of ourselves to think any thing as of ourselves; but our sufficiency is of God;"

Paul says our sufficiency is of God. It is from God. He is the only sufficient One.

As Paul said here, genuine Christians' sufficiency is from God Himself.
- 2 Corinthians 12:9

"And he said unto me, My grace is sufficient for thee: for my strength is made perfect in weakness. Most gladly therefore will I rather glory in my infirmities, that the power of Christ may rest upon me."

True Christians must rely on God's sufficient grace to help them.

2 Corinthians 2:17

"For we are not as many, which corrupt the word of God: but as of sincerity, but as of God, in the sight of God speak we in Christ."

Verses On Corrupt

Paul was not as many in his day who that corrupted the Words of God. In our day, true Christians should not side with the many, many modern Bible versions that corrupt God's Words such as the New American Standard Version, the American Standard Version, the New International Version, the English Standard Version, or even the New King James Version.

In my computer, I have access to sixty different foreign language versions. They use the wrong Hebrew, Masoretic, and Greek texts and "translate" very loosely from these false texts. There are 8,000 differences in the New Testament Greek texts which contain three hundred and fifty-six doctrinal passages that are wrong.

- **Matthew 6:19-21**

"Lay not up for yourselves treasures upon earth, where moth and rust doth corrupt, and where thieves break through and steal: But lay up for yourselves treasures in heaven, where neither moth nor rust doth corrupt, and where thieves do not break through nor steal: For where your treasure is, there will your heart be also."

Vessels on earth can corrupt, rust, and be stolen, but not the treasures in Heaven.

- **Matthew 7:17**

"Even so every good tree bringeth forth good fruit; but a corrupt tree bringeth forth evil fruit."

A good tree cannot bring forth evil fruit. Neither can a corrupt tree bring forth good fruit

- **Ephesians 4:29**

"Let no corrupt communication proceed out of your mouth, but that which is good to the use of edifying, that it may minister grace unto the hearers."

The language of genuine Christians should not be corrupt or evil, but should be true, honest, and edifying.

2 Corinthians Chapter Three

2 Corinthians 3:1

"Do we begin again to commend ourselves? or need we, as some *others*, epistles of commendation to you, or *letters* of commendation from you?"

Paul mentions three different kinds of commending: (1) commending himself; (2) commending the church; and (3) commending by the church.

- 2 Corinthians 10:12

"For we dare not make ourselves of the number, or compare ourselves with some that commend themselves: but they measuring themselves by themselves, and comparing themselves among themselves, are not wise."

Paul did not want to commend himself or brag about what he had accomplished for his Saviour. To do this is not wise.

- 2 Corinthians 10:18

"For not he that commendeth himself is approved, but whom the Lord commendeth."

The main thing is to have the Lord Jesus Christ commend those who work for Him, not they themselves. Self-commendation is foolish, not wise.

2 Corinthians 3:2

"Ye are our epistle written in our hearts, known and read of all men:"

Paul tells the genuine Christians at Corinth that they are his epistle, written in his heart. They are also known and read of all men. People read them now that they are true Christians rather than lost people. They are written in Paul's heart because they found the Saviour through his ministry.

- **Colossians 4:16**
"And when this epistle is read among you, cause that it be <u>read also in the church of the Laodiceans</u>; and that ye likewise read the *epistle* from Laodicea."

The church was to pass this letter on to those in Laodicea. The Bible is to be read by all genuine Christians. It should not be hidden or put on a shelf to collect dust.

- **1 Thessalonians 5:27**
"I charge you by the Lord <u>that this epistle be read unto all the holy brethren</u>."

Paul wanted his letter to the Thessalonian Christians to be read by all the true Christians. He wanted them to be profited, helped, and uplifted by it.

- **2 Thessalonians 2:15**
"Therefore, brethren, <u>stand fast, and hold the traditions which ye have been taught</u>, whether by word, or our epistle."

Paul wanted the genuine Christians at Thessalonica to stand fast and hold to the teachings that he had taught them either by his words when he visited them, or by his letters to them. Many, if not most, churches today are moving, drifting, and changing their theology, their Bibles, their hymns, their dress standards, and many other things. Paul asks this church to stand fast and hold the traditions that they were taught. Yesterday's truth is still truth today, and also truth tomorrow. They were to hold fast the traditions which they had been taught, including the deity of Christ, His bodily resurrection, His blood atonement, salvation by grace through faith, and all the other doctrines of the Bible.

- **2 Thessalonians 3:14**
"And if any man obey not our word by this epistle, <u>note that man, and have no company with him, that he may be ashamed</u>."

If somebody in that church (or any church even today) does not obey Paul's words in this letter to the genuine Christians at Thessalonica, three things should take place: (1) note or expose this person publicly; (2) have no fellowship with him or her; and (3) do this with the result that he or she might be ashamed.

2 Corinthians 3:3

"*Forasmuch as ye are* **manifestly declared to be the epistle of Christ ministered by us, written not with ink, but with the Spirit of the living God; not in tables of stone, but in fleshy tables of the heart.**"

Paul is speaking about the true Christians at Corinth who were led to Christ by him and received the Holy Spirit because of their genuine salvation.

Once a person is genuinely saved and becomes a true Christian, God the Holy Spirit indwells that person. That word, "*heart,*" occurs five hundred and ninety times in the King James Bible. The heart is very important.

- **1 Corinthians 6:19-20**
  "What? know ye not that your body is the temple of the Holy Ghost *which is* in you, which ye have of God, and ye are not your own? For ye are bought with a price: therefore glorify God in your body, and in your spirit, which are God's."

This is a verse that shows that those who are genuine Christians, really Christians, have God the Holy Spirit indwelling their bodies. These true Christians have two natures–their flesh and the indwelling Holy Spirit. Once a person becomes a true Christian, they do not belong to themselves. They have been bought with a price and are no longer their own. The price was paid by of the Lord Jesus Christ's death on the cross of Calvary.

Because of this, they should glorify God in their bodies. Their bodies are no longer their own.

- **1 Corinthians 2:4**
  "And my speech and my preaching was not with enticing words of man's wisdom, but in demonstration of the Spirit and of power:"

Paul said that his speech and preaching were by the power of the Holy Spirit of God. It was not with the words of his own wisdom.

- **1 Corinthians 3:16**
  "Know ye not that ye are the temple of God, and *that* the Spirit of God dwelleth in you?"

These genuine Christians were now the temple of God because God's Holy Spirit indwelled them.

- **1 John 1:9**
 "If we confess our sins, he is faithful and just to forgive us *our* sins, and to cleanse us from all unrighteousness."

The Greek Word used for *"confess"* here is HOMOLOGEO. It means to say the same thing about sins as God says and agree with Him that the genuine Christians have really sinned. If this is true, God is both faithful and just in forgiving their sins and cleansing them from all unrighteousness.

- **Galatians 5:16-17**
 "*This* I say then, Walk in the Spirit, and ye shall not fulfil the lust of the flesh. For the flesh lusteth against the Spirit, and the Spirit against the flesh: and these are contrary the one to the other: so that ye cannot do the things that ye would."

Since God's Holy Spirit indwells all genuine Christians, they are to walk in the power of the Holy Spirit so as to not fulfill the lusts of their flesh. These two natures are contrary one to the other. There are these two natures inside every true Christian's body. If God the Holy Spirit is controlling them, their flesh will take a back seat. If their flesh is controlling them, the Holy Spirit of God will take a back seat.

- **Ephesians 3:16**
 "That he would grant you, according to the riches of his glory, to be strengthened with might by his Spirit in the inner man;"

God wants to strengthen every true Christian by the Holy Spirit Who indwells them in their inner person.

- **Ephesians 4:30**
 "And grieve not the holy Spirit of God, whereby ye are sealed unto the day of redemption."

The Holy Spirit seals the genuine Christian until the day of redemption. He never leaves them, or forsakes them. They are sealed until the day their redeemed bodies are received. Known, unconfessed sin grieves God the Holy Spirit.

2 Corinthians 3:4

"And such trust have we through Christ to God-ward:"

I believe that trust is that God the Holy Spirit indwells those who are true Christians.

2 Corinthians 3:5

"Not that we are sufficient of ourselves to think any thing as of ourselves; but our sufficiency *is* of God;"

No genuine Christian is sufficient in their own selves, but their sufficiency comes from God. Their sufficiency must come from Him, not from themselves.

- **2 Corinthians 12:9**
  "And he said unto me, <u>My grace is sufficient for thee</u>: for my strength is made perfect in weakness. Most gladly therefore will I rather glory in my infirmities, that the power of Christ may rest upon me."

Paul was stoned at Lystra in the book of Acts, Chapter 14. Those who stoned him dragged him out of the city. I believe that he died for a little while. The Lord took him to Heaven on that occasion. Paul saw things in Heaven that no one had ever seen before. Then the Lord brought him back to earth to continue serving Him. So that he would not be exalted by the wonderful glories of Heaven that he had seen, God gave him a thorn in his flesh. We are not sure what that was. Paul asked three times for God to remove that "*thorn,*" but it was not removed. The Lord told him, "*My grace is sufficient for thee.*" Paul answered, "*most gladly therefore will I rather glory in my infirmities that the power of Christ may rest upon me.*" Paul wanted the inner power of God, regardless of his infirmity.

2 Corinthians 3:6

"Who also hath made us able ministers of the New Testament; not of the letter, but of the spirit: for the letter killeth, but the spirit giveth life."

God made Paul, and the other apostles, to be able ministers or servants of the New Testament by the power of God the Holy Spirit. Every genuine Christian should be God's servant. Many true Christians do not want to serve. They want to be the boss. They want to be the head honcho who is in charge. No, God wants to be in charge of things. He wants His true Christians to be His servants serving Him.

- **1 Corinthians 4:1**

  "Let a man so account of us, as of the ministers of Christ, and stewards of the mysteries of God."

Genuine Christians should be servants and stewards of the mysteries of God. A steward is one that takes care of his master's goods. The only way we can be stewards of what God has given to us in the Scriptures is to know them and defend the proper Hebrew, Aramaic, an Greek original language text and the English King James Bible as well as other proper language Bibles.

- **2 Corinthians 6:4**

  "But in all *things* approving ourselves as the ministers of God, in much patience, in afflictions, in necessities, in distresses,"

True Christians should be ministers and servants of God in patience, afflictions, necessities, and distresses.

- **2 Corinthians 11:15**

  "Therefore *it is* no great thing if his ministers also be transformed as the ministers of righteousness; whose end shall be according to their works."

This verse is talking about fake and phony ministers of the Devil. He has ministers and servants who pretend to be *"Christian,"* but who are not.

- **1 Timothy 1:12**

  "And I thank Christ Jesus our Lord, who hath enabled me, for that he counted me faithful, putting me into the ministry;"

God gave Paul strength, enabled him, and put him into the ministry who before was a Jewish Pharisee.

2 Corinthians 3:7

"But if the ministration of death, written *and* engraven in stones, was glorious, so that the children of Israel could not stedfastly behold the face of Moses for the glory of his countenance; which *glory* was to be done away:"

This verse is referring to the law of Moses which is called *"the ministration of death."* Various sins under the law led to physical death under the law of Moses such as cursing, adultery, homosexuality, and many other sins.

2 Corinthians Preaching Verse-By-Verse   47

- **Exodus 24:12**

"And the LORD said unto Moses, <u>Come up to me into the mount</u>, and be there: and I will give thee tables of stone, and a law, and commandments which I have written; that thou mayest teach them."

That is what the Lord told Moses to do and he did it.

- **Exodus 31:18**

"And he gave unto Moses, when he had made an end of communing with him upon mount Sinai, <u>two tables of testimony, tables of stone, written with the finger of God</u>."

God gave him these two tables of stone that He wrote.

- **Exodus 32:13**

"Remember Abraham, Isaac, and Israel, thy servants, to whom thou swarest by thine own self, and saidst unto them, <u>I will multiply your seed as the stars of heaven</u>, and all this land that I have spoken of will I give unto your seed, and they shall inherit *it* for ever."

This was a promise by God that He fulfilled partially and will complete the fulfillment at a later time.

- **Exodus 32:15**

"And Moses turned, and went down from the mount, and <u>the two tables of the testimony *were* in his hand</u>: the tables *were* written on both their sides; on the one side and on the other were they written."

The writing was the writing of God, engraven upon the tables, written on both sides.

- **Exodus 34:28-35**

"And he was there with the LORD forty days and forty nights; he did neither eat bread, nor drink water. And <u>he wrote upon the tables the words of the covenant</u>, the ten commandments. And it came to pass, when Moses came down from mount Sinai with the two tables of testimony in Moses' hand, when he came down from the mount, that Moses wist not that the skin of his face shone while he talked with him. And when Aaron and all the children of Israel saw Moses, behold, the skin of his face shone; and they were afraid to come nigh him. And Moses called unto them; and Aaron and all the rulers of the congregation returned unto him: and Moses talked with them. And afterward all the children of Israel came nigh: and he gave them in commandment all that the LORD had spoken with him in mount Sinai. And till Moses had done speaking with them, he put a vail on his face. But when Moses went in before the

LORD to speak with him, he took the vail off, until he came out. And he came out, and spake unto the children of Israel that which he was commanded. And the children of Israel saw the face of Moses, that the skin of Moses' face shone: and Moses put the vail upon his face again, until he went in to speak with him."

And so there was something about the law of Moses, even though it brought death, even though we could not keep it, the Israelites could not keep it. We are not now under any part of the law of Moses except the few parts that are written in the New Testament. There was something about it that was glorious because it was from the Lord. Moses had to put a vail over his face when he spoke to the Israelites after being on the mount with the Lord.

2 Corinthians 3:8

"How shall not the ministration of the spirit be rather glorious?"

If the law of Moses was glorious, what about the spirit of God in the New Testament. The Lord Jesus Christ was more glorious than Moses.

- **John 1:14**

"And the Word was made flesh, and dwelt among us, (and we beheld his glory, the glory as of the only begotten of the Father,) full of grace and truth."

The New Testament apostles, like John, beheld the glory of the Lord Jesus Christ.

- **John 17:5**

"And now, O Father, glorify thou me with thine own self with the glory which I had with thee before the world was."

He left the glory of God when He came from heaven to this earth. If the Lord Jesus Christ had kept the glory of God He would have to have had a vail like Moses had. His incarnation was a shield to His perfect glory. At the mount of transfiguration, Peter, James and John saw the glory of the Lord to a certain extent. His features became whiter than snow when He was on that mountain. He prayed the Father might glorify Him with the glory that He had before the world was.

- **John 17:22**

"And the glory which thou gavest me I have given them; that they may be one, even as we are one:"

True Christians have been given part of the glory of the Lord Jesus Christ.

- **John 17:24**
"Father, I will that they also, whom thou hast given me, be with me where I am; that they may behold my glory, which thou hast given me: for thou lovedst me before the foundation of the world."

On this earth, the apostles could not behold His glory. They'd be killed, if they saw the full glory of the Lord Jesus Christ. When they get glorified bodies, genuine Christians will be able to behold His glory in Heaven.

- **Acts 7:55**
"But he, being full of the Holy Ghost, looked up stedfastly into heaven, and saw the glory of God, and Jesus standing on the right hand of God,"

Just before they stoned Stephen to death he saw the glory of God. Stephen, the first Christian martyr, was able to see the glory of God before he died.

- **Romans 8:18**
"For I reckon that the sufferings of this present time *are* not worthy *to be compared* with the glory which shall be revealed in us."

Sufferings on this earth is not to be compared with the glory which will be seen in Heaven.

- **1 Corinthians 2:8**
"Which none of the princes of this world knew: for had they known *it*, they would not have crucified the Lord of glory."

Those who crucified the Lord Jesus Christ did not know of His Deity and power.

- **2 Corinthians 4:6**
"For God, who commanded the light to shine out of darkness, hath shined in our hearts, to *give* the light of the knowledge of the glory of God in the face of Jesus Christ."

He says, every one of those who are true Christians, have been given the knowledge of the glory of God in the face of Jesus Christ. He has shined this in their hearts.

2 Corinthians 3:9

"For if the ministration of condemnation *be* glory, much more doth the ministration of righteousness exceed in glory."

Paul is comparing the law of Moses with the New Testament grace of the Lord Jesus Christ. If the condemnation be glorious, Moses face shone because he saw the glory of the Lord, "*much more doth the ministration of righteousness exceed in* glory."

- **Romans 8:1**

"<u>There is therefore now no condemnation</u> to them which are in Christ Jesus, who walk not after the flesh, but after the Spirit."

No condemnation. Those who are true Christians and are in the Lord Jesus Christ, there is no more condemnation.

- **Romans 3:21-22**

"But now the righteousness of God without the law is manifested, being witnessed by the law and the prophets; Even <u>the righteousness of God *which is* by faith of Jesus Christ</u> unto all and upon all them that believe: for there is no difference:"

God says by genuinely trusting the Lord Jesus Christ as their Saviour, He gives them righteousness.

- **Romans 4:5**

"But to him that worketh not, but believeth on him that justifieth the ungodly, <u>his faith is counted for righteousness</u>."

What a wonderful verse that is. God gives righteousness to genuine Christians who have trusted in the finished work of His Son at Calvary. Their faith is counted for righteousness.

- **Ephesians 2:8-9**

"For <u>by grace are ye saved through faith</u>; and that not of yourselves: *it is* the gift of God: Not of works, lest any man should boast."

True salvation is by God's grace through true faith in the Lord Jesus Christ.

- **Romans 10:4**
   "For Christ *is* the end of the law <u>for righteousness to every one that believeth.</u>"

The Lord Jesus Christ is the end of the law of Moses. We are never to mix Mosaic law with the grace of the Lord Jesus Christ. Genuine and saving trust in the Lord Jesus Christ as their Saviour brings God's righteousness and pardon.

- **Romans 10:10**
   "For with the heart <u>man believeth unto righteousness</u>; and with the mouth confession is made unto salvation."

With the heart a person sincerely believes in what the Lord Jesus Christ has done for them. This alone brings salvation to them.

- **2 Corinthians 5:21**
   "For he hath made him *to be* sin for us, who knew no sin; that we might be <u>made the righteousness of God in him</u>."

God the Father made the Lord Jesus Christ to be sin for all mankind, so that those who believe and receive Him as their Saviour might be saved and be made righteous before God.

- **Galatians 2:21**
   "I do not frustrate the grace of God: for <u>if righteousness *come* by the law</u>, then Christ is dead in vain."

Righteousness could not have come by the law of Moses. If so, Christ's death would have been in vain.

- **Galatians 3:21**
   "*Is* the law then against the promises of God? God forbid: for <u>if there had been a law given which could have given life</u>, verily righteousness should have been by the law."

God's righteousness could not be received by keeping the law of Moses, but only by the substitutionary death of the Lord Jesus Christ and people is belief and trust in Him as their Saviour.

2 Corinthians 3:10

"For even that which was made glorious had no glory in this respect, by reason of the glory that excelleth."

It is talking about the law of Moses. Even though that law of Moses was by works, nobody could keep it. Iit had some glory. Of course, the law of grace, the Lord Jesus is greater glory than that.

For instance,
- **Exodus 24:12**
"And the LORD said unto Moses, <u>Come up to me into the mount</u>, and be there: and I will give thee tables of stone, and a law, and commandments which I have written; that thou mayest teach them."

He was to teach these to the people of Israel. Moses went up. His minister, Joshua, Moses went up to the mount of God. He said to the others,
- **Exodus 24:14-17**
"And he said unto the elders, Tarry ye here for us, until we come again unto you: and, behold, Aaron and Hur *are* with you: if any man have any matters to do, let him come unto them. And Moses went up into the mount, and a cloud covered the mount. And the glory of the LORD abode upon mount Sinai, and the cloud covered it six days: and the seventh day he called unto Moses out of the midst of the cloud. <u>And the sight of the glory of the LORD *was* like devouring fire</u> on the top of the mount in the eyes of the children of Israel.

The glory of the Lord, even in the giving of the law, the Lord's glory was there but there is greater glory of Christ, the Lord Jesus Christ in the New Testament. God's glory shone for Moses and the cloud covered it for six days "and the seventh day he called unto Moses out of the midst of the cloud."
- **Luke 2:9**
"And, lo, the angel of the Lord came upon them, and <u>the glory of the Lord shone round about them</u>: and they were sore afraid."

God's glory was manifested in the New Testament at the cross which showed greater glory than by Moses' law.
- **Luke 2:13-14**
"And suddenly there was with the angel a multitude of the heavenly host praising God, and saying, <u>Glory to God in the highest</u>, and on earth peace, good will toward men."

The Lord Jesus Christ's birth was filled with glory by these angels.
- **Luke 9:32**
"But Peter and they that were with him were heavy with sleep: and <u>when they were awake, they saw his glory</u>, and the two men who stood with him."

On the mount of Transfiguration, Peter, James and John saw the glory of the Lord Jesus Christ after they woke up.

2 Corinthians Preaching Verse-By-Verse

- **John 1:14**

"And the Word was made flesh, and dwelt among us, (and <u>we beheld his glory, the glory</u> as of the only begotten of the Father,) full of grace and truth."

John and the other apostles saw the glory of the Lord Jesus Christ.

- **John 17:5**

"And now, O Father, <u>glorify thou me with thine own self with the glory which I had with thee</u> before the world was."

The Lord Jesus Christ had glory with God the Father before He came to this earth.

2 Corinthians 3:11

"For if that which is done away *was* glorious, much more that which remaineth *is* glorious."

The glory of the Lord Jesus Christ is greater than the law of Moses which has gone away.

2 Corinthians 3:12

"Seeing then that we have such hope, we use great plainness of speech:"

Verses On Speech

Because of his hope, Paul used great plainness of speech.

- **1 Corinthians 2:4**

"And <u>my speech and my preaching *was* not with enticing words of man's wisdom</u>, but in demonstration of the Spirit and of power:"

Many preachers today speak with enticing words that trap people into false doctrines and theology.

- **1 Corinthians 4:19**

"But I will come to you shortly, if the Lord will, and will know, <u>not the speech of them which are puffed up, but the power</u>."

Paul wanted to go back to Corinth if it was God's will. When he went, he did not want to use puffed up speech, but the power of God the Holy Spirit.

- **2 Corinthians 7:4**

"<u>Great *is* my boldness of speech</u> toward you, great *is* my glorying of you: I am filled with comfort, I am exceeding joyful in all our tribulation."

Paul used boldness in speech as he was filled with comfort and joy.

- **John 3:16**
"For God so loved the world, that he gave his only begotten Son, that whosoever believeth in him should not perish, but have everlasting life."

This verse in John 3:16 speaks very plainly and completely denies the false hyper-Calvinist position of salvation.

- **2 Corinthians 10:10**
"For *his* letters, say they, *are* weighty and powerful; but *his* bodily presence *is* weak, and *his* speech contemptible."

Some thought Paul's speech was contemptible. This might have been caused by his thorn in the flesh, but it is not clear. What he wrote and spoke was Biblical and should be believed.

- **Colossians 4:6**
"Let your speech be alway with grace, seasoned with salt, that ye may know how ye ought to answer every man."

Genuine Christians should have gracious speech but it should be seasoned with salt. This would include items that should be used against those who are believing and teaching false doctrines.

- **Titus 2:8**
"Sound speech, that cannot be condemned; that he that is of the contrary part may be ashamed, having no evil thing to say of you."

True Christians' speech should be sound. It should be true to the teachings of the Bible, regardless of how many deny it or do not want to hear it. Many people use foul words and terms in their speech.

2 Corinthians 3:13

"And not as Moses, *which* put a vail over his face, that the children of Israel could not stedfastly look to the end of that which is abolished:"

Genuine Christians should not cover their faces with a vail as Moses did.

- **Exodus 34:33-35**
"And *till* Moses had done speaking with them, he put a vail on his face. But when Moses went in before the LORD to speak with him, he took the vail off, until he came out. His face shone because of the glory of the Lord.

- **Romans 6:14**
"For sin shall not have dominion over you: for ye are not under the law, but under grace."

True Christians are not under any part of the law of Moses.

- **Romans 7:4**
"Wherefore, my brethren, <u>ye also are become dead to the law by the body of Christ</u>; that ye should be married to another, *even* to him who is raised from the dead, that we should bring forth fruit unto God."
Dead to the law refers to the law of Moses.
- **Romans 7:6**
"But now <u>we are delivered from the law</u>, that being dead wherein we were held; that we should serve in newness of spirit, and not *in* the oldness of the letter."
True Christians are no longer under any part of the law of Moses.
- **Romans 10:4**
"For <u>Christ is the end of the law</u> for righteousness to every one that believeth."
What does "end" mean? It means the end. It means finished. Every saved, born-again Christian is no longer under any part of the law of Moses.
- **Galatians 3:24-25**
"Wherefore the law was our schoolmaster *to bring us* unto Christ, that we might be justified by faith."
That is, until Christ came, it is a schoolmaster, teaches unto Christ. But after that faith is come, we are no longer under a schoolmaster." Genuine Christians are no longer under any part of the law of Moses.

2 Corinthians 3:14

"But their minds were blinded: for until this day remaineth the same vail untaken away in the reading of the Old Testament; which *vail* is done away in Christ."

The Jewish minds were blinded. They have a vail over their minds when reading the Old Testament.

Verses On The Jews Being Blinded
- **John 12:40**
"<u>He hath blinded their eyes</u>, and hardened their heart; that they should not see with *their* eyes, nor understand with *their* heart, and be converted, and I should heal them."
The Israelites were blinded. There is blindness even today.

- **Romans 11:7-8**

"What then? Israel hath not obtained that which he seeketh for; but the election hath obtained it, and <u>the rest were blinded</u> (According as it is written, God hath given them the spirit of slumber, <u>eyes that they should not see</u>, and ears that they should not hear;) unto this day."

There were a few Jews, like Paul and the apostles, who came to the Lord Jesus Christ, but most of them were blinded.

2 Corinthians 3:15

"**But even unto this day, when Moses is read, the vail is upon their heart.**"

Verses On The Jews Not Understanding

- **Isaiah 53:5**

"But he *was* wounded for our transgressions, *he was* bruised for our iniquities: the chastisement of our peace *was* upon him; and with his stripes we are healed."

I am told that in the Jewish synagogues and temples, they never read Isaiah 53. It is because it says "*he was wounded for our transgressions,*" That is speaking of the Lord Jesus Christ, the Messiah. This is the Messiah, it is the Lord Jesus Christ. They do not want to read it. They are blinded.

- **Matthew 13:13-14**

"Therefore speak I to them in parables: because they <u>seeing see not; and hearing they hear not, neither do they understand</u>. And in them is fulfilled the prophecy of Esaias, which saith, By hearing ye shall hear, and shall not understand; and seeing ye shall see, and shall not perceive:"

Israel is blinded, even today. The vail is upon the heart and mind of many Jews today.

- **Acts 8:30-31**

"And Philip ran thither to *him*, and heard him read the prophet Esaias, and said, <u>Understandest thou what thou readest? And he said, How can I, except some man should guide me</u>? And he desired Philip that he would come up and sit with him."

And Philip joined the Eunuch and explained that Isaiah was talking about the Lord Jesus Christ Who died for our sins. This man accepted the Lord Jesus Christ as his Saviour and was baptized by Philip.

So, Israel was blinded, the vail was upon their heart, unto this very day, said Paul.

2 Corinthians 3:16

"Nevertheless when it shall turn to the Lord, the vail shall be taken away."

As we have mentioned before, during the Tribulation time, the vail over the eyes and hearts of the Jews will be taken away. Many will come to the Lord Jesus Christ as their Saviour. The Antichrist will be there and as soon as they come to Christ, he will slaughter them. Their vails will be taken away.

- **Zechariah 13:1**

"In that day there shall be a fountain opened to the house of David and to the inhabitants of Jerusalem for sin and for uncleanness."
- In this day, a fountain of faith will be opened to the Israelites.

- **Matthew 23:37-39**

"O Jerusalem, Jerusalem, *thou* that killest the prophets, and stonest them which are sent unto thee, how often would I have gathered thy children together, even as a hen gathereth her chickens under *her* wings, and ye would not! Behold, your house is left unto you desolate. For I say unto you, Ye shall not see me henceforth, till ye shall say, Blessed *is* he that cometh in the name of the Lord."

The eyes of the Jews were blinded when the Lord Jesus Christ was on earth, though He would have taken them in. But they refused Him.

- **Romans 11:23**

"And they also, if they abide not still in unbelief, shall be graffed in: for God is able to graff them in again."

Israel will one day be grafted in again if they no longer have unbelief in the Saviour.

- **Romans 11:25**

"For I would not, brethren, that ye should be ignorant of this mystery, lest ye should be wise in your own conceits; that blindness in part is happened to Israel, until the fulness of the Gentiles be come in."

Israel as a nation has been blinded, at least, "*in part.*"

- **Romans 11:26**

"And so all Israel shall be saved: as it is written, There shall come out of Sion the Deliverer, and shall turn away ungodliness from Jacob:"

When the Lord Jesus Christ returns, ungodliness will be taken away from Israel.

2 Corinthians 3:17

"Now the Lord is that Spirit: and where the Spirit of the Lord *is*, there *is* liberty."

Our nation was founded upon liberty expressed in the Declaration of Independence. Since that time, much of our former liberties have been lost by following the United Nations and by ceasing to practice the clear words of our United States Constitution. This is a very serious condition.

Verses On Liberty

- **Leviticus 25:10**

"And ye shall hallow the fiftieth year, and <u>proclaim liberty throughout *all* the land unto all the inhabitants thereof</u>: it shall be a jubile unto you; and ye shall return every man unto his possession, and ye shall return every man unto his family."

This verse is on our Liberty Bell. Many politicians, and others, have not followed the liberty that once was followed in our nation.

- **Isaiah 61:1**

"The Spirit of the Lord GOD *is* upon me; because the LORD hath anointed me to preach good tidings unto the meek; <u>he hath sent me</u> to bind up the brokenhearted, <u>to proclaim liberty to the captives</u>, and the opening of the prison to *them that are* bound;"

All true Christians should be thankful that the Lord Jesus Christ can deliver those who are bound for Hell when they truly trust the Saviour.

- **John 8:32**

"And ye shall know the truth, and <u>the truth shall make you free</u>."

True spiritual freedom comes when people receive the Lord Jesus Christ as their Saviour.

- **John 8:36**

"If the Son therefore shall make you free, <u>ye shall be free indeed</u>."

True spiritual freedom can only come to people who are genuine Christians.

- **Luke 4:18**
"The Spirit of the Lord *is* upon me, because he hath anointed me to preach the Gospel to the poor; he hath sent me to heal the brokenhearted, to preach deliverance to the captives, and recovering of sight to the blind, to set at liberty them that are bruised,"

The Lord Jesus Christ wanted to "*set at liberty*" those who are in bondage of some sort and deliver those in the bondage of sin.

- **Romans 8:21**
"Because the creature itself also shall be delivered from the bondage of corruption into the glorious liberty of the children of God."

True salvation brings the "*glorious liberty*" spoken of in this verse.

- **Galatians 5:1**
"Stand fast therefore in the liberty wherewith Christ hath made us free, and be not entangled again with the yoke of bondage."

Paul is talking about the law of Moses in this verse. Genuine Christians are to stay away from following the law of Moses and the bondage that this brings.

- **Romans 6:18**
"Being then made free from sin, ye became the servants of righteousness."

Paul is speaking here of being made free from the sin nature when true Christians are walking with the Lord Jesus Christ in accord with His will.

2 Corinthians 3:18

"But we all, with open face beholding as in a glass the glory of the Lord, are changed into the same image from glory to glory, *even* as by the Spirit of the Lord."

The Bible can transform genuine Christians by the indwelling Holy Spirit and they look diligently into God's Words in the proper Bible translation and closely following those Words..

Verses On Following The Bible

- **Luke 10:39**
"And she had a sister called Mary, which also sat at Jesus' feet, and heard his word."

Mary was to be commended because she chose to sit at Jesus' feet and hear His Words.

- **Luke 24:32**

 "And they said one to another, <u>Did not our heart burn within us</u>, while he talked with us by the way, and <u>while he opened to us the scriptures</u>?"
 This verse refers to the two people that the Lord Jesus Christ met after His bodily resurrection. They did not know that the Lord Jesus Christ was the One Who was talking with them. When He broke bread with them, they recognized from His hands that He had been crucified and that this was the bodily resurrected Lord Jesus Christ. As He talked with them about the cross and its meaning, their heart *"burned within"* them. These powerful Words of the Bible can make the hearts of true Christians burn within them as well.

- **Romans 12:2**

 "And be not conformed to this world: but <u>be ye transformed by the renewing of your mind</u>, that ye may prove what *is* that good, and acceptable, and perfect, will of God."
 This transformation can take place by reading and following the Bible's Words.

2 Corinthians Chapter Four

2 Corinthians 4:1

"Therefore seeing we have this ministry, as we have received mercy, we faint not;"

Paul was given a special ministry by the Lord Jesus Christ at his conversion by God's mercy. He was faithful in that ministry as all genuine Christians should be in the ministry God gives them.

Verses On Being Faithful To His Ministry

- **Acts 6:4**

"But we will give ourselves continually to prayer, and to the ministry of the word."

Paul received the ministry from the Lord Jesus Christ when he was saved and continued in it as all true Christians should do today.

- **Acts 20:24**

"But none of these things move me, neither count I my life dear unto myself, so that I might finish my course with joy, and the ministry, which I have received of the Lord Jesus, to testify the Gospel of the grace of God."

Paul was told not to go to Jerusalem because there were those who wanted to kill him. He wanted to fulfill the ministry given to him by the Lord Jesus Christ.

- **2 Corinthians 6:3**

"Giving no offence in any thing, that the ministry be not blamed:"

Paul did not want his ministry wrongly blamed.

- **Ephesians 4:12**

"For the perfecting of the saints, for the work of the ministry, for the edifying of the body of Christ:"

Paul wanted to fulfill the ministry his Saviour had given him.

- **Colossians 4:17**
"And say to Archippus, Take heed to the ministry which thou hast received in the Lord, that thou fulfil it."
Every true Christian should take heed to the ministry God has given them.
- **1 Timothy 1:12**
"And I thank Christ Jesus our Lord, who hath enabled me, for that he counted me faithful, putting me into the ministry;"
Paul was thankful that the Saviour put him into the ministry because He knew he would be faithful.
- **2 Timothy 4:5**
"But watch thou in all things, endure afflictions, do the work of an evangelist, make full proof of thy ministry."
Genuine Christians should use to the full whatever ministry the Lord might give them.

Verses On Mercy

- **Ephesians 2:4**
"But God, who is rich in mercy, for his great love wherewith he loved us,"
God's richness in mercy offers eternal life to every sinner who genuinely trusts the Lord Jesus Christ as their Saviour, even though they deserve to go to Hell.
- **1 Timothy 1:13**
"Who was before a blasphemer, and a persecutor, and injurious: but I obtained mercy, because I did *it* ignorantly in unbelief."
God showed his mercy on the Apostle Paul who was so wicked and corrupt.
- **1 Timothy 1:16**
"Howbeit for this cause I obtained mercy, that in me first Jesus Christ might shew forth all longsuffering, for a pattern to them which should hereafter believe on him to life everlasting."
Paul knew very well that God showed him mercy rather than judgment.
- **Hebrews 4:16**
"Let us therefore come boldly unto the throne of grace, that we may obtain mercy, and find grace to help in time of need."
True Christians should come boldly to the throne of grace to obtain God's mercy.

- **1 Peter 1:3**
"<u>Blessed be the God and Father</u> of our Lord Jesus Christ, which <u>according to his abundant mercy hath begotten us again unto a lively hope</u> by the resurrection of Jesus Christ from the dead,"
God's abundant mercy makes it possible for sinners to be born-again by true faith in the Lord Jesus Christ.

Verses On Faint

- **Isaiah 40:29-31**
"<u>He giveth power to the faint</u>; and to *them that have* no might he increaseth strength. Even the youths shall faint and be weary, and the young men shall utterly fall: But they that wait upon the LORD shall renew *their* strength; they shall mount up with wings as eagles; <u>they shall run, and not be weary;</u> *and* <u>they shall walk, and not faint</u>."
God says He can give power to genuine Christians who faint.

- **Luke 18:1**
"And he spake a parable unto them to *this end*, that <u>men ought always to pray, and not to faint</u>;"
Biblical Prayer to the Lord will enable His true Christians not to faint.

- **2 Corinthians 4:16**
"<u>For which cause we faint not</u>; but though our outward man perish, yet the inward *man* is renewed day by day."
Paul never fainted in the ministries that his Saviour gave him.

- **Galatians 6:9**
"And let us not be weary in well doing: for <u>in due season we shall reap, if we faint not</u>."
The reaping of well doing will be accomplished *if we faint not*.

- **Hebrews 12:3**
"For <u>consider him that endured such contradiction of sinners</u> against himself, <u>lest ye</u> be wearied and <u>faint in your minds</u>."
Considering the enduring of the Lord Jesus Christ will prevent fainting in the minds of true Christians.

- **Hebrews 12:5**
"And ye have forgotten the exhortation which speaketh unto you as unto children, My son, despise not thou the chastening of the Lord, <u>nor faint when thou art rebuked of him</u>:"
Genuine Christians should not faint when they are rebuked by the Lord.

2 Corinthians 4:2

"But have renounced the hidden things of dishonesty, not walking in craftiness, nor handling the word of God deceitfully; but by manifestation of the truth commending ourselves to every man's conscience in the sight of God."

Paul has renounced such things as dishonesty. Such renouncing today would include exposing various English Bible versions such the American Standard Verison, the New American Standard Version, the New International Version, the Revised Standard Version, the English Standard Version and many, many more.

Verses On Deceitful
- **Ephesians 4:14**

"That we *henceforth* be no more children, tossed to and fro, and carried about with every wind of doctrine, by the sleight of men, *and* cunning craftiness, whereby they lie in wait to deceive;"

People with modern Bible versions which are not based on the proper Hebrew, Aramaic, and Greek manuscripts and which are not translated accurately deceive those who read them.

- **Proverbs 14:25**

"A true witness delivereth souls: but a deceitful *witness* speaketh lies."

Though they will not admit it, deceitful witnesses speak lies.

- **Proverbs 27:6**

"Faithful *are* the wounds of a friend; but the kisses of an enemy *are* deceitful."

Nobody likes to be wounded, but wounds are faithful and clear. However, when enemies give their kisses, this is deceitful. So with the kiss by Judas Iscariot on the Lord Jesus Christ.

- **Jeremiah 17:9**

"The heart is deceitful above all things, and desperately wicked: who can know it?"

Every single person born of Adam has a deceitful heart. Even those who are born-again, their hearts are part of their old flesh and therefore deceitful.

- **Jeremiah 48:10**
"Cursed be he that doeth the work of the LORD deceitfully, and cursed be he that keepeth back his sword from blood."
Satan's ministers pretend to do the work of the Lord, but do it in a deceitful manner. This is true of Satan's ministers. He has his lost ministers in many, many pulpits of the world.

2 Corinthians 11:13
"For such are false apostles, deceitful workers, transforming themselves into the apostles of Christ."
These deceitful workers are fakes, phonies, and disgusting. There are many such around the world.

- **Ephesians 4:22**
"That ye put off concerning the former conversation the old man, which is corrupt according to the deceitful lusts;"
The old natures of humans are corrupt and deceitful.

- **Hebrews 3:13**
"But exhort one another daily, while it is called To day; lest any of you be hardened through the deceitfulness of sin."
Sin is a very deceitful thing. It hardens people against the Lord.

2 Corinthians 4:3

"But if our Gospel be hid, it is hid to them that are lost:"

The Gospel of Christ is the good news that the Lord Jesus Christ came into the world to seek and to save those who are lost. Those who are lost must realize they are lost and bound for Hell. That is the first part of the Gospel. Secondly, they must realize that the Lord Jesus Christ died for their sins and the sins of the whole world. If they do not believe He died for their sins and that they must sincerely trust Him as their Saviour, they are lost.

- **Psalms 119:176**
"I have gone astray like a lost sheep; seek thy servant; for I do not forget thy commandments."
Realizing that a person is lost is the first step of their realizing need to be saved.

- **Ezekiel 34:16**
"I will seek that which was lost, and bring again that which was driven away, and will bind up that which was broken, and will strengthen that which was sick: but I will destroy the fat and the strong; I will feed them with judgment."
Like Ezekiel, we should have an interest in seeking the lost and giving them the Gospel message of our Saviour.

- **Matthew 10:6**

"But <u>go rather to the lost sheep</u> of the house of Israel."

Lost sheep must be found and lost sinners must come to the Saviour and be saved.

- **Matthew 15:24**

"But he answered and said, <u>I am not sent but unto the lost sheep of the house of Israel</u>."

That is why the Lord Jesus Christ came into this world. He went first to lost Israel and they rejected Him. Then He went to the lost Gentiles.

- **Matthew 18:11**

"For <u>the Son of man is come to save that which was lost</u>."

Saving lost people is why the Lord Jesus Christ came into this world and died on the cross.

- **Luke 15:4**

"What man of you, having an hundred sheep, if he lose one of them, doth not leave the ninety and nine in the wilderness, and <u>go after that which is lost</u>, until he find it?"

And that is what we have to do to those that are lost. They do not think they are lost but they are lost. People that are without Christ, the only genuine Saviour, can be saved if they truly trust Him.

- **Luke 15:32**

"It was meet that we should make merry, and be glad: for this <u>thy brother</u> was dead, and is alive again; and <u>was lost, and is found</u>."

The older brother wondered why his father was so merry. It was because his younger brother was lost and now was found.

- **Luke 19:10**

"For <u>the Son of man is come to seek and to save that which was lost</u>."

This is why the Lord Jesus Christ came into this world. It was to save with eternal life those lost people who believe on Him as their Saviour.

2 Corinthians 4:4

"In whom the god of this world hath blinded the minds of them which believe not, lest the light of the glorious Gospel of Christ, who is the image of God, should shine unto them."

This is referring back to the lost people in the previous verse. Satan, the god of this world, blinded the minds lest Christ's glorious Gospel should shine on them. Blind minds are more serious even than blind eyes.

Verses On Satan, The god Of This World
- **Matthew 25:41**

"Then shall he say also unto them on the left hand, Depart from me, ye cursed, into everlasting fire, prepared for the devil and his angels:"

Hell's Lake of Fire was prepared for Satan and his angels.

- **Luke 4:8**

"And Jesus answered and said unto him, Get thee behind me, Satan: for it is written, Thou shalt worship the Lord thy God, and him only shalt thou serve."

When the Lord Jesus Christ was in the wilderness forty days and nights, Satan tried to tempt him to sin, but the Saviour rebuked him.

- **Luke 22:3**

"Then entered Satan into Judas surnamed Iscariot, being of the number of the twelve."

Satan entered into one of the disciples that the Lord Jesus Christ chose, Judas Iscariot. Judas was not saved. He was lost. Satan cannot enter into genuine Christians. He can influence them greatly, but he cannot indwell them. The Holy Spirit of God indwells true Christians.

- **John 8:44**

"Ye are of *your* father the devil, and the lusts of your father ye will do. He was a murderer from the beginning, and abode not in the truth, because there is no truth in him. When he speaketh a lie, he speaketh of his own: for he is a liar, and the father of it."

The Lord Jesus Christ was speaking to the Pharisees who were children of the Devil.

- **Acts 26:18**
"To open their eyes, *and* to turn them from darkness to light, and *from* the power of Satan unto God, that they may receive forgiveness of sins, and inheritance among them which are sanctified by faith that is in me."

Paul sought to turn the lost people of his day from Satan's power unto the power of God.

- **Ephesians 4:27**
"Neither give place to the devil."

Genuine Christians should not give the Devil any room or space in their lives.

- **Ephesians 6:11**
"Put on the whole armour of God, that ye may be able to stand against the wiles of the devil."

Only by true Christians using God's armor can they stand against the Devil's strategies and tricks.

- **1 Corinthians 7:5**
"Defraud ye not one the other, except *it be* with consent for a time, that ye may give yourselves to fasting and prayer; and come together again, that Satan tempt you not for your incontinency."

When genuine Christians who are married violate God's rules for married love in this verse, Satan might tempt and test them.

- **2 Corinthians 2:11**
"Lest Satan should get an advantage of us: for we are not ignorant of his devices."

True Christians should not be ignorant of Satan's devices to take advantage of them.

- **2 Corinthians 11:14**
"And no marvel; for Satan himself is transformed into an angel of light."

Satan is the darkest creature in the world, but he is able to be transformed into an angel of light. This fools and deceives many people.

- **1 Thessalonians 2:18**
"Wherefore we would have come unto you, even I Paul, once and again; but Satan hindered us."

Satan is able to hinder people like he hindered Paul several times.

- **1 Timothy 3:7**
"Moreover he must have a good report of them which are without; lest he fall into reproach and the snare of the devil."

Paul is talking about the qualifications of deacons, here. They must have a good report of the non-Christians so as not to fall into the Devil's snare.

- **James 4:7**
"Submit yourselves therefore to God. Resist the devil, and he will flee from you."

Always resist the Devil so that he will flee from you. Do not ever say yes or agree with him.

- **1 Peter 5:8**
"Be sober, be vigilant; because your adversary the devil, as a roaring lion, walketh about, seeking whom he may devour:"

Be vigilant about the roaring lion Devil.

- **Revelation 12:9**
"And the great dragon was cast out, that old serpent, called the Devil, and Satan, which deceiveth the whole world: he was cast out into the earth, and his angels were cast out with him."

Satan has these four names and deceives the whole world.

- **Revelation 20:10**
"And the devil that deceived them was cast into the lake of fire and brimstone, where the beast and the false prophet *are*, and shall be tormented day and night for ever and ever."

The Devil will be cast into the lake of fire and be tormented day and night for ever and ever.

Verses On Light

- **John 1:4**
"In him was life; and the life was the light of men."

The Lord Jesus Christ is the light of men.

- **John 1:7**
"The same came for a witness, to bear witness of the Light, that all *men* through him might believe."

John the Baptist came to bear witness of the Saviour Who is the Light.

- **John 3:19**
"And this is the condemnation, that light is come into the world, and men loved darkness rather than light, because their deeds were evil."

Because of their evil deeds, men love darkness rather than light.

- **John 8:12**
"Then spake Jesus again unto them, saying, <u>I am the light of the world</u>: he that followeth me shall not walk in darkness, but shall have the light of life."

One of the Names for the Lord Jesus Christ is the Light of the world.

- **John 12:46**
"<u>I am come a light into the world</u>, that whosoever believeth on me should not abide in darkness."

The Lord Jesus Christ came as a Light into the world.

- **Acts 26:18**
"To open their eyes, *and* <u>to turn *them* from darkness to light</u>, and *from* the power of Satan unto God, that they may receive forgiveness of sins, and inheritance among them which are sanctified by faith that is in me."

God wants every one in the world, through trusting His Son, to turn from their Satan's darkness into His Light.

- **1 Peter 2:9**
"But ye *are* a chosen generation, a royal priesthood, an holy nation, a peculiar people; that ye should shew forth the praises of him who hath <u>called you out of darkness into his marvellous light</u>:"

True Christians have been called out from their darkness into the marvelous Light of the Lord Jesus Christ.

2 Corinthians 4:5

"**For we preach not ourselves, but Christ Jesus the Lord; and ourselves your servants for Jesus' sake.**"

Paul, as a servant, was not preaching himself. He was preaching the Lord Jesus Christ. That is what every Bible-believing, genuine Christian should do. They should preach about the Lord Jesus Christ, not about themselves.

2 Corinthians 4:6

"**For God, who commanded the light to shine out of darkness, hath shined in our hearts, to *give* the light of the knowledge of the glory of God in the face of Jesus Christ.**"

Paul was talking to the true Christians at Corinth. The hearts of those who are genuinely saved, have God's light.

Verses On Light And Darkness
- **Genesis 1:3**

"And God said, <u>Let there be light</u>: and there was light."
The whole world was in darkness at creation, and God said let there be light and it was made by Him.
- **Isaiah 9:2**

"<u>The people that walked in darkness have seen a great light</u>: they that dwell in the land of the shadow of death, <u>upon them hath the light shined</u>."
The great Light was the Lord Jesus Christ Himself.
- **Acts 26:18**

"To open their eyes, *and* <u>to turn *them* from darkness to light</u>, and *from* the power of Satan unto God, that they may receive forgiveness of sins, and inheritance among them which are sanctified by faith that is in me."
God is interested in turning people from darkness to light.
- **Romans 13:12**

"The night is far spent, the day is at hand: let us therefore cast off the works of darkness, and <u>let us put on the armour of light</u>."
Every born-again, saved, genuine Christian should cast off all those works of darkness and put on God's armour of His Light.
- **Ephesians 5:8**

"For ye were sometimes darkness, but <u>now *are ye* light in the Lord: walk as children of light</u>:"
Once true Christians turn to the Light of the world, the Lord Jesus Christ, they should walk as children His Light.

Verses On Darkness
- **Ephesians 5:11**

"And <u>have no fellowship with the unfruitful works of darkness</u>, but rather reprove *them*."
Reprove means to shine the light upon the works of darkness. We seek to do that in various ways. We do not fellowship with darkness but reprove and expose it. Though people that are being exposed do not like to be exposed, they should be exposed regardless.
- **Colossians 1:13**

"Who hath <u>delivered us from the power of darkness</u>, and hath translated *us* into the kingdom of his dear Son:"
Only born-again, saved, genuine Christians have been delivered from the power of darkness.

- **2 Peter 2:4**
"For if God spared not the angels that sinned, but cast *them* down to hell, and <u>delivered *them* into chains of darkness</u>, to be reserved unto judgment;"
Angels that sinned were delivered into chains of darkness to be judged.

2 Corinthians 4:7

"But we have this treasure in earthen vessels, that the excellency of the power may be of God, and not of us."

The treasure of God's salvation is in earthen vessels or vessels of clay. This shows that the power of true Christians is of God and not from them.

Verses On Treasure

- **Proverbs 15:6**
"<u>In the house of the righteous *is* much treasure</u>: but in the revenues of the wicked is trouble."
Those who have the righteousness of the Lord Jesus Christ have much spiritual treasure.

- **Proverbs 15:16**
"Better *is* little with the fear of the LORD than <u>great treasure and trouble therewith</u>."
Little with the Lord is better than great treasure and much trouble along with it.

- **Matthew 6:20-21**
"But <u>lay up for yourselves treasures in heaven</u>, where neither moth nor rust doth corrupt, and where thieves do not break through nor steal: For <u>where your treasure is, there will your heart be also</u>."
Treasures in Heaven are far more helpful to true Christians rather than treasures on earth no matter how great they are.

- **Luke 12:21**
"So *is* <u>he that layeth up treasure for himself</u>, and is not rich toward God."
God is far better for us than any earthly treasure we can gather.

2 Corinthians 4:8

"*We are* troubled on every side, yet not distressed; *we are* perplexed, but not in despair;"

The Greek Word for "*troubled*" means "*to be pressed in, straightened out in a narrow place. To be in distress. In a narrow place, cramped, and reduced to straights.*" The Greek Word for "*perplexed*" means: "*without resources, to be left wanting, to be at a loss.*" There are a number of **verses on these** words.

Verses On Troubled And Perplexed

- **John 14:1**

"Let not your heart be troubled: ye believe in God, believe also in me."

The Lord Jesus Christ told His disciples not to let their hearts be troubled. He was going back to His Father's Home in Heaven.

- **John 14:27**

"Peace I leave with you, my peace I give unto you: not as the world giveth, give I unto you. Let not your heart be troubled, neither let it be afraid."

The Saviour told his disciples not to have their hearts troubled or be afraid.

- **2 Corinthians 7:5**

"For, when we were come into Macedonia, our flesh had no rest, but we were troubled on every side; without *were* fightings, within *were* fears."

Paul and his followers were troubled on every side when coming to Macedonia. There were fightings without and fears within.

- **2 Corinthians 7:6**

"Nevertheless God, that comforteth those that are cast down, comforted us by the coming of Titus;"

Though Paul and his companions were cast down and troubled they were comforted by Titus.

- **2 Timothy 2:9**

"Wherein I suffer trouble, as an evil doer, *even* unto bonds; but the word of God is not bound."

Paul was writing from a Roman prison. It was his last letter before Rome beheaded him. This certainly was great "*trouble.*"

- **1 Peter 3:14**
  "But and if ye suffer for righteousness' sake, happy *are ye*: and be not afraid of their terror, <u>neither be troubled</u>;"

Do not be troubled by the terrors of people. God is able to help you in any circumstances.

- **2 Samuel 22:7**
  "<u>In my distress I called upon the LORD</u>, and cried to my God: and he did hear my voice out of his temple, and my cry *did enter* into his ears."

David called upon the Lord in his distress and cried to his God and God heard him.

- **1 Kings 1:29**
  "And the king sware, and said, *As* the LORD liveth, that hath <u>redeemed my soul out of all distress</u>,"

There are wonderful things that God can do, including helping the genuine Christians in all their distress.

- **Psalms 18:6**
  "<u>In my distress I called upon the LORD, and cried unto my God: he heard my voice</u> out of his temple, and my cry came before him, *even* into his ears."

This verse is similar to 2 Samuel 22:7 above.

- **Psalms 25:17**
  "<u>The troubles of my heart are enlarged</u>: *O* <u>bring thou me out of my distresses</u>."

Prayer by true Christians is always to be made in their troubles and in their distresses.

- **Psalms 107:6**
  "Then <u>they cried unto the LORD in their trouble, *and* he delivered them out of their distresses</u>."

That is the proper place for genuine Christians to cry when in trouble or distress.

- **Psalms 120:1**
  "<u>In my distress I cried unto the LORD</u>, and he heard me."

The Lord always hears them when true Christians cry unto Him.

- **Isaiah 25:4**
  "For thou hast been a strength to the poor, <u>a strength to the needy in his distress, a refuge from the storm</u>, a shadow from the heat, when the blast of the terrible ones *is* as a storm *against* the wall."

The Lord is a strength for needy true Christians in their distresses and storms.

- **Romans 8:35**
"<u>Who shall separate us from the love of Christ</u>? *shall tribulation, or <u>distress</u>, or <u>persecution</u>, or famine, or nakedness, or <u>peril</u>, or sword?*"
None of these things mentioned above can separate genuine Christians from the love of Christ.
- **2 Corinthians 6:4**
"But in all *things* <u>approving ourselves as the ministers of God</u>, in much patience, <u>in afflictions, in necessities, in distresses</u>,"
Paul wanted to be a minister of God in all troubles that might come his way.
- **2 Corinthians 12:10**
"Therefore <u>I take pleasure in infirmities, in reproaches, in necessities, in persecutions, in distresses for Christ's sake</u>: for when I am weak, then am I strong."
Paul took pleasure in all these difficult things mentioned for the sake of the Lord Jesus Christ.

2 Corinthians 4:9

"Persecuted, but not forsaken; cast down, but not destroyed;"

Paul was victorious in all these difficulties that came in his ministry for the Saviour. The Greek Word for "*persecuted*" means "*to pursue in a hostile manner, pressed down, against people.*" The Greek Word for "*forsaken*" means "*totally abandoned, utterly forsaken.*" The Greek Word for "cast down" means "*thrown back, put into a lower place.*" Though Paul experienced all of these adversities, he was not destroyed in his faith and service for His Saviour.

Verses On Persecution
- **Matthew 5:10**
"Blessed *are* they which are <u>persecuted for righteousness' sake</u>: for theirs is the kingdom of heaven."
Though unpleasant, this persecution is to be expected from unrighteous people.

- **Matthew 5:11**
"Blessed are ye, when *men* shall revile you, and persecute *you*, and shall say all manner of evil against you falsely, for my sake."

To have people revile, persecute, and speak evil against you falsely for the sake of the Lord Jesus Christ is to be blessed according to this verse.

- **Matthew 5:12**
"Rejoice, and be exceeding glad: for great *is* your reward in heaven: for so persecuted they the prophets which were before you."

True Christians and churches today are persecuted like the true prophets of old in many different areas.

- **John 5:16**
"And therefore did the Jews persecute Jesus, and sought to slay him, because he had done these things on the sabbath day."

The Jews were going to kill the Lord Jesus Christ because he was performing miracles on the sabbath day.

- **John 15:20**
"Remember the word that I said unto you, The servant is not greater than his lord. If they have persecuted me, they will also persecute you; if they have kept my saying, they will keep yours also."

Genuine Christians will be persecuted just like the Lord Jesus Christ was.

- **Acts 8:1**
"And Saul was consenting unto his death. And at that time there was a great persecution against the church which was at Jerusalem; and they were all scattered abroad throughout the regions of Judaea and Samaria, except the apostles."

Before Saul became a Christian, he and others made a great persecution of the churches.

- **Acts 9:4-5**
"And he fell to the earth, and heard a voice saying unto him, Saul, Saul, why persecutest thou me? And he said, Who art thou, Lord? And the Lord said, I am Jesus whom thou persecutest: *it is* hard for thee to kick against the pricks."

The Lord Jesus Christ asked Paul from Heaven why he was persecuting Him.

- **Acts 22:4**
"And I persecuted this way unto the death, binding and delivering into prisons both men and women."

Paul admitted that he persecuted the Christian way very strongly.

- **Acts 26:11**
"And I punished them oft in every synagogue, and compelled *them* to blaspheme; and being exceedingly mad against them, I persecuted *them* even unto strange cities."

Paul's persecution of genuine Christians is outlined clearly in this verse.

- **Romans 8:35**
"Who shall separate us from the love of Christ? *shall* tribulation, or distress, or persecution, or famine, or nakedness, or peril, or sword?"

No amount of persecution can separate a genuine Christian from the love of Christ.

- **Galatians 1:13**
"For ye have heard of my conversation in time past in the Jews' religion, how that beyond measure I persecuted the church of God, and wasted it:"

Paul admitted that he persecuted the church beyond measure.

- **Galatians 1:23**
"But they had heard only, That he which persecuted us in times past now preacheth the faith which once he destroyed.

Before his conversion, Paul persecuted Christians greatly.

- **2 Timothy 3:12**
"Yea, and all that will live godly in Christ Jesus shall suffer persecution."

All godly Christians will suffer persecution.

Verses On Forsaken

- **Psalms 27:10**
"When my father and my mother forsake me, then the LORD will take me up."

When mothers and fathers forsake us, the Lord will rescue true Christians.

- **Psalms 71:9**
"Cast me not off in the time of old age; forsake me not when my strength faileth."

David prayed that God would not forsake him when he was old.

- **Psalms 71:18**

"Now also when I am old and grayheaded, O God, forsake me not; until I have shewed thy strength unto *this* generation, *and* thy power to every one *that* is to come."

David did not want God to forsake him until he had served Him successfully.

- **2 Timothy 4:10**

"For Demas hath forsaken me, having loved this present world, and is departed unto Thessalonica; Crescens to Galatia, Titus unto Dalmatia."

Demas forsook Paul because he loved the world more than the Lord Jesus Christ.

- **Hebrews 13:5**

"*Let your* conversation *be* without covetousness; *and be* content with such things as ye have: for he hath said, I will never leave thee, nor forsake thee."

The Lord Jesus Christ will never forsake a genuine Christian.

Verses On Cast Down

- **Psalms 37:24**

"Though he fall, he shall not be utterly cast down: for the LORD upholdeth *him with* his hand."

God's true followers might fall, but will not be utterly be cast down.

- **2 Corinthians 7:6**

"Nevertheless God, that comforteth those that are cast down, comforted us by the coming of Titus;"

God comforts the genuine Christians who are cast down.

Verses On Destroy

- **Psalms 11:3**

"If the foundations be destroyed, what can the righteous do?"

One of the very important foundations is the Words of God.

- **Proverbs 29:1**

"He, that being often reproved hardeneth *his* neck, shall suddenly be destroyed, and that without remedy."

Reproof, if honest and true, should be listened to and acted upon favorably. If not, the person will be destroyed.

- **Isaiah 9:16**

"For the leaders of this people cause *them* to err; and *they that are* led of them are destroyed."

Those who follow erring leaders will be destroyed.

- **Luke 17:29**
"But the same day that Lot went out of Sodom <u>it rained fire and brimstone from heaven, and destroyed</u> *them* <u>all</u>."
Except for a few people, Sodom was destroyed by fire and brimstone from Heaven.

2 Corinthians 4:10

"Always bearing about in the body the dying of the Lord Jesus, that the life also of Jesus might be made manifest in our body."

Verses About True Christians Dying With Christ
Paul says here, to the Christians there in Corinth, "*bearing about in the body <u>the dying of the Lord Jesus</u>,*"
- **Galatians 2:20a**
"<u>I am crucified with Christ</u>: nevertheless I live;"
Every true Christian died with Christ. We were in Christ at His death.
- **Romans 6:8**
"Now <u>if we be dead with Christ</u>, we believe that we shall also live with him:"
Genuine Christians died with Christ.
- **Galatians 6:14**
"But God forbid that I should glory, save in the cross of our Lord Jesus Christ, by whom the world is crucified unto me, and I unto the world."

Another very important verse. The world hates the cross. They despised the Lord Jesus Christ and crucified him. It is a very serious situation but he says you should glory in the cross and the Lord Jesus Christ. That is the one whose got the victory, the one that died for the sins of the world on the cross of Calvary. You should glory in it. Paul says that the life of Jesus might be manifest in our bodies.

2 Corinthians 4:11

"For we which live are alway delivered unto death for Jesus' sake, that the life also of Jesus might be made manifest in our mortal flesh."

True Christians are delivered unto death for the sake of their Lord Jesus Christ so that Christ's life might be manifest in their flesh.

2 Corinthians 4:12

"So then death worketh in us, but life in you."

Death works in genuine Christians, but the life of the Lord Jesus Christ works in these Christians.

If you add them up, you will find **twenty-five problems** like death and difficulties that came to Paul in his life.

- **2 Corinthians 11:23**

"Are they ministers of Christ? (I speak as a fool) I *am* more; in labours more abundant, in stripes above measure, in prisons more frequent, in deaths oft."

- **2 Corinthians 11:24**

"Of the Jews five times received I forty *stripes* save one."

- **2 Corinthians 11:25**

"Thrice was I beaten with rods, once was I stoned, thrice I suffered shipwreck, a night and a day I have been in the deep;"

- **2 Corinthians 11:26**

"*In* journeyings often, *in* perils of waters, *in* perils of robbers, *in* perils by *mine own* countrymen, *in* perils by the heathen, *in* perils in the city, *in* perils in the wilderness, *in* perils in the sea, *in* perils among false brethren;"

- **2 Corinthians 11:27**

"In weariness and painfulness, in watchings often, in hunger and thirst, in fastings often, in cold and nakedness."

2 Corinthians 4:13

"We having the same spirit of faith, according as it is written, I believed, and therefore have I spoken; we also believe, and therefore speak;"

Notice the words, "*as it is written*." These Word are in the perfect tense in the Greek language. This speaks of the Bible preservation of the original Hebrew, Aramaic, and Greek Words of the Old and New Testaments which Words underlie the King James Bible which accurately translated these Words into English.

- **Psalms 116:10**
"I believed, therefore have I spoken: I was greatly afflicted:" The Psalmist believed God's Words and therefore spoke about them, if when he was afflicted. Today, most churches, colleges, seminaries (even the former Fundamentalist groups) no longer believe or teach that God's original Words have been preserved until this day. They hate it, and despise it.
- **Psalms 107:2**
"Let the redeemed of the LORD say so, whom he hath redeemed from the hand of the enemy;" These truths should be proclaimed and defended by those who have been redeemed.
- **1 Peter 3:15**
"But sanctify the Lord God in your hearts: and be ready always to give an answer to every man that asketh you a reason of the hope that is in you with meekness and fear:" True Christians should be prepared to give answers to those who differ with the truth with meekness and fear.

2 Corinthians 4:14

"Knowing that he which raised up the Lord Jesus shall raise up us also by Jesus, and shall present *us* with you."

The proper Greek text has been used in the King James Bible. It says clearly that God Who raised up the Lord Jesus bodily from death shall also raise up genuine Christians **"by Jesus."** Every one of the versions and translations that are not founded on the Received New Testament Greek Text, as our King James Bible is, have a tremendous, gigantic, doctrinal error in this verse. nstead of reading **"by Jesus,"** they read **"with Jesus."** By using the false Gnostic critical Greek text, and the false words of **"with Jesus"** they deny the Lord Jesus Christ is able to raise the true Christians from the dead. They also deny that, if the genuine Christians will not be raised until the Lord Jesus Christ is raised, He has not yet been raised and will not be raised until the rapture of the born-again Christians.

This serious doctrinal error is taught by such false translations as the ASV, NASV, RSV, Holman Study Bible, The Common English Version, the Darby version, the ESV, the NKJV, the New Century Version, the Latin Vulgate, and many, many more versions based on the Critical Gnostic Greek text.

Dr. Jack Moorman's book lists 356 doctrinal passages also found in these false New Testaments, like the Westcott and Hort and Nestle-Aland Greek editions.

2 Corinthians 4:15

"For all things *are* for your sakes, that the abundant grace might through the thanksgiving of many redound to the glory of God."

Verses On Grace

- **2 Corinthians 8:9**

"For ye know the grace of our Lord Jesus Christ, that, though he was rich, yet for your sakes he became poor, that ye through his poverty might be rich."

The Lord Jesus Christ's grace brought the offer of salvation to the sinful world.

- **Ephesians 1:7**

"In whom we have redemption through his blood, the forgiveness of sins, according to the riches of his grace;"

God has great riches of His grace that He can provide for true Christians who trust Him.

- **Ephesians 2:5**

"Even when we were dead in sins, hath quickened us together with Christ, (by grace ye are saved;)"

God's grace has provided salvation for those who trust the Lord Jesus Christ as their Saviour.

- **Ephesians 2:7**

"That in the ages to come he might shew the exceeding riches of his grace in *his* kindness toward us through Christ Jesus."

God's exceeding riches of His grace will be showed in the coming ages.

- **Ephesians 2:8-10**

"For by grace are ye saved through faith; and that not of yourselves: *it is* the gift of God: Not of works, lest any man should boast."

No one can be saved except through God's grace by genuinely trusting His Son as their Saviour.

- **Hebrews 4:16**

"Let us therefore come boldly unto the throne of grace, that we may obtain mercy, and find grace to help in time of need."

It is from the throne of grace, that genuine Christians can obtain God's mercy and grace.

Verses On Thanksgiving
- **Psalms 95:2**

"Let us come before his presence with thanksgiving, and make a joyful noise unto him with psalms."

Genuine Christians should be thankful Christians.

- **Psalms 100:4**

"Enter into his gates with thanksgiving, *and* into his courts with praise: be thankful unto him, *and* bless his name."

It is a wonderful thing for which genuine Christians can be thankful for what they have.

- **Philippians 4:6**

"Be careful for nothing; but in every thing by prayer and supplication with thanksgiving let your requests be made known unto God."

Prayer and thanksgiving should be part of every true Christian's life.

- **Colossians 2:7**

"Rooted and built up in him, and stablished in the faith, as ye have been taught, abounding therein with thanksgiving."

Genuine Christians should have an abundance of thankfulness to the Lord Jesus Christ.

2 Corinthians 4:16

"For which cause we faint not; but though our outward man perish, yet the inward *man* is renewed day by day."

Though the "*outward man*" might get weaker and weaker as we live longer, yet the "*inward man*" of the genuine Christian can be "*renewed day by day*" by following God's Words daily, praying, and walking in the Lord's will.

Verses On Fainting
- **Proverbs 24:10**

"*If* thou faint in the day of adversity, thy strength *is* small."

If the strength of genuine Christians is small, they will undoubtedly faint when adversity comes upon them. They must stand firm for the Lord, whatever the cost might be.

- **Galatians 6:9**

"And let us not be weary in well doing: for in due season we shall reap, if we faint not."

True Christians should not be weary in well doing. Good that is defined in the Bible, will reap rewards if they do not faint.

2 Corinthians 4:17

"For our light affliction, which is but for a moment, worketh for us a far more exceeding *and* eternal weight of glory;"

Paul calls these twenty-five different problems he has undergone (listed in 2 Corinthians 4:11) *"light affliction."* Such afflictions are for only a moment compared with eternity where they work toward an eternal weight of glory.

Verses On Afflictions

- **1 Thessalonians 1:6**

"And ye became followers of us, and of the Lord, having received the word in much affliction, with joy of the Holy Ghost:"

Though these genuine Christians received the Words of God with much affliction, there was joy of the Holy Spirit also connected with it.

- **Hebrews 11:25**

"Choosing rather to suffer affliction with the people of God, than to enjoy the pleasures of sin for a season;"

Better to suffer affliction with God's people than enjoy temporary sinful pleasures.

- **James 5:10**

"Take, my brethren, the prophets, who have spoken in the name of the Lord, for an example of suffering affliction, and of patience."

These prophets were examples not only of suffering affliction, but of their patience that went along with the affliction.

2 Corinthians 4:18

"While we look not at the things which are seen, but at the things which are not seen: for the things which are seen *are* temporal; but the things which are not seen *are* eternal."

Those who are genuine Christians, should be looking, not only at the things they can see. They should also consider eternal things that they cannot see.

- **John 20:25**
  "The other disciples therefore said unto him, We have seen the Lord. But he said unto them, Except I shall see in his hands the print of the nails, and put my finger into the print of the nails, and thrust my hand into his side, I will not believe."

Thomas was there at the second evening service after the bodily resurrection of the Lord Jesus Christ. He missed the first evening service after His resurrection. The other apostles told Thomas that they had seen the Saviour after His bodily resurrection, but Thomas did not believe them.

- **John 20:29**
  "Jesus saith unto him, Thomas, because thou hast seen me, thou hast believed: blessed are they that have not seen, and yet have believed."

The apostles met on Sundays, the first day of the week. They met on Sundays just like we meet on Sundays. Thomas was there on that Sunday when the Lord Jesus Christ's resurrected body appeared right through the closed door. His resurrected body was able to do this. Thomas was there and he saw Him. He did not do as he said he would do but said *"My Lord and my God."* Thomas believed only by seeing, not by faith alone.

- **1 Corinthians 2:9**
  "But as it is written, Eye hath not seen, nor ear heard, neither have entered into the heart of man, the things which God hath prepared for them that love him."

The "*eye hath not seen,*" the things which God hath prepared for human beings. These things must be revealed by the Words of God.

- **Colossians 2:18**
  "Let no man beguile you of your reward in a voluntary humility and worshipping of angels, intruding into those things which he hath not seen, vainly puffed up by his fleshly mind,"

A true Christian should not be fooled by "*intruding into those things which he hath not seen.*" They should not be trying to change such things as Heaven, Hell, the resurrection of the saved, and many other things.

- **Hebrews 11:1**
  "Now <u>faith</u> is the substance of things hoped for, <u>the evidence of things not seen</u>."

Faith is what brings to life and reality things that true Christians cannot see with their eyes. This includes things such as the Lord Jesus Christ's presence in Heaven, His being seated at the right hand of God, His bodily return at the Rapture of genuine Christians, and many, many other important things.

- **Hebrews 11:7**
  "<u>By faith Noah, being warned of God of things not seen as yet</u>, moved with fear, prepared an ark to the saving of his house; by the which he condemned the world, and became heir of the righteousness which is by faith."

Noah had faith that the universal flood God warned him about would come to pass. He obeyed God's orders to build an ark to save alive certain ones He wanted to spare from death.

Seven pairs of clean animals came into that ark and a pair of all the rest of the animals. Noah, his wife, his three sons and their three wives–entered the ark and were spared. He might have offered others to enter, but they did not go in because of their unbelief.

- **Hebrews 11:27**
  "<u>By faith he forsook Egypt</u>, not fearing the wrath of the king: for he endured, as seeing him who is invisible."

Moses forsook Egypt as *"seeing Him Who is invisible."* He was used, though not perfect, in leading the Israelites in the wilderness for forty years.

- **1 Peter 1:8**
  "<u>Whom having not seen, ye love</u>; in whom, though now ye see *him* not, yet believing, ye rejoice with joy unspeakable and full of glory:"

Genuine Christians love the Lord Jesus Christ, even though they have never seen Him. My wife's father, R. O. Sanborn, used to quote this verse as he led in prayer in our local church.

2 Corinthians Chapter Five

2 Corinthians 5:1

"For we know that if our earthly house of *this* tabernacle were dissolved, we have a building of God, an house not made with hands, eternal in the heavens."

Many people do not believe there is an intermediate body for genuine Christians. I believe the Scriptures are clear about this teaching. It is different than their resurrected body that they will have when the Lord Jesus Christ returns at the rapture. It is a special body, an intermediate body, that they receive at their death.

This verse pictures a building of God in the heavens, we have which true Christians have immediately when they die. Not until the rapture, when the Lord Jesus Christ returns, will they receive their resurrected bodies from the grave.

Verses On Life

- **Genesis 2:7** And the LORD God formed man *of* the dust of the ground, and breathed into his nostrils the breath of life; and man became a living soul.

Just dust, that is all we are.

- **Job 10:9**

"Remember, I beseech thee, that thou hast made me as the clay; and wilt thou bring me into dust again?"

Yes, He will bring us into dust. He made us of clay. Just clay vessels very meek and mild.

- **Psalms 90:9**

"For all our days are passed away in thy wrath: we spend our years as a tale *that is told*."

Just a story. And when someone ends a story that is it. It is a tale that is told.

- **Psalms 90:10**
  "The days of our years _are_ threescore years and ten; and if by reason of strength _they be_ fourscore years, yet _is_ their strength labour and sorrow; for it is soon cut off, and we fly away."

The life ends here at 70 or 80 in this verse. Some live longer of course. We have 88 so far. And my wife has 89. And I guess Anthony has even more than that.

- **Psalms 90:12**
  "So teach _us_ to number our days, that we may apply _our_ hearts unto wisdom."

Since our life is brief we have to be taught to number our days. Genuine Christians do not know the number of our days, so we should value and use our days wisely for the Lord Jesus Christ.

- **Psalms 102:11**
  "My days _are_ like a shadow that declineth; and I am withered like grass."

David realized his days were like a shadow that soon vanished away. When the sun goes down on life, the shadow goes down forever.

- **Psalms 144:4**
  "Man is like to vanity: his days _are_ as a shadow that passeth away."

Again life is like a shadow that passes away soon. Once the light goes the shadow goes. It passes away.

- **Ecclesiastes 6:12**
  "For who knoweth what is good for man in this life, all the days of his vain life which he spreadeth as a shadow? for who can tell a man what shall be after him under the sun?"

Here is another verse on life's length like a shadow. This is the third verse on shadows.

- **Ecclesiastes 8:13**
  "But it shall not be well with the wicked, neither shall he prolong _his_ days, _which are_ as a shadow; because he feareth not before God."

The wicked's days are especially like a shadow. They do not seem to care that they will die. Some of them when they die we are told that they yell and shout and scream. Maybe that is when they discover there is a hell.

2 Corinthians 5:2

"For in this we groan, earnestly desiring to be clothed upon with our house which is from heaven:"

"*In this*"that is in this body, *we,* now it is talking about believers, genuine Christians, not the unsaved people. Christians, we groan earnestly desiring to be clothed upon with our house, ' which is from heaven. This body is the Christian's house. After a Christian dies they don't just float around like a spirit in the heavens somewhere. There is a unit. There is a house for us. We are not told what kind of house, the type of it, the shape of it. There is some kind of intermediate body. They desire to be clothed with their house from Heaven which would be their intermediate body that is talked about here. They do not wait until the rapture. This is a house immediate upon death. Some place to dwell in heaven.

Verses On True Christians' Resurrected Bodies
- 1 Thessalonians 4:14-17

"For if we believe that Jesus died and rose again, even so them also which sleep in Jesus will God bring with him. For this we say unto you by the word of the Lord, that we which are alive *and* remain unto the coming of the Lord shall not prevent them which are asleep <u>For the Lord himself shall descend from heaven with a shout, with the voice of the archangel, and with the trump of God: and the dead in Christ shall rise first: Then we which are alive *and* remain shall be caught up together with them in the clouds, to meet the Lord in the air: and so shall we ever be with the Lord</u>."

That speaks of the rapture. Those who sleep in Jesus are those who have died, that are genuine Christians. That speaks of the rapture. Those who have died, their bodies will be resurrected and raised up and glorified.

- **1 Thessalonians 4:15**

"For this we say unto you by the word of the Lord, that we which are alive *and* remain unto the coming of the Lord shall not prevent them which are asleep."

That speaks of those of us who are in the grave. The dead in Christ will rise and get their resurrected bodies from the grave. It is not that temporary house or body in verse 2. At the rapture those alive will be taken and changed. Together we will go to meet the Lord in the air. The heavenly house has nothing to do with that resurrected body. It is a separate body. It is an intermediate body. Not a resurrected body at all. In 1 Corinthians 15, it is very clear, our God has given a body,

- **1 Corinthians 15:38**

"But <u>God giveth it a body as it hath pleased him, and to every seed his own body</u>."

All true Christians will have their own resurrected bodies.

- **1 Corinthians 15:42-44**

"So also is the resurrection of the dead. It is sown in corruption; <u>it is raised in incorruption</u>: It is sown in dishonour; <u>it is raised in glory</u>: it is sown in weakness; <u>it is raised in power</u>: It is sown a natural body; <u>it is raised a spiritual body</u>. There is a natural body, and there is a spiritual body."

This is the rapture. These are some of the differences between the natural bodies and the Christians' resurrected bodies. But before this resurrected body, genuine Christians will have an intermediate body.

2 Corinthians 5:3

"If so be that being clothed we shall not be found naked."

God does not want Genuine Christians after they died to be "*naked*" in Heaven. He wants each genuine Christian to be a definable unity. We are not sure what kind of a body that will be, but it will last for them until their permanent and glorified body is given at their rapture by the Lord Jesus Christ.

2 Corinthians 5:4
"For we that are in *this* tabernacle do groan, being burdened: not for that we would be unclothed, but clothed upon, that mortality might be swallowed up of life."
True Christians are not just spirits, but they will be clothed upon, with their special intermediate bodies. True Christians will be clothed with these bodies until they receive their resurrected bodies at the rapture of the Lord Jesus Christ.

2 Corinthians 5:5
"Now he that hath wrought us for the selfsame thing *is* God, who also hath given unto us the earnest of the Spirit."
Paul is still speaking of genuine Christians, not unbelievers. He has given every one of them th earnest of God the Holy Spirit. "*Earnest*" means sort of a down-payment for their state in Heaven with their resurrected bodies and all of their eternal blessings. Some people say, "But I don't feel the Holy Spirit within me." We do not have to feel the Holy Spirit. We just have to believe the Bible.

Verses On Sealing
- **2 Corinthians 1:22**

"<u>Who hath also sealed us</u>, and given the earnest of the Spirit in our hearts."
Every true Christian is indwelled by the Holy Sprit. And then the fight is on between our old flesh which we will never lose till we stand before Christ, and the Holy Spirit.

- **Ephesians 1:13**

"In whom ye also *trusted*, after that ye heard the word of truth, the Gospel of your salvation: in whom also <u>after that ye believed, ye were sealed with that holy Spirit of promise</u>,"
All genuine Christians have been sealed by the Holy Spirit. They are saved for eternity and can never lose their salvation, though they can lose their fellowship with the Lord if they do not walk according to the Bible and the Holy Spirit. The sealing by the Holy Spirit cannot be broken. If we walk in the Spirit we will not fulfill the lusts of the flesh.

2 Corinthians 5:6

"Therefore *we are* always confident, knowing that, whilst we are at home in the body, we are absent from the Lord:"

Paul was confident that he could not be "*at home*" in his body and with the Lord in Heaven at the same time. When he was in his earthly body, he was absent from the Lord in Heaven.

- **Philippians 1:23**

"For I am in a strait betwixt two, having a desire to depart, and to be with Christ; which is far better:"

Paul did not want to stay around on earth in his natural body. He knew what Heaven was because when he was stoned at Lystra and died, he went to Heaven and experienced its glory. He wanted to go there, but he knew it was best for the Philippians for him to stay to minister to them and to many others.

2 Corinthians 5:7

"(For we walk by faith, not by sight:)"

No genuine Christian living today has seen the Lord Jesus Christ. They must walk by faith.

Verses On Faith

- **Hebrews 11:1**

"Now faith is the substance of things hoped for, the evidence of things not seen."

This is the Biblical definition of "*faith*." In a real sense, it is seeing the unseen. Faith has evidence.

- **Hebrews 11:6-7**

"But without faith *it is* impossible to please *him*: for he that cometh to God must believe that he is, and *that* he is a rewarder of them that diligently seek him. By faith Noah, being warned of God of things not seen as yet, moved with fear, prepared an ark to the saving of his house; by the which he condemned the world, and became heir of the righteousness which is by faith."

Without faith, it is impossible to please God. Without genuine faith in the Lord Jesus Christ, no one can please God. The Lord Jesus Christ died for the sins of the entire world. To be redeemed and become a true Christian person is to follow the Bible's truths especially in the following three areas:

2 Corinthians Preaching Verse-By-Verse

1. People must believe they are sinners in God's sight and cannot go to Heaven, but are destined to the Lake of Fire in Hell.

2. People must believe that the Lord Jesus Christ died in their place to atone for their sins on the cross to save them from Hell and take them to Heaven when they die.

3. People must genuinely believe on, receive, and accept the Lord Jesus Christ as their Saviour Who died on the cross, in their place, to atone for their sins.

Noah had faith in God's Words that there would be a universal flood of water that would destroy all land and air life except those who were safe by going into the giant boat that Noah would construct. After it had rained and the flood waters were all over the earth, God shut the door of the ark so that no one else could enter and be spared death by drowning.

- **John 10:9**

"<u>I am the door: by me if any man enter in, he shall be saved</u>, and shall go in and out, and find pasture."

The Lord Jesus Christ is the only Door to Heaven whereby people must truly trust to go to Heaven.

- **Hebrews 11:8**

"<u>By faith Abraham</u>, when he was called to go out into a place which he should after receive for an inheritance, <u>obeyed; and he went out</u>, not knowing whither he went."

By faith in God's words to him, he went out in obedience to the Lord to a strange foreign country.

- **Hebrews 11:17**

"<u>By faith Abraham, when he was tried, offered up Isaac</u>: and he that had received the promises offered up his only begotten *son*,"

By faith in God's promises, Abraham was willing to offer up his on, Isaac. Though at the last minute, Isaac was spared, God still counted Abraham's willingness to offer Isaac, God considered that Abraham had "*offered up his only begotten son.*" Abraham believed God was able to raise up Isaac from the dead.

2 Corinthians 5:8

"**We are confident, I** *say***, and willing rather to be absent from the body, and to be present with the Lord.**"

When Paul was stoned at Lystra and died, he went to Heaven. From this experience, he was very willing to be absent from his body and be present with the Lord. But he knew that he had more work to do for the Lord Jesus Christ on earth before going to Heaven.

Verses On Heaven
- **Philippians 1:23**

"For I am in a strait betwixt two, <u>having a desire to depart, and to be with Christ; which is far better</u>:"
Paul mentions how being with the Lord Jesus Christ in Heaven is far better than being on earth.
- **John 14:1-3**

"Let not your heart be troubled: ye believe in God, believe also in me. In my Father's house are many mansions: if *it were* not *so*, I would have told you. I go to prepare a place for you. And if I go and prepare a place for you, <u>I will come again, and receive you unto myself; that where I am, *there* ye may be also</u>."
The Lord Jesus Christ **will** come again for all the genuine Christians, in the rapture, to take them to Heaven. He will also take them to Heaven at their death if they die before the Lord Jesus Christ has not returns in the rapture. At many funerals of lost, non-true Christian people, the presiding pastors wrongly put the dead person in Heaven. Only genuine Christians go to Heaven upon their death.
- **2 Corinthians 12:2**

"I knew a man in Christ above fourteen years ago, (whether in the body, I cannot tell; or whether out of the body, I cannot tell: God knoweth;) <u>such an one caught up to the third heaven</u>."
Paul is speaking here of his being stoned at Lystra mentioned in Acts 14. He died and was taken to the third Heaven.

- 1 John 3:2

"Beloved, now are we the sons of God, and it doth not yet appear what we shall be: but we know that, <u>when he shall appear, we shall be like him; for we shall see him as he is.</u>" The genuine Christians are going to be like the Lord Jesus Christ in Heaven when He appears at the rapture. At that time, they will have resurrected bodies and will be like their Saviour.

- **Revelation 21:1-4**

"And I saw a new heaven and a new earth: for the first heaven and the first earth were passed away; and there was no more sea. And I John saw the holy city, new Jerusalem, coming down from God out of heaven, prepared as a bride adorned for her husband. And I heard a great voice out of heaven saying, Behold, the tabernacle of God *is* with men, and he will dwell with them, and they shall be his people, and <u>God himself shall be with them, *and be* their God. And God shall wipe away all tears from their eyes; and there shall be no more death, neither sorrow, nor crying, neither shall there be any more pain: for the former things are passed away.</u>"

2 Corinthians 5:9

"Wherefore we labour, that, whether present or absent, we may be accepted of him."

That should be the goal of every genuine Christian, to be accepted of the Lord Jesus Christ. They should labor to be accepted of Him. This is very important.

2 Corinthians 5:10

"For we must all appear before the judgment seat of Christ; that every one may receive the things *done* in *his* body, according to that he hath done, whether *it be* good or bad."

This "*we*" is referring to every true Christian, who has trusted the Lord Jesus Christ as their Saviour. It does not refer to non-Christians. They will not appear before the judgment seat of Christ, but before the Great White Throne Judgment and be sent to Hell's Lake of Fire.

The purpose of the Judgment Seat of Christ is that everyone "*may receive the things done in his body.* 1 Corinthians 3 explains this judgement in detail.

Verses On Judging
- **Romans 14:10**

"But <u>why dost thou judge thy brother</u>? or why dost thou set at nought thy brother? for we shall all stand before the judgment seat of Christ."

Genuine Christians should not judge each other. That is up to Lord Jesus Christ at the Judgement Seat of Christ.

- **1 Corinthians 4:5**

"Therefore <u>judge nothing before the time, until the Lord come</u>, who both will bring to light the hidden things of darkness, and will make manifest the counsels of the hearts: and then shall every man have praise of God."

True Christians should be patient and wait for the Saviour to judge these Christians.

Verses On Fellowship With Christ
- **Philippians 1:20**

"According to my earnest expectation and *my* hope, that in nothing I shall be ashamed, but *that* with all boldness, as always, *so* now also <u>Christ shall be magnified in my body</u>, whether *it be* by life, or by death."

Paul wanted to have such fellowship with the Lord Jesus Christ that He might be magnified in his body, whether by life or by death.

- **1 John 1:6-10**

"If we say that we have fellowship with him, and walk in darkness, we lie, and do not the truth: But <u>if we walk in the light, as he is in the light, we have fellowship one with another</u>, and the blood of Jesus Christ his Son cleanseth us from all sin. If we say that we have no sin, we deceive ourselves, and the truth is not in us. If we confess our sins, he is faithful and just to forgive us *our* sins, and to cleanse us from all unrighteousness. If we say that we have not sinned, we make him a liar, and his word is not in us."

Fellowship with the Saviour comes to pass when genuine Christians walk in the light of God's Words.

2 Corinthians 5:11

"Knowing therefore the terror of the Lord, we persuade men; but we are made manifest unto God; and I trust also are made manifest in your consciences."

Verses On The Terror Of The Lord

- **Genesis 35:5**

"And they journeyed: and <u>the terror of God was upon the cities that *were* round about them</u>, and they did not pursue after the sons of Jacob."

As Jacob journeyed toward Bethel the terror of God was upon some of the people in the cities where he journeyed.

- **Jeremiah 32:21**

"And <u>hast brought forth thy people Israel out of the land of Egypt</u> with signs, and with wonders, and with a strong hand, and with a stretched out arm, and <u>with great terror</u>;"

Israel's miraculous exit from Egypt was with a strong hand and great terror.

Verses On Witnessing

- **Psalms 107:2**

"<u>Let the redeemed of the LORD say *so*</u>, whom he hath redeemed from the hand of the enemy;"

Genuine Christians should tell those who are not Christians about the Gospel of the Lord Jesus Christ. All you can do is tell the truth about the Lord Jesus Christ Who died for their sins, realizing that they are sinners, and truly trust and believe on Him as their Saviour.

- **Romans 1:16**

"For <u>I am not ashamed of the Gospel of Christ: for it is the power of God unto salvation to every one that believeth</u>; to the Jew first, and also to the Greek."

Paul was not ashamed of the Gospel about the Lord Jesus Christ. All genuine Christians should not be ashamed of that good news either. This good news should be shared with all people whether Jews or Gentiles.

2 Corinthians 5:12

"For we commend not ourselves again unto you, but give you occasion to glory on our behalf, that ye may have somewhat to *answer* them which glory in appearance, and not in heart."

Paul did not want to brag on himself but he did want to tell the Corinthians a little about himself so that if people asked about him they had somewhat to answer. The people he was speaking to were people that were glorying in their appearance and not in their hearts. The heart is the most important thing to glory in. The heart is the inside of us. It is the most important part of us. It is the soul, the spirit, the heart. Some people glory just in that which is seen on the outside.

For example, the Lord said to Samuel, whom am I going to get for the king? Who should be the right king?

- **1 Samuel 16:7**

"But the LORD said unto Samuel, Look not on his countenance, or on the height of his stature; because I have refused him: for *the LORD seeth* not as man seeth; for man looketh on the outward appearance, but the LORD looketh on the heart."

Countenance means his face and his looks. That is true. Man looks on the outward appearance. Jesse's first son just looked like a king. But God said, "*the LORD seeth* not as man seeth; I have refused him". "[T]he LORD looketh on the heart." That is true. Man does look on the outward appearance. What do you look like? What are we dressed like? How do we act? Is our hair combed? Is our face alright? Are they handsome or ugly or beautiful or whatever? God looks upon the heart. He looks inside of us.

- **John 7:24**

"Judge not according to the appearance, but judge righteous judgment."

A lot of people say we are not supposed to judge anything. No, that is false. The scriptures tell us to judge but not according to the appearance. Judge righteous judgment. We are to have righteous judgment based upon the scriptures, the Word of God and truth when we judge. For with what judgment we judge, we shall be judged as it says in Matthew 7:1. In 1 Corinthians 10 and verse 7 Paul reprimanded the Corinthian Christians.

- **2 Corinthians 10:7**

"Do ye look on things after the outward appearance? If any man trust to himself that he is Christ's, let him of himself think this again, that, as he is Christ's, even so *are we* Christ's."

Look not after the outward appearance. That is what they were doing and that is what Paul was reprimanding them for.

Verse 10 talks about Paul's letter,

- **2 Corinthians 10:10**

"For *his* letters, say they, *are* weighty and powerful; but *his* bodily presence is weak, and *his* speech contemptible."

These Corinthian Christians were looking at Paul's presence. I do not know why he was weak. He probably looked small. Maybe he had a speech impediment. We do not know. His speech was contemptible. They did not respect Paul. God says some people are glorying in appearance, concerned about what they look like rather than in the heart. God wants them to glory in the heart.

2 Corinthians 5:13

"For whether we be beside ourselves, *it is* to God: or whether we be sober, *it is* for your cause."

These are interesting terms. Strange that Paul would say this. "[W]hether we be beside ourselves," That is EXISTAMI, the Greek word means "to be out of one's mind, to be crazy." Well, people thought he was crazy. Paul was not crazy. Maybe people think we are crazy. That is what that Greek word means, "beside ourselves, crazy." That is how God sees them. God is the one who is serving. Notice, "whether we be sober." That word SUFRONEO "in a sound mind, not crazy." He says, "it is for your cause." So either way you look at it, whether Paul is considered to be crazy, or of a sound mind, it is very important for the sake of the Lord and the sake of the people to whom he is speaking. Its an interesting sentence there, an interesting phrase and contrast.

2 Corinthians 5:14

"For the love of Christ constraineth us; because we thus judge, that if one died for all, then were all dead:"

The love of Christ constraineth us. That word "constraineth" is SUNEXO. It means to hold us together, to compress us, as compress us on every side. Paul said, The Lord Jesus Christ loves me. You love me because I love Him. He constrains us to do many things for him for the good. We judge "that if one died for all." Now notice, this is speaking of the Lord Jesus Christ, who died for all the sins of the whole world. This is putting the negative to the hyper-Calvinists heresy. We have many friends, Christian friends, that are hyper-Calvinists, that say Christ only died for the elect, a small, little group of people. The rest of you sinners out there, he did not die for you. LIE. Absolute lie. Heresy. "If one died for all." The Lord Jesus died for the sins of the whole world. It does not mean everyone is saved. You have to genuinely trust him to be saved but he paid the penalty for your sins. Then all were dead.

Now notice, all were dead, "dying with Christ," as it says in scripture,

- **Galatians 2:20**

    "I am crucified with Christ: nevertheless I live; yet not I, but Christ liveth in me: and the life which I now live in the flesh I live by the faith of the Son of God, who loved me, and gave himself for me."

Crucified with Christ. Everyone that is genuinely saved was there at the cross. Physically we were not there but in God's eyes, we died with Christ. That is what dying with Christ means.

- **Matthew 14:22**

    "And straightway Jesus constrained his disciples to get into a ship, and to go before him unto the other side, while he sent the multitudes away."

They probably did not want to get in the ship. He constrained them, he urged them, constrained them to get into the ship and go to the other side while he sent the multitudes away. He wanted the disciples on the other side. They did not want to go. He constrained them.

- **Luke 24:29**
"But they constrained him, saying, Abide with us: for it is toward evening, and the day is far spent. And he went in to tarry with them."

They constrained him. This is the resurrected Saviour with the two on the road to Emmaus. They came to the house. They constrained him and said abide with us for it is toward evening and the day is long spent. He did abide with them.

- **Acts 16:15**
"And when she was baptized, and her household, she besought us, saying, If ye have judged me to be faithful to the Lord, come into my house, and abide *there*. And she constrained us."

Lydia was the lady that was welcoming the apostles to come in and stay with them and abide. Wonderful hospitality that Lydia had and they went in and stayed with them.

Another verse on constrain,

- **Acts 28:19**
"But when the Jews spake against *it*, I was constrained to appeal unto Caesar; not that I had ought to accuse my nation of."

The Jews wanted to kill Paul. They wanted to bring him to Jerusalem and kill him, murder him on the way. That was why he appealed to Caesar that he should be released from Roman imprisonment. He was constrained because the Jews were against him. They would have killed him. Paul made an appeal to Caesar. Now Caesar was not concerned but the law was. Roman law in those days was a fair law apparently. Paul appealed to Caesar and he was justified. Caesar justified him, let him loose and released him from that first Roman imprisonment as we know.

- **1 Peter 5:2**
"Feed the flock of God which is among you, taking the oversight *thereof*, not by constraint, but willingly; not for filthy lucre, but of a ready mind;"

That is what a pastor, bishop, elder should do, feed the flock, not with food but spiritual food, and as an overseer of the local congregation. A lot of churches, have a bunch of deacons and they will rule the whole show. Deacons rule the pastor. Horrible! Deacon rule is not scriptural rule. A deacon is to be a servant. It is the pastor (bishop, elder) that takes the oversight. They are to be servants. They are there to help him. Now, notice, not by constraint. A man is not to be pressured into taking the oversight and to feed the flock.

Secondly, not only is it not to be by constraint, but not for filthy lucre. No pastor is to take the oversight to feed the flock because of money. We have pictures, all over the world, millionaire pastors, for the sake of lucre. Pastors are to be of a willing but ready mind.

- **Ephesians 2:1**

"And you *hath he quickened*, who were dead in trespasses and sins;"

Now these are some of the things, constraint and dying with Christ.

2 Corinthians 5:15

"And *that* he died for all, that they which live should not henceforth live unto themselves, but unto him which died for them, and rose again."

Notice he died for all. There again. Unlimited atonement. I am glad that in Dallas seminary, even in those early days, Dr. Chafer, the founder and first President, my teacher for four years, believed and taught the unlimited atonement. He was a Calvinist but he was only a four-point Calvinist. He took away the "L", limited atonement and changed it to "U", unlimited atonement. He died for all the sins of the world and those that trust him can be saved. Only those who genuinely trust him. "They which live" those that are living for Christ, those that are genuinely saved, "should not henceforth", after being saved, after being genuine Christians, not live unto themselves, "but unto him which died for them, and rose again." Now that Gospel song, "Living for Jesus"

"Living for Jesus a life that is true,
    Striving to please Him in all that I do;

Living for the Lord Jesus. That should be the goal of every genuine Christian.

- **Philippians 1:20**
"According to my earnest expectation and *my* hope, that in nothing I shall be ashamed, but *that* with all boldness, as always, *so* now also Christ shall be magnified in my body, whether *it be* by life, or by death."

After Paul was saved, after he became a genuine Christian, lived for Christ. Whether by life or by death, he did not care. We want to live for Christ. And if the FEMA camps come to get us and we mistakenly go with them in the bus, instead of staying home and saying NO, I am going to stay here. If we mistakenly go with them on the bus and they take us to the camps. And the United Nations, whether it is China or Russia, or whoever it is, may kill us, help us to be faithful unto death in that situation. Paul says, "whether it be by life, or by death" that Christ might be magnified in my body. "For to me to live is Christ and to die is gain."

- **2 Corinthians 5:9**
"Wherefore we labour, that, whether present or absent, we may be accepted of him."

That should be the goal of every born-again Christian, to be accepted of the Lord Jesus.

2 Corinthians 5:16

"Wherefore henceforth know we no man after the flesh: yea, though we have known Christ after the flesh, yet now henceforth know we *him* no more."

It could be Paul, even before he was saved, had known about the Lord Jesus Christ, but now he is risen, he is in heaven. In Acts chapter 9, Paul saw him, the Lord Jesus, in heaven. Saw him, not after the flesh, but after the Spirit.

- **Acts 9:5a**
"And he said, Who art thou, Lord? And the Lord said, I am Jesus whom thou persecutest:"

And this event led him to Christ and he was saved. The Lord Jesus now was in heaven and no longer in the flesh on earth.

2 Corinthians 5:17

"Therefore if any man *be* in Christ, *he is* a new creature: old things are passed away; behold, all things are become new."

Thirteen new things belong to concerned and dedicated genuine Christians. It is important that we see these thirteen new things. These are only for genuine Christians. A lot of people just call themselves Christians in words. These are for genuine, born again, saved Christians. If you are reading this and have never genuinely trusted the Lord Jesus as Saviour, realize you are a sinner, and Christ died for you. Believe on him and trust in him. If you are not a genuine Christians, these promises are not for you. I urge you to trust the Lord, that they may be. Notice these thirteen things.

The first new thing,
- **John 3:3**

   Jesus answered and said unto him, Verily, verily, I say unto thee, Except a man be born again, he cannot see the kingdom of God.

Born again, the new birth. Those who are genuine Christians have been born again.
- **1 Peter 1:23**

   "Being born again, not of corruptible seed, but of incorruptible, by the word of God, which liveth and abideth for ever."

So, we have a new birth, if we are genuine Christians.

A second new thing, "if any man be in Christ," a new creature, a new relationship.
- **Galatians 4:6**

   "And because ye are sons, God hath sent forth the Spirit of his Son into your hearts, crying, Abba, Father."

We have a new relationship. Now, before we were genuine Christians, if we are genuine Christians today, Satan was our Father. Genuine Christians have a new Father, a new relationship. God, heavenly Father, is our Father. Abba, Father.

A third new thing, about a genuine Christian, a new fellowship.

- **1 Corinthians 1:9**
"God is faithful, by whom ye were called unto the fellowship of his Son Jesus Christ our Lord."

People that are lost, if you are here today or listening on the internet that are lost, you have no fellowship with the Lord. Only those who are genuinely saved have fellowship with the Lord Jesus Christ. A new fellowship.

- **1 John 1:3**
"That which we have seen and heard declare we unto you, that ye also may have fellowship with us: and truly our fellowship is with the Father, and with his Son Jesus Christ."

Only genuine Christians can have true fellowship with the Father and with the Son.

The fourth new thing. A new cleansing.

- **1 John 1:7**
"But if we walk in the light, as he is in the light, we have fellowship one with another, and the blood of Jesus Christ his Son cleanseth us from all sin."

If we are a genuine Christian, the blood of Christ has cleansed us from all sin.

- **1 John 1:9**
"If we confess our sins, he is faithful and just to forgive us our sins, and to cleanse us from all unrighteousness."

This is for genuine Christians, believers, if we confess our sins. A new cleansing.

A fifth new thing, if we are genuine Christians, is a new song.

- **Psalms 40:3**
"And he hath put a new song in my mouth, even praise unto our God: many shall see it, and fear, and shall trust in the LORD."

- **Psalms 96:1**
"O sing unto the LORD a new song: sing unto the LORD, all the earth."

The disciples in prison, sang a new song at midnight,

- **Acts 16:30**
"And brought them out, and said, Sirs, what must I do to be saved?"

A new song. Revelation says only those that are saved know that song.

A sixth thing, a new thing genuine Christians have. A new name.
- **Isaiah 62:2**

"And the Gentiles shall see thy righteousness, and all kings thy glory: and thou shalt be called by a new name, which the mouth of the LORD shall name."
- **Revelation 2:17**

"He that hath an ear, let him hear what the Spirit saith unto the churches; To him that overcometh will I give to eat of the hidden manna, and will give him a white stone, and in the stone a new name written, which no man knoweth saving he that receiveth it."

A new name. A genuine Christian has a new name. It is a Christian name, not the old heathen name.

Then a seventh new thing. A new freedom. Only genuine Christians have this new freedom.
- **John 8:36**

"If the Son therefore shall make you free, ye shall be free indeed."

A new freedom. Not enslaved by the old flesh, the world, the devil.
- **Romans 6:22**

"But now being made free from sin, and become servants to God, ye have your fruit unto holiness, and the end everlasting life."
- **Galatians 5:1**

"Stand fast therefore in the liberty wherewith Christ hath made us free, and be not entangled again with the yoke of bondage."

A new freedom in Christ. No longer a slave by the world, the flesh and the devil. Only for genuine Christians.

An eighth new thing for genuine Christians. We have a new friend.
- **Proverbs 18:24**

"A man *that hath* friends must shew himself friendly: and there is a friend *that* sticketh closer than a brother."

The friend is the Lord.

- **John 15:15**
"Henceforth I call you not servants; for the servant knoweth not what his lord doeth: but I have called you friends; for all things that I have heard of my Father I have made known unto you."

These are genuine Christians. It is not speaking of those who are not genuine Christians, those that have never trusted Christ. This does not apply to you. If you have been genuinely born again, saved, if you have trusted the Lord Jesus, you have a new friend. The Lord Jesus is your friend. If you have rejected him, never trusted him genuinely, he is your enemy, not your friend. He is your enemy. He will be your judge at the Great White Throne Judgment. Serious business. You either make him a friend, or if he stays as your enemy, he is the one who will judge you in the end.

The ninth new thing for those genuine Christians, a new companion.

- **1 Corinthians 6:19**
"What? know ye not that your body is the temple of the Holy Ghost *which* is in you, which ye have of God, and ye are not your own?"

The Holy Spirit of God is indwelling genuine Christian bodies. We have a new companion, the Spirit of God, who goes with us wherever we go and that is a new, good thing.

A tenth new thing for genuine Christians is a new service.

Romans 12:1
"I beseech you therefore, brethren, by the mercies of God, that ye present your bodies a living sacrifice, holy, acceptable unto God, *which* is your reasonable service."

There is a new service.

- **1 Corinthians 6:20**
"For ye are bought with a price: therefore glorify God in your body, and in your spirit, which are God's."

A new service for genuine Christians. Lost people do not have any of this service but genuine Christians do.

An eleventh new thing for genuine Christians. A new deliverance.

- **2 Corinthians 1:10**
"Who delivered us from so great a death, and doth deliver: in whom we trust that he will yet deliver *us*;"

He delivered us from hell, from the Lake of Fire and spiritual death in the second death.

- **Galatians 1:4**
  "Who gave himself for our sins, that he might deliver us from this present evil world, according to the will of God and our Father:"

He will deliver us from this world.

- **Colossians 1:13**
  "Who hath delivered us from the power of darkness, and hath translated *us* into the kingdom of his dear Son:"

Genuine Christians are delivered from the power of darkness and translated into the kingdom of his dear Son.

- **1 Thessalonians 1:10**
  "And to wait for his Son from heaven, whom he raised from the dead, *even* Jesus, which delivered us from the wrath to come."

Only genuine Christians will be delivered from the wrath to come. Two wraths. The one is the tribulation wrath. The Lord will deliver us from that wrath. The pretribulation rapture of the church will deliver from the wrath to come, the tribulation. The Lord will deliver us from the hell of fire, the Lake of Fire. This is the second wrath. Only genuine Christians will be delivered from the Lake of Fire, from wrath to come.

The twelfth new thing for genuine Christians, a new person.

- **Galatians 6:15**
  "For in Christ Jesus neither circumcision availeth any thing, nor uncircumcision, but a new creature."

A new creature. A new person.

- **Ephesians 4:24**
  "And that ye put on the new man, which after God is created in righteousness and true holiness."

A new creation. A new person, if we are genuine Christians.

The thirteenth and final thing, we have a new destination. Genuine Christians have a new destination. We are born sinners. If we do nothing, our destination is hell and ultimately the Lake of Fire. Millions and billions of people all around the world that have a destination in the Lake of Fire because they have done nothing about their sin. We have people in this country, who go to church, Baptist church, Presbyterian church, Lutheran church, Catholic church, you name it, but they do nothing with the Lord Jesus Christ. They have never trusted him as their Saviour and so, their destination is the Lake of Fire. They may call themselves Christians, but God knows their heart. If they are not genuine, they are going to the Lake of Fire.

Our new destination, heaven, is for genuine Christians only.
- **John 14:2**
"In my Father's house are many mansions: if *it were* not so, I would have told you. I go to prepare a place for you."
- **John 14:3**
"And if I go and prepare a place for you, I will come again, and receive you unto myself; that where I am, *there* ye may be also."

Prepare a place for you. That is only for genuine Christians, not the unsaved people. The place for the unsaved people, those who have never accepted the Lord Jesus genuinely as their Saviour, the place prepared for the devil and his angels, is the place prepared for them. That is their destination, that is the Lake of Fire. That is hell for all of eternity. His destination is hell. The Lord Jesus spoke more about hell then any other person in the whole New Testament. It is real.

This is the high priestly prayer,
- **John 17:24**
"Father, I will that they also, whom thou hast given me, be with me where I am; that they may behold my glory, which thou hast given me: for thou lovedst me before the foundation of the world."

Now this is the destination of every genuine Christian. A place in heaven.
- **2 Corinthians 5:8**
"We are confident, *I say*, and willing rather to be absent from the body, and to be present with the Lord."

That is the destination of genuine Christians, a place with the Lord.
- **Philippians 1:23**
"For I am in a strait betwixt two, having a desire to depart, and to be with Christ; which is far better:"

Paul knew where his destination was. He knew it was heaven, itself. He did not have to worry about where he was going when he died. He knew heaven was far better than anything on earth.

So these thirteen things taken from that verse, 2 Corinthians 5:17 belong to the genuinely saved person. "Therefore If any man be in Christ, he is a new creature: old things are passed away; behold, all things are become new." We may not act like new creatures but God says, in his books, every genuine Christian is a new creature. A new creation. Old things have passed away, all things have become new, as far as God is concerned.

2 Corinthians 5:18

"And all things *are* of God, who hath reconciled us to himself by Jesus Christ, and hath given to us the ministry of reconciliation;"

Those who are genuine Christians have been reconciled to God by the Lord Jesus. Reconciled, no longer a stranger, no longer against God. Notice, after a person has been reconciled to God by genuine faith in Christ, a genuine Christian, God gives to that person a "ministry of reconciliation;" We have to tell others about the Lord Jesus Christ, tell others that they are sinners and lost. They do not like to hear that but if they do not hear that they are sinners, agree that they are sinners, they cannot go to heaven. Only those that recognize they are sinners, go to heaven. After they recognize they are sinners, they must recognize the Lord Jesus Christ as their Saviour. They must realize that the Lord Jesus Christ died for their sins. They can still go to hell. They must trust the Lord Jesus, believe on him as their Saviour and receive his everlasting right to forgiveness. Only those. That is the ministry of reconciliation. Only then are they reconciled. The Lord Jesus Christ died for the lost sinners. They must trust him and believe on the Lord Jesus Christ and be saved. And then they are reconciled.

2 Corinthians 5:19

"To wit, that God was in Christ, reconciling the world unto himself, not imputing their trespasses unto them; and hath committed unto us the word of reconciliation."

God the Father was in Christ, his Son, reconciling the world unto himself, "not imputing their trespasses unto them;" The provision was made. That does not mean the whole world has been reconciled to him. God is reconciled to the world. A sinner must be reconciled to God by genuine faith in the Lord Jesus. But God has made the first move. The Lord Jesus was sent from heaven. He took upon himself the sins of the world. That is the only way that God could be reconciled with this wicked world. Now it is up to us, each person, to trust the Lord Jesus Christ to be reconciled to him. That will take care of joint reconciliation between both the Father and the sinner. And has committed unto us the word of reconciliation. He has given unto us the Gospel message to tell others about this word of reconciliation and

getting them to be saved and going to heaven. Now there is no imputation of sin,
- **Psalms 32:2**
"Blessed is the man unto whom the LORD imputeth not iniquity, and in whose spirit *there* is no guile."

When we are in Christ, trusting him as our Saviour, God does not impute unto us sin, wickedness and corruption. Our sins have been placed upon the Lord Jesus Christ. He buried the sins. If we trust him, he bore our sins.
- **Romans 4:8**
"Blessed is the man to whom the Lord will not impute sin."

God does not impute sin to those who have genuinely trusted the Saviour, who died for those sins. Trust in him. Believe in him. Become righteous before him. It is mportant indeed that we have this word of reconciliation. And then tell others about the Saviour.

2 Corinthians 5:20

"Now then we are ambassadors for Christ, as though God did beseech *you* by us: we *pray* you in Christ's stead, be ye reconciled to God."

Notice the "we," all the genuine Christians. He is not talking about unsaved people. They are not the ambassadors of anybody but the devil. Unsaved people are ambassadors to the devil. I do not care what religious ambassadors, whatever they are, whatever the religion is. Those who are genuine Christians have been converted into becoming ambassadors for Christ. An ambassador is someone who represents a foreign country. An ambassador to China from the United States is appointed to China, to represent the United States of America. An ambassador to Japan, represents the United States of America. An ambassador for Christ, is one a genuine Christian who has been saved representing the Lord Jesus Christ.

Notice, "ambassadors for Christ, as though God did beseech you by us: we pray you in Christ's stead, be ye reconciled to God." God has been reconciling the world by the death of his Son." It does not mean everyone is saved. It does not mean that. As far as God is concerned, he made the first move in sending his Son to this world that die for the sins of the world. That is the first move in reconciling the whole world to Himself. Now, it is our move. Our move. Every person that lives on this earth must ask what have we done. Have we accepted the Saviour, the Lord Jesus Christ? Are we now reconciled to Him? By trusting the Lord

Jesus, who died for our sins, that is our step. That is our move. Believe on the Lord Jesus Christ and thou shalt be saved and thy house. Be ye reconciled. That is the message of a true ambassador for Christ.

The Lord Jesus told his disciples about being ambassadors,
- **Mark 16:15**
"And he said unto them, Go ye into all the world, and preach the Gospel to every creature."

All the world. Not just the elect, some little elect group, but to every creature. The Gospel should be preached to every creature because every creature is lost. He needs Christ.

This message is repeated,
- **Acts 1:8**
"But ye shall receive power, after that the Holy Ghost is come upon you: and ye shall be witnesses unto me both in Jerusalem, and in all Judaea, and in Samaria, and unto the uttermost part of the earth."

The Lord Jesus told his disciples and apostles, they would be witnesses unto him and ambassadors to the uttermost part of the earth.

Paul was in prison when he wrote the epistles of Ephesians,, Galatians, Ephesians, Philippians and Colossians. He often mentions his bonds.
- **Ephesians 6:20**
"For which I am an ambassador in bonds: that therein I may speak boldly, as I ought to speak."

Preaching Christ, he is an ambassador, in bonds. He is in bonds because he is an ambassador of Christ. He is in prison because he is a Christian. God permits this wicked world to imprison Christians because they are Christians, and will be ambassadors, we hope, in bonds. Ambassadors of Christ should speak boldly, and being good witnesses wherever we may be in our bondage.

2 Corinthians 5:21

"For he hath made him *to be* sin for us, who knew no sin; that we might be made the righteousness of God in him."

What a wonderful Gospel verse this is in the last verse, twenty-one. He, *that is God, the Father,* "hath made him" *that is, God, the Son,* "to be sin for us," *the whole world, in our place, in our stead.* Now, that is something. To have a sinless Saviour be made sin for us. All the sins, of all the world, all mankind, from Adam to the end of the world, were placed by the Father onto

God, the Son, the Lord Jesus Christ, on the cross. He made Him sin for us. Horrible, horrible thing for a sinless Saviour to be made sin in our place. Notice, he "who knew no sin;" He was sinless and spotless. Many, many verses teach us the Lord Jesus was sinless. The Father knew the only way sin could be completely atoned for was to put the sins of the world on his own Son. The Son had to be perfect, had to be God Himself. The Lord Jesus, God the Son, had to be infinite because only an infinite person could pay the infinite price for the sins of the whole world. The Son accepted the sins of all mankind and then suffered their infinite punishment. Sins can be forgiven because God has been satisfied. He became sin for us, who knew no sin.

Now, notice the purpose, that those who trust the Lord Jesus Christ "that we might be made"sinless in the books of heaven. We still sin but in the books of heaven, that we, who trust the Lord Jesus Christ and profess him, are "made the righteousness of God in him." In the books of heaven, those who have genuinely trusted the Lord Jesus as Saviour, I mean, genuinely in the heart, not the head only, they have declared to be totally, 100%, absolutely, impeccable, sinless and righteous. Not a sin on those books.

Now what we'd better do on this earth is to shoot at that goal, to be impeccable and sinless in all that we can. Nobody can achieve that. We are not sinlessly perfect, but that is the goal. We have been made the righteousness of God, only in Him, in the Lord Jesus Christ, not in ourselves, nor by our church, nor in baptism nor anything else that we can do or say. We have been made righteous not by rituals but only in Christ. What a tremendous Gospel verse.

Verses on Christ burying our sins,
- **John 1:29**

"The next day John seeth Jesus coming unto him, and saith, Behold the Lamb of God, which taketh away the sin of the world."

Our sins are taken away. They are not just covered KUPHAR as in the Old Testament. He taketh away the sin of the world.

- **Hebrews 9:26**

"For then must he often have suffered since the foundation of the world: but now once in the end of the world hath he appeared to put away sin by the sacrifice of himself."

There is no repetition about that like the Roman Catholics heretically teach. In every single mass, he dies as the priest falsely, heretically says this bread becomes his body. Heresy! You cannot make a bread into a body. He takes a cup and that becomes the blood of Christ. Heresy! Then he dies and if you take that cup, you are saved, you are born again-absolute heresy. That is not what Christ did. He appeared ONCE at the end of the world, put away sin by the sacrifice of himself. One sacrifice, never to be repeated. No masses, nothing at all for repetition.

- **1 Peter 2:24**

"Who his own self bare our sins in his own body on the tree, that we, being dead to sins, should live unto righteousness: by whose stripes ye were healed."

Who bare our sins in his own body. That is what the Lord Jesus did, sins of the whole world.

- **1 John 3:5**

"And ye know that he was manifested to take away our sins; and in him is no sin."

There are some other verses that have to do with the Lord Jesus giving genuine Christians his righteousness. It says we are "made the righteousness of God in him."

- **Genesis 15:6**

And he believed in the LORD; and he counted it to him for righteousness.

The righteousness came for Abraham by genuine faith in the Lord.

- **Romans 3:22**

"Even the righteousness of God *which is* by faith of Jesus Christ unto all and upon all them that believe: for there is no difference:"

Righteousness comes by genuine faith in the Lord Jesus Christ. That is the only way we can get God's righteousness.

- **Romans 4:3**

"For what saith the scripture? Abraham believed God, and it was counted unto him for righteousness."

It was credited unto him and counted unto him for righteousness by faith. Only by faith in Christ can they receive righteousness of God.

- **Romans 9:30**

"What shall we say then? That the Gentiles, which followed not after righteousness, have attained to righteousness, even the righteousness which is of faith."

The only way we can be righteous before God is by genuine faith in the Lord Jesus Christ.

- **Romans 10:4**
"For Christ is the end of the law for righteousness to every one that believeth."
What about those who do not believe in the Lord Jesus. They do not have a righteous standing before God.
- **Romans 10:10**
"For with the heart man believeth unto righteousness; and with the mouth confession is made unto salvation."
We confess that we are righteous once we have been saved. Believe with the heart, not with the head, with the heart, individuals, men and women, boys and girls, believe unto righteousness.
- **Galatians 3:6**
"Even as Abraham believed God, and it was accounted to him for righteousness."
There again, Abraham, repeated over and over, "believed God and it was counted to him for righteousness."
- **Philippians 3:9**
"And be found in him, not having mine own righteousness, which is of the law, but that which is through the faith of Christ, the righteousness which is of God by faith:"
A righteous standing before God by genuine faith in the Lord Jesus Christ. That is the only way we can attain it. Christ paid for it. He is the one who gives it to us by faith in him.
- **Hebrews 11:7**
"By faith Noah, being warned of God of things not seen as yet, moved with fear, prepared an ark to the saving of his house; by the which he condemned the world, and became heir of the righteousness which is by faith."
He became an heir, of course, by faith. Trusting. He looked forward to the cross of Calvary; forward to the Lord Jesus dying for the sins of the world, and received righteousness by faith, just like Abraham did.
- **James 2:23**
"And the scripture was fulfilled which saith, Abraham believed God, and it was imputed unto him for righteousness: and he was called the Friend of God."
He did it by faith. Trusting God by faith and so those who come to the Lord Jesus Christ by genuine faith, God can give righteousness. That is what verse twenty-one says. "He" that is God, the Father, "hath made him to be" that is, God, the Son," sin for us" and that is everyone that has ever lived, he "who knew no sin;" the Lord Jesus "that we might be made" those who trust the Lord Jesus by genuine faith, "that we might be made" not that we

do anything "made the righteousness of God in him." In Christ alone, genuinely by faith, can we be made, in the books of heaven, absolute, total, one hundred percent, righteous.

And so, this last part of chapter five, these thirteen new things belong to genuine Christians. Only genuine Christians have every one of these thirteen new things. And every genuine Christians has all thirteen of these new things. Not a one is missing, not a single one. If you want these things and you are not absolutely positive you are a genuine Christian, those that are in this audience this morning, those listening on the internet, you want to make positive that you are a genuine Christian and receive these wonderful things, including, especially, a new destination in heaven.

2 Corinthians Chapter Six

2 Corinthians 6:1

"We then, as workers together *with him*, beseech *you* also that ye receive not the grace of God in vain."

This "*we*" is speaking of genuine Christians. They are workers together with their Saviour. If they do not work for Him, it is like receiving salvation in vain without any useful purpose.

Verses On In Vain

- **Psalms 127:1**

"Except the LORD build the house, they labour in vain that build it: except the LORD keep the city, the watchman waketh but in vain."

The Lord must build the house and help the watchman with the city.

- **Mark 7:7**

"Howbeit in vain do they worship me, teaching *for* doctrines the commandments of men."

The Lord Jesus Christ is referring to the religious Pharisees of His day. Their worship is in vain.

- **1 Corinthians 15:10**

"But by the grace of God I am what I am: and his grace which *was bestowed* upon me was not in vain; but I laboured more abundantly than they all: yet not I, but the grace of God which was with me."

Paul did not waste his life. He labored for his Saviour once he was saved. His salvation was not in vain.

- **1 Corinthians 15:58**

"Therefore, my beloved brethren, be ye stedfast, unmoveable, always abounding in the work of the Lord, forasmuch as ye know that your labour is not in vain in the Lord."

Anything true Christians do for the Lord is not in vain.

- **Philippians 2:16**
"Holding forth the word of life; that I may rejoice in the day of Christ, that I have not run in vain, neither laboured in vain."
If genuine Christians labour for the Lord Jesus Christ, it is not in vain, but has a godly purpose.

2 Corinthians 6:2

"(For he saith, I have heard thee in a time accepted, and in the day of salvation have I succoured thee: behold, now *is* the accepted time; behold, now *is* the day of salvation.)"

Before anybody can have any Christian ministry, they must be a partaker of God's salvation. Without salvation there can be no valid Christian ministry.

Verses On Salvation
- **Isaiah 49:8**
"Thus saith the LORD, In an acceptable time have I heard thee, and in a day of salvation have I helped thee: and I will preserve thee, and give thee for a covenant of the people, to establish the earth, to cause to inherit the desolate heritages;"
God's salvation must precede any person's ministry of any kind.
- **Luke 19:9-10**
"And Jesus said unto him, This day is salvation come to this house, forsomuch as he also is a son of Abraham. For the Son of man is come to seek and to save that which was lost."
The Lord Jesus Christ was talking about Zacchaeus, a short man who was watching Him while he was up in the tree. The Lord saw him and told him to come down because He was going to his house.
- **Acts 4:12**
"Neither is there salvation in any other: for there is none other name under heaven given among men, whereby we must be saved."
This verse is quite clear. There is no other Name. No Baptist name, no Presbyterian name, no Roman Catholic name, no Lutheran name, no Methodist name, no Episcopal name, no other name of any kind--None other Name but that of the Lord Jesus Christ.

- **Romans 1:16**
"For I am not ashamed of the Gospel of Christ: for it is the power of God unto salvation to every one that believeth; to the Jew first, and also to the Greek."
Salvation is only to those who genuinely believe in the Lord Jesus Christ as their Saviour.
- **2 Corinthians 7:10**
"For godly sorrow worketh repentance to salvation not to be repented of: but the sorrow of the world worketh death."
Sometimes godly sorrow precedes salvation.
- **Titus 2:11**
"For the grace of God that bringeth salvation hath appeared to all men,"
It is God's grace that brought about the possibility for every person who ever lived to receive His eternal salvation if His conditions for that salvation are met.
- **Hebrews 2:3**
"How shall we escape, if we neglect so great salvation; which at the first began to be spoken by the Lord, and was confirmed unto us by them that heard *him*;"
If people neglect God's great salvation by refusing to genuinely trust the Lord Jesus Christ as their Saviour, their destination will be Hell's Lake of Fire for all eternity. They cannot escape it.
- **Hebrews 5:9**
"And being made perfect, he became the author of eternal salvation unto all them that obey him;"
The Lord Jesus Christ is the Author of eternal salvation to those who genuinely obey and trust Him as their Saviour.

2 Corinthians 6:3

"Giving no offence in any thing, that the ministry be not blamed:"

Verses On Offence

Those that are true Christians should not give offence to others against the Words of God. Truth offends but each true Christian should be careful not to give offence in things that are not Biblically necessary to bring out. The ministry should not be blamed for things that genuine Christians be causing others to be offended by. This is not an easy task.

- **Acts 24:16**

  "And herein do I exercise myself, <u>to have always a conscience void of offence</u> toward God, and *toward* men."

Paul tried to be void of offense not only to men, but also against God Himself. It is very difficult not to offend. Offences might be caused by how we look, what we say, where we go, what we believe, other things as well.

- **1 Corinthians 10:32**

  "<u>Give none offence, neither to the Jews, nor to the Gentiles, nor to the church of God:</u>"

True Christians should seek to give none offence to any of these three groups: to Jews, to Gentiles, or to the church of God.

- **Philippians 1:10**

  "That ye may approve things that are excellent; <u>that ye may be sincere and without offence</u> till the day of Christ;"

This is to be the goal for genuine Christians' ministries by not offending people if they can help it. It is difficult but that is what God wants and this should be their goal.

Verses On Ministry

- **Acts 6:4**

  "But <u>we will give ourselves</u> continually to prayer, and <u>to the ministry of the word</u>."

This is to be the ministry of the Words of God. It is to be the ministry of the Scriptures, the Words of God, rather than other things. It should be the right Words of God. In our English language, the proper Words of God would be found in the King James Bible which is accurately translated from the preserved and proper underlying Hebrew, Aramaic, and Greek words that underlie that Bible. The modern Bible versions pervert the New Testament Greek text in 8,000 places. There are 356 of these places that involve important doctrinal passages. We must reject such Bible perversions.

- **Acts 20:24**

  "But none of these things move me, neither count I my life dear unto myself, <u>so that I might finish my course with joy, and the ministry, which I have received of the Lord Jesus,</u> to testify the Gospel of the grace of God."

That ministry of Paul must be continued. I feel that way as a minister of the Lord Jesus Christ that I have received of my Saviour.

- **Colossians 4:17**
"And say to Archippus, Take heed to the ministry which thou hast received in the Lord, that thou fulfil it."

Archippus was reminded to take heed to fulfill the ministry he received of his Saviour. He was not to cease fulfilling his ministry, nor should any genuine Christian today.

- **1 Timothy 1:12**
"And I thank Christ Jesus our Lord, who hath enabled me, for that he counted me faithful, putting me into the ministry;"

The Lord Jesus Christ counted Paul faithful to Him and therefore put him into the ministry for his Saviour.

- **2 Timothy 4:5**
"But watch thou in all things, endure afflictions, do the work of an evangelist, make full proof of thy ministry."

Pastor Timothy was commanded by Paul to watch all around at various things, endure afflictions of what sort they might be, do the work of an evangelist, and make full proof of his ministry. These were important duties of this or any pastor.

2 Corinthians 6:4

"But in all *things* approving ourselves as the ministers of God, in much patience, in afflictions, in necessities, in distresses,"

Paul wanted to be approved by God as His minister in these four areas: (1) patience; (2) afflictions; (3) necessities, and (4) distresses.

Verses On Patience

- **2 Corinthians 12:12**
"Truly the signs of an apostle were wrought among you in all patience, in signs, and wonders, and mighty deeds."

The signs of an apostle were showed the true Christians at Corinth in patience.

- **Hebrews 10:36**
"For ye have need of patience, that, after ye have done the will of God, ye might receive the promise."

Every genuine Christian needs patience.

- **Hebrews 12:1b-2**

"... and <u>let us run with patience the race that is set before us</u>, Looking unto Jesus the author and finisher of *our* faith; who for the joy that was set before him endured the cross, despising the shame, and is set down at the right hand of the throne of God."

True Christians must run their races that are set before them looking unto the Lord Jesus Christ.

The second area of genuine Christians approving themselves as ministers of God, is "*in afflictions*." That Greek Word means things that are strongly pressing upon them.

Verses On Afflictions

- **Acts 20:23**

"Save that the Holy Ghost witnesseth in every city, saying that <u>bonds and afflictions abide me</u>."

Paul knew what he was getting into when he went to these places. Bonds and afflictions were coming to him.

- **1 Thessalonians 3:3**

"That <u>no man should be moved by these afflictions</u>: for yourselves know that we are appointed thereunto."

No true Christian should be moved by these afflictions to cause them to betray their Saviour.

- **2 Timothy 1:8**

"Be not thou therefore ashamed of the testimony of our Lord, nor of me his prisoner: but be thou partaker of the afflictions of the Gospel according to the power of God;"

Do not be ashamed of me, Timothy. Be a partaker of the afflictions. It is going to come. He warned him about it.

- **2 Timothy 3:11**

"Persecutions, <u>afflictions, which came unto me at Antioch, at Iconium, at Lystra</u>; what persecutions I endured: but out of *them* all the Lord delivered me."

The Lord delivered him out of all these afflictions.

- **2 Timothy 4:5**

"But watch thou in all things, <u>endure afflictions</u>, do the work of an evangelist, make full proof of thy ministry."

The third area of true Christians approving themselves as God's ministers is in "*necessities*." This Greek Word indicates calamities and straits.

The fourth area of true Christians approving themselves as God's ministers is "*distresses*." The Greek Word indicates various calamities and extreme affliction.

- **2 Corinthians 12:10**
"Therefore I take pleasure in infirmities, in reproaches, in necessities, in persecutions, in distresses for Christ's sake: for when I am weak, then am I strong."
Like Paul, true Christians should take pleasure in all these difficult problems for the sake of the Lord Jesus Christ.

2 Corinthians 6:5

"In stripes, in imprisonments, in tumults, in labours, in watchings, in fastings;"

Paul refers to *"stripes"* which are beatings. We have not yet been beaten. We may be beaten. The early Christians were. Paul was, many times he suffered afflictions. We today, as genuine Christians, must be ministers of God, even when we are being beaten. If you think that is easy, try it sometime. I am sure it is not easy.

Notice the sixth area of proving ourselves as ministers of God, *"in imprisonments."* Having been in many prisons, as Paul was, he knew what sorrow that could bring. This may come for true Christians today by being put into FEMA camps.

One of our friend's pastor is up there in a FEMA camp in Grayling, Michigan. They say that Fort Dix is going to be transformed into a FEMA camp. Who is going to be in the FEMA camps? These apostate preachers have been trained to falsify the word of God and use wrongly Romans 13:1-4. They misapply these verses which clearly say that only biblical kind of government should be obeyed, not government that is against the principles of the Bible.

The government in Romans 13 rewards the good and punishes the bad. Genuine Christians must obey God rather than men. That is what Paul did in the New Testament. That is what the apostles did. It is what we have to do.

If the FEMA bus comes to take you to the FEMA camp, do not go. Stay out of the bus. Say, thank you very much but I have enough food here, you go on. Stay out of the FEMA buses.

Verses On Stripes

- **Acts 16:33**
"And he took them the same hour of the night, and washed *their* stripes; and was baptized, he and all his, straightway."
Paul was beaten in Philippi. When the Philippian jailer asked what he must do to be saved, he washed the stripes of Paul and Silas.

- **2 Corinthians 11:23-24**
"Are they ministers of Christ? (I speak as a fool) I *am* more; in labours more abundant, in stripes above measure, in prisons more frequent, in deaths oft. Of the Jews five times received I forty *stripes* save one.""
Paul was beaten many times as one of the faithful disciples of the Lord Jesus Christ.

Verses On Labors
The word for "*labours*" indicates very serious work.
- **2 Corinthians 11:23**
"Are they ministers of Christ? (I speak as a fool) I *am* more; in labours more abundant, in stripes above measure, in prisons more frequent, in deaths oft."
Paul's labors were abundant, not just very few in number.

Paul had many "*watchings*" as well. The Greek word for "*watch*" involves sleeplessness. You cannot sleep. You just watch. You can sleep even in sleeplessness, where you have no offence and approve yourselves as the ministers of God.

2 Corinthians 6:6
"By pureness, by knowledge, by longsuffering, by kindness, by the Holy Ghost, by love unfeigned,"

All these different things are part of godly living by genuine Christians. Pureness. God wants believers, when they serve the Lord, to be pure, not sinful, wicked, and corrupt with the world.
- **1 Timothy 4:12**
"Let no man despise thy youth; but be thou an example of the believers, in word, in conversation, in charity, in spirit, in faith, in purity."
True Christians must be pure.

Verses On Knowledge
I believe the word "*knowledge*" refers to what is found in the Words of God. Genuine Christians must know the Words from God's Book, the Bible, in order to be able and loyal servants of their Saviour.
- **Romans 10:2**
"For I bear them record that they have a zeal of God, but not according to knowledge."
True and Biblical zeal must be accompanied by sound Biblical knowledge.

Patience is different from longsuffering. Those two Greek synonyms are used in the Greek New Testament. Trench's excellent book makes a clear distinction between these two. Patience has to do with putting up with **things** and **circumstances** that go wrong. Longsuffering has to do with putting up with people who often go wrong. Putting up with people is often very difficult. Many times it is much easier to put up with things and circumstances rather than putting up with people.

- **Galatians 5:22**

"But the fruit of the Spirit is love, joy, peace, longsuffering, gentleness, goodness, faith,"

Longsuffering enables genuine Christians who are controlled by God the Holy Spirit to put up with people.

- **Colossians 1:11**

"Strengthened with all might, according to his glorious power, unto all patience and longsuffering with joyfulness;"

God can strengthen true Christians with longsuffering.

- **Colossians 3:12**

"Put on therefore, as the elect of God, holy and beloved, bowels of mercies, kindness, humbleness of mind, meekness, longsuffering;"

In Colossians 1:11, both of these terms are used, in the same verse, patience and longsuffering. Patience, putting up with things and circumstances, longsuffering, putting up with people, with joyfulness.

- **2 Timothy 3:10**

"But thou hast fully known my doctrine, manner of life, purpose, faith, longsuffering, charity, patience,"

Paul knew how to put up with people. He had to. So many people were against him. They wanted to put him in prison. They wanted to beat him. They wanted to take different views than he had.

- **2 Timothy 4:2**

"Preach the word; be instant in season, out of season; reprove, rebuke, exhort with all longsuffering and doctrine."

That is what a preacher must do if he preaches God's Words faithfully. He must preach the right Words. In English, it is the King James Bible which is an accurate translation from the preserved Hebrew, Aramaic, and Greek texts.

The right Bible should be preached in season and out of season. In other words, all the time. Reprove, when it is necessary. Rebuke, when it is necessary. Exhort, when it is necessary with all longsuffering, putting up with people.

This should be done by kindness. As a Pastor serves, he should do it in a kind way. Is it always easy to be kind? No. It is sometimes difficult to be kind. When you differ with somebody, it is sometimes easier to be unkind.

Now notice, this other thing, it is to be done "*by the Holy Ghost.*" Genuine Christians, as ministers of God, must be guided, controlled, and filled by the Spirit of God. It should all be done "*by love unfeigned.*" *Unfeigned* means sincere, not hypocritical, and without any hypocrisy.

- **1 Peter 1:22**

"Seeing ye have purified your souls in obeying the truth through the Spirit unto unfeigned love of the brethren, *see that ye* love one another with a pure heart fervently:"

This is a part of the proper ministry. It must be with a pure heart and fervently.

2 Corinthians 6:7

"By the word of truth, by the power of God, by the armour of righteousness on the right hand and on the left,"

By the Word of God, the Word of truth. We have to be using the right words, otherwise you won't have the right truth. As I have said before, in the New Testament alone, there are 8,000 differences between the Gnostic Greek Test and the new versions and the texts that underlie our King James Bible. Many of them are minor but there are 356 doctrinal passages that are different. You have to have the right Words, the Word of truth, as you approve ourselves as ministries of God, those that are genuine Christians.

Verses On The Power Of God

Notice number eighteen, "*by the power of God,*" Not by our power, not by what we do, what we say, what we think but if we are approving ourselves as ministers of God, it must be by God's power, working through us.

- **Romans 1:16**

"For I am not ashamed of the gospel of Christ: for it is the power of God unto salvation to every one that believeth; to the Jew first, and also to the Greek."

The power of God is within the Gospel of Jesus Christ, dying for the sins of the world.

- **1 Corinthians 1:18**
"For the preaching of the cross is to them that perish foolishness; but unto us which are saved it is the power of God."
The preaching the cross to unsaved is foolishness, but to the genuine Christians, it is the power of God.
- **1 Corinthians 1:24**
"But unto them which are called, both Jews and Greeks, Christ the power of God, and the wisdom of God."
It's a title for the Lord Jesus Christ, the power of God.
- **1 Corinthians 2:5**
"That your faith should not stand in the wisdom of men, but in the power of God."
That's where the true Christians faith should stand.
- **2 Timothy 1:8**
"Be not thou therefore ashamed of the testimony of our Lord, nor of me his prisoner: but be thou partaker of the afflictions of the gospel according to the power of God;"
Those afflictions were helped to endure by the power of God.
- **1 Peter 1:5**
"Who are kept by the power of God through faith unto salvation ready to be revealed in the last time."
Genuine Christians are kept saved for all eternity. Methodists are wrong. The holiness people are wrong. And many other groups are wrong in saying they can lose their salvation.

Verses On The True Christians' Armour

The nineteenth area, "*by the armour of righteousness on the right hand and on the left,*" The armour of righteousness. True Christians have God's armor. They have a righteous standing before God. That's armour. It should be put on.
- **Ephesians 6:11**
"Put on the whole armour of God, that ye may be able to stand against the wiles of the devil."
Armour must be put on before it can be profitable.
- **Ephesians 6:13**
"Wherefore take unto you the whole armour of God, that ye may be able to withstand in the evil day, and having done all, to stand."
Genuine Christians' armor is very important. They should make use of it daily.

2 Corinthians 6:8

"By honour and dishonour, by evil report and good report: as deceivers, and yet true;"

Again, number twenty-one by honour, if we're in good shape and everything we are doing is good, where we shall honor the Lord. We should be good ministers, put ourselves as ministers to the Lord. Some people think that we are honorable. Some people think we are dishonorable. If they think we're honorable, still be good ministers of the Lord in that particular area but if it's number twenty-two, to dishonour, ATIMIA of one who is defamed, still maintain good ministry, approving yourselves as ministers of God. Even if people defame you, you still have to be a good minister of God.

Now notice number twenty-three, by evil report. Evil and good report. Good report is EUPHEMIA which is praise. Be a good minister and people will praise you. Don't let it go to your head, don't get egotistical about it, don't get proud about it, arrogant about it but serve the Lord with your ministry, whether it is by evil report or by good report.

As deceivers. Some people may think we are deceiving people by making salvation simply by genuine faith in Christ. Still keep your ministry, no matter if people think you are deceived. That word is PLANOS, misleading people, leading people into error. No. We are not leading people into error by following the Bible. We are leading people into the truth. That's why we have to be faithful in our ministry. Notice, we have the truth. We are truth ALATHEIS loving the truth, speaking the truth and using the truth.

2 Corinthians 6:9

"As unknown, and yet well known; as dying, and, behold, we live; as chastened, and not killed;"

First, unknown. A lot of people that are genuine Christians are not known by others like people in foreign countries, we don't know anything about them. But if they're just saved, genuine people and they have to live their ministry for the Lord, even though they may be unknown. Most of us are unknown to the hierarchs in this country. Probably all of us are unknown to the hierarchs of the country but still keep our ministries faithful, approving ourselves as good ministers. Yet well known, we're well known to each other. We are well known of the Lord. The Lord knows us. Genuine Christians, he knows us well. We are to be ministers, ministering unto him. Now notice, as dying. Paul knew what that was. We don't know yet what that is, as dying. Acts 14, in Lystra, they stoned Paul, dragged him out of the city. We believe he was dead, as dying, and yet the Lord raised him up again, took him to heaven, showed the glories of heaven. He couldn't speak about it. Had to be very quiet about it, given revelations. He was given a thorn in the flesh. He knew what dying was.

Now none of us, as yet, that are here in the room, know of dying. One day, some of us, will die. Who knows who it is going to be. It could be some of us in here. It could be some of the others. Age has no first or second place sometimes, does it? Sometimes you die as a baby, die as a two-year-old, three-year-old. Whatever the age, even as dying, we must approve ourselves as ministers of God. May we have a testimony on our death, as Paul did in his death, a testimony for our Saviour, our Lord Jesus Christ.

Is it possible, you say, to die as a Christian and have a testimony for the Lord? I tell you, it is for most people. He has commanded us. These are rules for approving ourselves as ministers of God. Many Christians don't have that testimony.

My wife's father, for example, had that testimony. He did not say a word in his death. He was in a wheel chair, he had one leg missing, could not say a word. At his death, we were told by the neighbor, that Dad Sanborn had a smile on his face. As far as we know, the neighbor was lost, he was not saved. He knew who my father-in-law was. Dad died as an approved minister. He died, but he served.

I have heard on the other hand, people when they die are ornery, wicked, bitter, crying out, cursing, angry, yelling and screaming. You have not died yet. I have not died yet. When we do, remember God wants us to continue to be an approved minister of his, serving the Lord Jesus Christ and a good witness. May that be our case, as dying. As we read Paul died but yet he lived. The Lord raised him up again. Gave him a great ministry. Paul never forgot that.

Now notice, number thirty-one. Chasten. Sometimes God has to chasten and discipline us who are genuine Christians, just as we, on occasion, discipline our own children. Not that we hate the children, because we discipline. We want them to be grown up and be obedient to the Lord. If they don't obey the parents, they won't obey the Lord. And so we sometimes have to discipline our children. Four sons and a daughter, five all together.

We started out at first with the three boys. They came together every two, two and a half years. They were very close in age and did a lot of fighting. And I disciplined them. Then Dan came along a little bit later. Not too bad for discipline and so on. He was a pretty good boy. The only thing I remember about Pastor Dan. I won't tell about it. We used to have a little table there but anyway, I won't tell about it. He was a good son. Not like our first three because the first three were together, fighting, fighting, fighting. He was all by himself. He was a good son. Praise the Lord. The best son we had. Really, I'm not kidding you. Praise God he's our assistant pastor as well. Good pastor and a good son. Praise the Lord.

So, chasten, sometimes we have to. Sometimes the Lord has to chasten us. You notice, it says in the book of Hebrews, the Old Testament as well, "whom the Lord loveth he chasteneth," He loves us to be obedient to him. He wants us to grow up unto him, he wants us to honor him and this chastening is not for our evil. It's for our good. We have to always think about that and the Lord chastens different people different ways. That's what we have to realize. We are worth more after the chastening.

- **Hebrews 12:6**

"For whom the Lord loveth he chasteneth, and scourgeth every son whom he receiveth."

Whom the Lord loveth. I remember, we have a picture, after I spanked little Dick. Dick my third son. A little white-haired boy. He was there. I was kneeled down onto him. He was crying. I always asked my sons after I chastened them, why did Dad spank you? Lest they forget, they said the truth, "Because you loved me. Because you loved me." I tell them that all the time. Sometimes they forget, why are you disciplining me? You do not remember it is because of love. Praise God. Everyone of our sons and daughter, they turned out well for the Lord. They are saved and born again. Praise God for it. That is the goodness of chastening, that we may be better, not worse, but better.

So, when the Lord chastens us, let us be sure to thank Him. Do not be angry with Him. Thank Him. Ask, "How can I be better because your chastening hand is upon me?" And he will bless us more.

Well, this is the thirty-two different areas of approving ourselves as ministers of God. May we be approved in every one of these. It's not easy to remember all of them. Thirty-two. May God give us, those who are genuine Christians, approved ministry for the Lord Jesus Christ, without fail for Jesus sake.

2 Corinthians 6:10

"As sorrowful, yet alway rejoicing; as poor, yet making many rich; as having nothing, and *yet* possessing all things."

If you are a genuine Christian, many times you are sorrowful.

Verses On Sorrow

- **Genesis 3:16**

'Unto the woman he said, I will greatly multiply thy sorrow and thy conception; in sorrow thou shalt bring forth children; and thy desire *shall be* to thy husband, and he shall rule over thee. And unto Adam he said, Because thou hast hearkened unto the voice of thy wife, and hast eaten of the tree, of which I commanded thee, saying, Thou shalt not eat of it: cursed *is* the ground for thy sake; in sorrow shalt thou eat *of* it all the days of thy life;"

Sorrow in child birth was a judgment on Eve for her sin. It has been passed down to all mothers in the future.

- **Exodus 3:7**

"And the LORD said, I have surely seen the affliction of my people which *are* in Egypt, and have heard their cry by reason of their taskmasters; for I know their sorrows;"

God knew Israel's sorrow in Egypt and is also familiar with all the sorrows of genuine Christians and others today.

- **John 16:6**

"But because I have said these things unto you, sorrow hath filled your heart."

The disciples had sorrow because the Lord Jesus Christ was going Home to Heaven and leaving them.

Verses On Joy And Rejoicing

- **John 16:20**

"Verily, verily, I say unto you, That ye shall weep and lament, but the world shall rejoice: and ye shall be sorrowful, but your sorrow shall be turned into joy."

The Lord Jesus Christ was talking about His death on the cross of

Calvary. The world would rejoice, but His disciples would weep. At His bodily resurrection, their sorrow turned to joy.

- **John 14:28**

"Ye have heard how I said unto you, I go away, and come *again* unto you. If ye loved me, ye would rejoice, because I said, I go unto the Father: for my Father is greater than I."

He was going to leave the disciples who would rejoice because He was going to His and their Father.

- **Acts 5:41**

"And they departed from the presence of the council, rejoicing that they were counted worthy to suffer shame for his name."

There was joy in the presence of shame.

- **Romans 5:2**

"By whom also we have access by faith into this grace wherein we stand, and rejoice in hope of the glory of God."

Hope in heaven, genuine Christians can rejoice.

From prison, Paul said,

- **Philippians 4:4**

"Rejoice in the Lord alway: *and* again I say, Rejoice."

Rejoicing can take place even in prison where Paul was when he wrote Philippians. If you are genuine Christian, there can be joy anywhere.

- **1 Thessalonians 5:16**

"Rejoice evermore."

True Christians can have joy continually.

- **1 Peter 1:8**

"Whom having not seen, ye love; in whom, though now ye see *him* not, yet believing, ye rejoice with joy unspeakable and full of glory:"

Having not seen the Lord Jesus Christ, there still can be unspeakable joy.

Verses On Poor

There were many genuine Christians in Paul's day and many today as well.

- **Matthew 5:3**

"Blessed *are* the poor in spirit: for theirs is the kingdom of heaven."

The true Christians might be poor in spirit, but they are bound for the riches of Heaven.

2 Corinthians Preaching Verse-By-Verse

- **2 Corinthians 8:9**
"For ye know the grace of our Lord Jesus Christ, that, <u>though he was rich, yet for your sakes he became poor, that ye through his poverty might be rich</u>."

The Lord Jesus Christ was rich in Heavenly glory, but He became poor by dying for the sins of the world on the cross to bring riches to the genuine Christians who trust Him.

- **James 2:5**
"Hearken, my beloved brethren, <u>Hath not God chosen the poor of this world rich in faith</u>, and heirs of the kingdom which he hath promised to them that love him?"

Poverty was great in the early church and today, many genuine Christians are poor as well.

Verses On Riches

- **Romans 10:12**
"For there is no difference between the Jew and the Greek: for <u>the same Lord over all is rich unto all that call upon him</u>."

The Lord is rich to all that sincerely call on Him through faith in His Son.

- **Romans 11:33**
"<u>O the depth of the riches both of the wisdom and knowledge of God</u>! how unsearchable *are* his judgments, and his ways past finding out!"

God is rich in both wisdom and knowledge. A very good verse indeed.

- **2 Corinthians 8:9**
"For ye know the grace of our Lord Jesus Christ, that, <u>though he was rich</u>, yet for your sakes he became poor, <u>that ye through his poverty might be rich</u>."

True Christians are rich in the Lord Jesus Christ.

- **Ephesians 3:8**
"Unto me, who am less than the least of all saints, is this grace given, <u>that I should preach among the Gentiles the unsearchable riches of Christ</u>;"

The Lord Jesus is rich and he gives genuine Christians His spiritual riches.

- **James 2:5**
"Hearken, my beloved brethren, Hath not God chosen the <u>poor of this world rich in faith</u>, and heirs of the kingdom which he hath promised to them that love him?"

Though true Christians might be poor in this world, they are rich in faith.

Verses On Having Very Little Yet Having Many Things

- **Romans 8:32**

"He that spared not his own Son, but delivered him up for us all, how shall he not with him also freely give us all things?"

God has given genuine Christians "*all things*" of eternal value.

- **1 Corinthians 3:21**

"Therefore let no man glory in men. For all things are yours;"

It is speaking of true Christians.

- **1 Timothy 6:17**

"Charge them that are rich in this world, that they be not highminded, nor trust in uncertain riches, but in the living God, who giveth us richly all things to enjoy;"

Genuine Christians have richly things to enjoy.

- **2 Peter 1:3**

"According as his divine power hath given unto us all things that *pertain* unto life and godliness, through the knowledge of him that hath called us to glory and virtue:"

True Christians have many wonderful things from God.

2 Corinthians 6:11

"O *ye* Corinthians, our mouth is open unto you, our heart is enlarged."

Paul was going to talk to these true Christians at Corinth in straight and clear words. These genuine Corinthians at Corinth were not separated unto the Lord as they should have been. They were disobedient in this vital area.

2 Corinthians 6:12

"Ye are not straitened in us, but ye are straitened in your own bowels."

That word for "*straitened*" in the Greek means "*being in a narrow place, being compressed and cramped.*" Paul said he had not done anything against them, but due to their lack of Biblical separation from evil, they had hurt themselves.

These Corinthian people were very seriously in trouble with the Lord Jesus Christ due to their lack of separation from evil. They were not following the Scriptures in many areas. Many Christians, today, do not follow the Scriptures in this area of Bible separation either. So they are straightened or cramped as to proper service for their Saviour.

"*Bowels*" is a Hebrew Word for the seat of tender affections, especially kindness, benevolence, and compassion. Paul is very seriously concerned about their status of not walking with the Lord and in this area of proper Bible separation.

2 Corinthians 6:13

"Now for a recompence in the same, (I speak as unto *my* children,) be ye also enlarged."

They are going to be recompensed by not following the Word of God as far as Bible separation is concerned. He is building this thing up before he gets to verse fourteen where he is very specific. He speaks like he would to his own children. When you talk to your children, you talk a little bit differently than you talk to general people. You speak right out in clear and specific terms. Children have things to learn. They have to be obedient. Paul is not trying to gloss things over. He is trying to be very clear.

2 Corinthians 6:14

"Be ye not unequally yoked together with unbelievers: for what fellowship hath righteousness with unrighteousness? and what communion hath light with darkness?"

Being a negative in the Greek present tense, it means that these Corinthian genuine Christians were to stop being unequally yoked together with unbelievers. They were doing this and Paul ordered them to stop it. A *"yoke"* is a strong bond that should not be true between genuine Christians whose spiritual Father is God, and non-Christians whose spiritual father is Satan.

The first two questions Paul asks the true Christians at Corinth are: (1) *"What fellowship hath righteousness with unrighteousness?"* And (2) *"What communion hath light with darkness?"* Because of these two questions, (1) there can be no real fellowship between righteousness and unrighteousness and (2) there can be no communion between light and darkness.

There are two general areas of Bible separation that are commanded in the Bible: (1) personal separation, and (2) organizational separation.

Personal separation involves the separation of every true Christian from personal sins and wickedness of any kind, especially that are clearly specified in the Bible or any other kind of unclean substances or habits not mentioned in the Bible. Among many other things, this would include fornication, adultery, lying, homosexuality, watching or listening to wicked and sinful movies, or television shows and many other things.

Organizational separation involves separation from groups, whether church groups, or other groups that teach or practice either doctrines, ideas, or practices that are contrary to or forbidden by the Bible. This would include liberal, apostate or compromised churches or groups such as the National Council of Churches, the World Council of Churches, the National Association of Evangelicals, or any other church or group that is not Biblical in doctrine and practice.

Verses On Yokes

- **1 Kings 19:19**

  "So he departed thence, and found Elisha the son of Shaphat, who *was* plowing *with* twelve yoke *of oxen* before him, and he with the twelfth: and Elijah passed by him, and cast his mantle upon him."

Twelve yoke of oxen were joined together and plowing. A yoke is something that joins together.

- **Job 1:3**

  "His substance also was seven thousand sheep, and three thousand camels, and five hundred yoke of oxen, and five hundred she asses, and a very great household; so that this man was the greatest of all the men of the east."

The oxen were yoked or joined together.

- **Isaiah 58:6**

  "*Is* not this the fast that I have chosen? to loose the bands of wickedness, to undo the heavy burdens, and to let the oppressed go free, and that ye break every yoke?"

There is another verse on yoking,

- **Jeremiah 51:23**

  "I will also break in pieces with thee the shepherd and his flock; and with thee will I break in pieces the husbandman and his yoke of oxen; and with thee will I break in pieces captains and rulers."

The oxen were joined together.

2 Corinthians Preaching Verse-By-Verse

- **Matthew 11:29-30**

"<u>Take my yoke upon you</u>, and learn of me; for I am meek and lowly in heart: and ye shall find rest unto your souls. For my yoke *is* easy, and my burden is light."

The Lord Jesus Christ told His followers to be joined together with Him and His Words and actions. That is a proper yoke.

- **Galatians 5:1**

"Stand fast therefore in the liberty wherewith Christ hath made us free, and <u>be not entangled again with the yoke of bondage</u>."

Do not be joined with bondage.

Verses On Fellowship

- **Psalms 94:20**

"<u>Shall the throne of iniquity have fellowship with thee</u>, which frameth mischief by a law?"

There should be no fellowship with any iniquity or evil.

- **1 Corinthians 10:20**

"But I *say*, that the things which the Gentiles sacrifice, they sacrifice to devils, and not to God: and <u>I would not that ye should have fellowship with devils</u>."

Genuine Christians should not have fellowship with devils.

- **Ephesians 5:11**

"And <u>have no fellowship with the unfruitful works of darkness</u>, but rather reprove *them*."

True Christians should not join in fellowship with the works of darkness and sin, but reprove them.

- **1 John 1:3**

"That which we have seen and heard declare we unto you, that ye also may have fellowship with us: and truly our fellowship *is* with the Father, and with his Son Jesus Christ."

Those that are genuine Christians, the fellowship is with the Father and with the Son.

- **1 John 1:6-7**

"If we say that we have fellowship with him, and walk in darkness, we lie, and do not the truth: But <u>if we walk in the light</u>, as he is in the light, <u>we have fellowship one with another</u>, and the blood of Jesus Christ his Son cleanseth us from all sin."

Fellowship can be made with two people who are walking in the light of the Bible.

Verses On Communion
- **1 Corinthians 10:16**
"The cup of blessing which we bless, is it not <u>the communion of the blood of Christ</u>? The bread which we break, is it not <u>the communion of the body of Christ</u>?"

At communion services, there is a joining together of genuine Christians with the body and blood of Christ.

- **2 Corinthians 13:14**
"The grace of the Lord Jesus Christ, and the love of God, and <u>the communion of the Holy Ghost, *be* with you all</u>. Amen."

Only true Christians can have fellowship and communion with the Holy Spirit.

Verses On Darkness And Light
- **Ephesians 5:8**
"For <u>ye were sometimes darkness</u>, but now *are ye* <u>light</u> in the Lord: walk as children of light:"

There is a gigantic difference between darkness and light.

- **1 Thessalonians 5:5**
"<u>Ye are all the children of light</u>, and the children of the day: <u>we are not of the night, nor of darkness</u>."

Genuine Christians are called by God light, not darkness.

- **1 Peter 2:9**
"But ye *are* a chosen generation, a royal priesthood, an holy nation, a peculiar people; that ye should shew forth the praises of him who hath <u>called you out of darkness into his marvellous light</u>:"

True Christians have been called out of darkness into God's light. There should be no communion or fellowship between light and darkness.

Verses On Darkness
- **John 8:12**
"Then spake Jesus again unto them, saying, I am the light of the world: <u>he that followeth me shall not walk in darkness</u>, but shall have the light of life."

There is to be no communion or fellowship with darkness of doctrine or life.

- **John 12:46**
"I am come a light into the world, that <u>whosoever believeth on me should not abide in darkness</u>."

Separation demands that people do not abide in darkness of doctrine or life.

- **Acts 26:18**
"To open their eyes, *and* to turn *them* from darkness to light, and *from* the power of Satan unto God, that they may receive forgiveness of sins, and inheritance among them which are sanctified by faith that is in me."

Paul wanted to turn people from darkness to light.

- **Romans 13:12**
"The night is far spent, the day is at hand: let us therefore cast off the works of darkness, and let us put on the armour of light."

Bible separation casts off the works of darkness.

- **Ephesians 5:8**
"For ye were sometimes darkness, but now *are ye* light in the Lord: walk as children of light:"

Every person is born in sin and darkness.

- **Ephesians 5:11**
"And have no fellowship with the unfruitful works of darkness, but rather reprove *them*."

There should be zero fellowship with the works of darkness.

- **Colossians 1:13**
"Who hath delivered us from the power of darkness, and hath translated *us* into the kingdom of his dear Son:"

God delivered true Christians from the power of darkness.

- **1 Peter 2:9**
"But ye *are* a chosen generation, a royal priesthood, an holy nation, a peculiar people; that ye should shew forth the praises of him who hath called you out of darkness into his marvellous light:"

Genuine Christians have been called out of darkness. They should stay away from it.

2 Corinthians 6:15

"And what concord hath Christ with Belial? or what part hath he that believeth with an infidel?"

In this verse, Paul asks two more questions of the genuine Christians at Corinth. The second and third question Paul asks about separation are these; (2) *What concord hath Christ with belial?* (3) *What part hath he that believeth with an infidel?* Because of these questions, it can be stated that (1) there can be no concord between Christ and Belial. And (2) there can be no part between the one who believes and an infidel.

Verses On Belial
- **Judges 19:22**

"*Now* as they were making their hearts merry, behold, the men of the city, <u>certain sons of Belial, beset the house round about, *and* beat at the door</u>, and spake to the master of the house, the old man, saying, <u>Bring forth the man that came into thine house, that we may know him</u>."

These were homosexual sons of Belial. They were Satanic men. They wanted to have sex with this guest.

- **1 Samuel 2:12**

"Now <u>the sons of Eli *were* sons of Belial; they knew not the L<small>ORD</small></u>."

Eli was a priest. He did not raise his children right. They were sons of Belial.

- **1 Samuel 25:25**

"Let not my lord, I pray thee, regard this man of Belial, *even* Nabal: for as his name *is*, so *is* he; Nabal *is* his name, and folly *is* with him: but I thine handmaid saw not the young men of my lord, whom thou didst send."

Nabal was a man of Belial, a man of Satan.

- **1 Kings 21:13**

"And <u>there came in two men, children of Belial</u>, and sat before him: and the men of Belial witnessed against him, *even* against Naboth, in the presence of the people, saying, Naboth did blaspheme God and the king. Then they carried him forth out of the city, and stoned him with stones, that he died."

Children of Belial were children of the devil. There can be no fellowship between Christ and Belial.

There should be a solid separation between genuine Christians and those who deny the Lord Jesus Christ and are infidels who deny any part of the Christian faith and doctrines.

2 Corinthians 6:16

"And what agreement hath the temple of God with idols? for ye are the temple of the living God; as God hath said, I will dwell in them, and walk in *them*; and I will be their God, and they shall be my people."

The fifth question about Biblical separation is: (5) "*What agreement hath the temple of God with idols?*" Every genuine Christian who is "*the temple of the living God*" has no agreement with idols which are instruments of Satan, who are the temples of the Devil.

Verses On Agreement
- 2 Kings 18:31

"Hearken not to Hezekiah: for thus saith the king of Assyria, Make an agreement with me by a present, and come out to me, and *then* eat ye every man of his own vine, and every one of his fig tree, and drink ye every one the waters of his cistern:"

This person was told to make an agreement with him rather than with King Hezekiah.

- Isaiah 28:15

"Because ye have said, We have made a covenant with death, and with hell are we at agreement; when the overflowing scourge shall pass through, it shall not come unto us: for we have made lies our refuge, and under falsehood have we hid ourselves:"

No one should be in agreement with death and hell.

- Isaiah 28:18

"And your covenant with death shall be disannulled, and your agreement with hell shall not stand; when the overflowing scourge shall pass through, then ye shall be trodden down by it."

The agreement with God and hell should not stand.

Verses On Temples
- 1 Corinthians 3:16-17

"Know ye not that ye are the temple of God, and *that* the Spirit of God dwelleth in you? If any man defile the temple of God, him shall God destroy; for the temple of God is holy, which *temple* ye are."

Every true Christian is considered to be a temple of God because God the Holy Spirit indwells them.

- **1 Corinthians 6:19-20**
"What? know ye not that your body is the temple of the Holy Ghost *which* is in you, which ye have of God, and ye are not your own? For ye are bought with a price: therefore glorify God in your body, and in your spirit, which are God's."

The bodies of genuine Christians are the temple of the Holy Spirit Which is in them.

- **Ephesians 2:21**
"In whom all the building fitly framed together groweth unto an holy temple in the Lord:"

All the true Christians are like a building called a holy temple in the Lord.

Verses On Idols

- **2 Kings 23:24**
"Moreover the *workers with* familiar spirits, and the wizards, and the images, and the idols, and all the abominations that were spied in the land of Judah and in Jerusalem, did Josiah put away, that he might perform the words of the law which were written in the book that Hilkiah the priest found in the house of the LORD."

King Josiah put away these idols and so should separated true Christians. We are not to have any fellowship with idols and idolatry. This includes the Roman Catholic church with its idols and picture of Mary and their saints.

- **Psalms 96:5**
"For all the gods of the nations *are* idols: but the LORD made the heavens."

The gods of many nations are idols.

- **Psalms 106:38**
"And shed innocent blood, *even* the blood of their sons and of their daughters, whom they sacrificed unto the idols of Canaan: and the land was polluted with blood."

The Israelites killed their children and sacrificed them to idols which was a terrible thing.

- **Psalms 115:4-7**
"Their idols *are* silver and gold, the work of men's hands. They have mouths, but they speak not: eyes have they, but they see not: They have ears, but they hear not: noses have they, but they smell not: They have hands, but they handle not: feet have they, but they walk not: neither speak they through their throat."

This is absolutely useless to worship any idols.
- **1 Corinthians 12:2**

"Ye know that ye were Gentiles, <u>carried away unto these dumb idols</u>, even as ye were led."

The Corinthian church was following heathen idols.
- **1 Thessalonians 1:9**

"For they themselves shew of us what manner of entering in we had unto you, and how <u>ye turned to God from idols</u> to serve the living and true God;"

The Thessalonians did right in turning to God from idols to serve the living and true God. That is what everyone should do, turn to God and turn your backs against these many idols and idol worship.
- **1 John 5:21**

"Little children, <u>keep yourselves from idols</u>. Amen."

Whether they be inanimate idols, or human idols, true Christians should be separated from them.

2 Corinthians 6:17

"Wherefore come out from among them, and be ye separate, saith the Lord, and touch not the unclean *thing*; and I will receive you,"

Verses fourteen and fifteen talk about the serious problems concerning sins and evils all around the genuine Christians who are living today and those who were living in days and years gone by, yesterday. This verse gives a command for all true Christians which, if followed, will provide God's proper Biblical solution to these problems.

True Christians should have nothing in common with unrighteousness, with darkness, with Belial, with infidels, or with idolaters.

Wherefore, if this is true and is practiced by these genuine Christians, they should follow God's solution to these problems and "*come out from among them*" and separate yourselves from them. This should be practiced in both personal separation as well as organizational separation.

The next part of verse seventeen is: "*touch not the unclean thing*." When God's Word says "*touch not*," He means no close fellowship, no close relationship with these people. Do not marry them. Do not have close business relationships with them.

I am not talking about going to the meat market and buying meat from a non-Christian person. I am not talking about going to the drug store to get some prescriptions. I am talking about close and continuing fellowship with apostates and non-Christian unbelievers.

"*Touch not the unclean thing.*" Touch them not. Do not keep close relationships with them. Do not say, "*Oh, they are my friends.*" God says, do not touch unclean things. If you want to give them the Gospel about the Lord Jesus Christ, but do not dwell with them. Do not stay with them. Do not eat with them. Do not keep close company with them. "*Touch not the unclean thing.*"

Notice the last part of this verse "*and I will receive you,*" God wants to receive clean-cut, genuine Christian people, separated from uncleanness, separated from touching unclean people and unclean things.

Verses On Come Out
- **Numbers 9:1**

"And the LORD spake unto Moses in the wilderness of Sinai, in the first month of the second year after they were come out of the land of Egypt, saying,"

Israel was told by God to come out of Egypt, and they came out.

- **Revelation 18:4**

"And I heard another voice from heaven, saying, Come out of her, my people, that ye be not partakers of her sins, and that ye receive not of her plagues."

That is God's command in Revelation for His people to come out from these people and do not be partakers of her sins.

Verses On Separation
- **Genesis 13:9**

"*Is* not the whole land before thee? separate thyself, I pray thee, from me: if *thou wilt take* the left hand, then I will go to the right; or if *thou depart* to the right hand, then I will go to the left."

Abraham told Lot to separate from him. Lot was going the wrong way.

- **Genesis 13:11**

"Then Lot chose him all the plain of Jordan; and Lot journeyed east: and they separated themselves the one from the other."

They separated because there were too many cattle and so they separated.

- **Leviticus 20:24**
"But I have said unto you, Ye shall inherit their land, and I will give it unto you to possess it, a land that floweth with milk and honey: <u>I am the LORD your God, which have separated you from other people</u>."

God is a separatist. It is one of the titles of the Lord. That word is not in many people's vocabulary. I am the Lord that separates you from other people. He is a separatist. In the book of Genesis, God created both darkness and light and separated them from each other.

- **Numbers 16:21**
"<u>Separate yourselves from among this congregation</u>, that I may consume them in a moment."

God told Moses and Aaron this before He slew many of the ungodly people around them.

- **1 Kings 8:53**
"For <u>thou didst separate them from among all the people of the earth, to be thine inheritance</u>, as thou spakest by the hand of Moses thy servant, when thou broughtest our fathers out of Egypt, O Lord GOD."

God took the people of Israel, even though they sinned against Him, and separated them to be his people.

- **Nehemiah 9:2**
"And <u>the seed of Israel separated themselves from all strangers</u>, and stood and confessed their sins, and the iniquities of their fathers."

At this time, Israel separated themselves from all strangers.

- **Nehemiah 10:28**
"And the rest of the people, the priests, the Levites, the porters, the singers, the Nethinims, and <u>all they that had separated themselves from the people of the lands unto the law of God</u>, their wives, their sons, and their daughters, every one having knowledge, and having understanding;"

This was a separated group of the people of the land. They were separated unto the Lord.

- **Nehemiah 13:3**
"Now it came to pass, <u>when they had heard the law, that they separated from Israel all the mixed multitude</u>."

They heard what God said in His Word and they separated from the heathen.

- **Isaiah 52:11**
"<u>Depart ye, depart ye, go ye out from thence, touch no unclean *thing*</u>; go ye out of the midst of her; be ye clean, that bear the vessels of the LORD."

This is where Paul got this phrase, "*touch not the unclean thing.*"

- **Matthew 25:32**
"And before him shall be gathered all nations: and <u>he shall separate them one from another</u>, as a shepherd divideth *his* sheep from the goats:"

At this judgment, the Lord Jesus Christ will separate the sheep from the goats.

- **Romans 1:1**
"Paul, a servant of Jesus Christ, called *to be* an apostle, separated unto the Gospel of God,"

He was a separated man.

- **Hebrews 7:26**
"For <u>such an high priest became us, *who is*</u> holy, harmless, undefiled, <u>separate from sinners</u>, and made higher than the heavens;"

The Lord Jesus believed in Bible separation. He was separate from close contact or fellowship with sinners.

Verses On Uncleanness

- **Numbers 19:11**
"He that toucheth the dead body of any man <u>shall be unclean seven days.</u>"

If you touch a dead body, that makes you unclean.

- **Numbers 19:13**
"<u>Whosoever toucheth the dead body</u> of any man that is dead, and purifieth not himself, defileth the tabernacle of the LORD; and that soul shall be cut off from Israel: because the water of separation was not sprinkled upon him, <u>he shall be unclean</u>; his uncleanness *is* yet upon him."

Touching a dead body made the person unclean.

- **Isaiah 52:11**
"Depart ye, depart ye, go ye out from thence, <u>touch no unclean *thing*</u>; go ye out of the midst of her; <u>be ye clean</u>, that bear the vessels of the LORD."

These were Levites who were not to touch any unclean thing.

2 Corinthians 6:18

"And will be a Father unto you, and ye shall be my sons and daughters, saith the Lord Almighty."

If true Christians will follow these preceding verses and commands regarding separation from unclean and evil people and things, then God promised to be a real and helpful Father unto them. If genuine Christians refuse to follow personal separation from sin, or refuse to follow organizational separation and get themselves tied into the National Council or World Council of Churches, or National Association of New Evangelicals, or the Emerging Church, God will judge you and not be a real and helpful Father to you.

Verses On Father

- **Jeremiah 3:19c**

"... and I said, <u>Thou shalt call me, My father; and shalt not turn away from me</u>."

God can be the real Father to true Christians who are separated from sin trusting Him.

- **Jeremiah 31:1**

"At the same time, saith the LORD, will I be the God of all the families of Israel, and <u>they shall be my people</u>."

He is the Father to genuine Christians,

- **Romans 8:15b**

"... but <u>ye have received the Spirit of adoption</u>, whereby <u>we cry, Abba, Father</u>."

He is a real Father to true Christians who are separated from sin and unto Him.

- **Galatians 4:6**

"And <u>because ye are sons</u>, God hath sent forth the Spirit of his Son into your hearts, <u>crying, Abba, Father</u>."

Genuine Christians have God as their Father, but their separation from evil makes Him their close Father.

- **1 John 1:3**

"That which we have seen and heard declare we unto you, that ye also may have fellowship with us: and truly our fellowship *is* with the Father, and with his Son Jesus Christ."

If we are not separated from wickedness and sin and unbelief, God cannot be a genuine, real, close father to us.

2 Corinthians Chapter Seven

2 Corinthians 7:1

"Having therefore these promises, dearly beloved, let us cleanse ourselves from all filthiness of the flesh and spirit, perfecting holiness in the fear of God."

The genuine Christians have all of God's promises. Because of this Paul urges them to cleanse themselves from all filthiness of both the flesh and the spirit. This includes not only sins of the flesh, but also the sins of the human spirit, including what goes on in their hearts, soul, minds, and thoughts.

God wants true Christians to perfect holiness by both reading, studying, and following His Words. That is the only way they can perfect holiness before God.

Verses On God's Promises

- **2 Corinthians 1:20**

"For all the promises of God in him *are* yea, and in him Amen, unto the glory of God by us."

- **Hebrews 10:36**

"For ye have need of patience, that, after ye have done the will of God, ye might receive the promise."

There is a great need of patience, because God does not always answer His promises immediately.

- **2 Peter 1:4**

"Whereby are given unto us exceeding great and precious promises: that by these ye might be partakers of the divine nature, having escaped the corruption that is in the world through lust."

By these promises, genuine Christians are able to keep themselves from all wickedness and evil of the flesh and spirit.

- **Matthew 23:26**

"*Thou* blind Pharisee, cleanse first that *which is* within the cup and platter, that the outside of them may be clean also."

Inward cleansing, as well as outward cleansing is needed.

- **Ephesians 5:26**

"That he might sanctify and cleanse it with the washing of water by the word,"

The words of God are his cleansing agents that can cleanse the true Christians from sins if followed and used.

- **James 4:8**

"Draw nigh to God, and he will draw nigh to you. Cleanse your hands, ye sinners; and purify your hearts, ye double minded."

Cleansed hands and purified hearts of genuine Christians are wanted by the Lord.

- **1 John 1:7**

"But if we walk in the light, as he is in the light, we have fellowship one with another, and the blood of Jesus Christ his Son cleanseth us from all sin."

The shed blood of the Lord Jesus Christ is a cleansing Agent.

- **1 John 1:9**

"If we confess our sins, he is faithful and just to forgive us our sins, and to cleanse us from all unrighteousness."

When true Christians agree with God that they have sinned, then God can and will cleanse them from their sins.

Verses On Holiness

- **Psalms 29:2**

"Give unto the LORD the glory due unto his name; worship the LORD in the beauty of holiness."

Many churches house many kinds of wickedness, corruption and unbelief. God wants holiness to be in His worship in churches and in homes.

- **Psalms 96:9**

"O worship the LORD in the beauty of holiness: fear before him, all the earth."

True Christians must worship the Lord in holiness, not in sinfulness and compromise.

- **Romans 6:19**

"I speak after the manner of men because of the infirmity of your flesh: for as ye have yielded your members servants to uncleanness and to iniquity unto iniquity; even so now yield your members servants to righteousness unto holiness."

These genuine Christians formerly served uncleanness and iniquity, but now should yield themselves to God's holiness.

- **Romans 6:22**
"But now being made free from sin, and become servants to God, <u>ye have your fruit unto holiness</u>, and the end everlasting life."

These are true Christians who were made free from the practice of sin and now had their fruit unto holiness.

- **1 Thessalonians 3:13**
"To the end <u>he may stablish your hearts unblameable in holiness before God</u>, even our Father, at the coming of our Lord Jesus Christ with all his saints."

God wants genuine Christians to be unblameable in holiness before Him.

- **1 Thessalonians 4:7**
"For <u>God hath not called us unto uncleanness, but unto holiness</u>."

God has called every true Christian away from uncleanness unto holiness.

- **Titus 2:3**
"<u>The aged women likewise, that *they be* in behaviour as becometh holiness</u>, not false accusers, not given to much wine, teachers of good things;"

God wants aged genuine Christian to have holiness in their behavior.

- **Hebrews 12:10**
"For they verily for a few days chastened *us* after their own pleasure; but he for *our* profit, that *we* might be partakers of his holiness.

The Lord chastens genuine Christians for our profit. Not for His pleasure but in order that they may be partakers of His holiness.

2 Corinthians 7:2

"Receive us; we have wronged no man, we have corrupted no man, we have defrauded no man."

Paul wanted to be received by the true Christians at Corinth. He had not either wronged, corrupted, or corrupted anyone. Although he had written a very strong letter to them how they should not have accepted the incest of one of their church members.

Verses On Wrong
- **Acts 25:10**

"Then said Paul, I stand at Caesar's judgment seat, where I ought to be judged: to the Jews have <u>I done no wrong</u>, as thou very well knowest."

Paul did no wrong against Caesar.

- **Philemon 1:18**

"<u>If he hath wronged thee</u>, or oweth *thee* ought, put that on mine account;"

If Onesimus had wronged Philemon, his master, Paul wanted him to put what Onesimus owed on Paul's account. He would pay for it.

Verses On Corrupt
- **Genesis 6:12**

"And <u>God looked upon the earth, and, behold, it was corrupt</u>; for <u>all flesh had corrupted his way</u> upon the earth."

This is why God judged the whole earth with a universal flood. Noah obeyed the Lord by building a huge ark which saved Noah's family and many animals. Other people were invited, but did not believe the flood would come. God then shut the door.

- **Exodus 32:7**

"And the LORD said unto Moses, Go, get thee down; for <u>thy people</u>, which thou broughtest out of the land of Egypt, <u>have corrupted *themselves*</u>:"

Moses was up on Mount Sinai, receiving the Law while Aaron was beneath the mountain leading the people into idolatry and corruption.

- **Judges 2:19**

"And it came to pass, <u>when the judge was dead, *that* they returned, and corrupted *themselves* more than their fathers</u>, in following other gods to serve them, and to bow down unto them; they ceased not from their own doings, nor from their stubborn way."

The Israelites did not follow their judges for very long. They followed the judge while he was living and then went back into corruption and sin.

- **2 Corinthians 11:3**
"But I fear, lest by any means, as the serpent beguiled Eve through his subtilty, so your minds should be corrupted from the simplicity that is in Christ."
Minds of even true Christians can be corrupted from the simplicity that is in Christ. They must be ware of this possibility.

Verses On Defraud
- **Leviticus 19:13**
"Thou shalt not defraud thy neighbour, neither rob *him*: the wages of him that is hired shall not abide with thee all night until the morning."
Defraud means *"to take advantage of someone, to overreach."* Genuine Christians should pay what they owe people. In the Old Testament, it was a day by day pay. The workers did not wait for a week or a month. They got paid at the end of every day.
- **1 Samuel 12:3**
"Behold, here I *am*: witness against me before the LORD, and before his anointed: whose ox have I taken? or whose ass have I taken? or whom have I defrauded? whom have I oppressed? or of whose hand have I received *any* bribe to blind mine eyes therewith? and I will restore it you."
Samuel had not defrauded anyone. He had a good witness before he left being the leader of Israel.
- **1 Samuel 12:4**
"And they said, Thou hast not defrauded us, nor oppressed us, neither hast thou taken ought of any man's hand."
Samuel had a good testimony. It is sad that his sons went astray. Therefore, his sons could not be prophets.
- **Mark 10:19**
"Thou knowest the commandments, Do not commit adultery, Do not kill, Do not steal, Do not bear false witness, Defraud not, Honour thy father and mother."
This man wanted to go to heaven by his good works, which is impossible to do.
- **1 Corinthians 7:5**
"Defraud ye not one the other, except *it be* with consent for a time, that ye may give yourselves to fasting and prayer; and come together again, that Satan tempt you not for your incontinency."
Now this is a verse regarding proper married love. Neither the husbands nor the wives were to defraud their partners sexual love except for these four conditions mentioned in this verse.

- **1 Thessalonians 4:6**

"That no *man* go beyond and defraud his brother in *any matter*: because that the Lord *is* the avenger of all such, as we also have forewarned you and testified."

The Lord is the avenger of those who defraud his fellow true Christian.

2 Corinthians 7:3

"I speak not *this* to condemn *you*: for I have said before, that ye are in our hearts to die and live with *you*."

Paul was not writing this letter to condemn the genuine Christians at Corinth. He wrote a letter condemning this incestuous man that should not have had his father's wife. Paul told them that they should put him out of the church rather than glorying and exalting him wrongly.

Verses On Condemn

- **John 3:17**

"For God sent not his Son into the world to condemn the world; but that the world through him might be saved."

God the Father sent His Son into the world not to condemn the world, but by saving the souls of those who genuinely trust the Lord Jesus Christ as their Saviour.

- **John 8:11**

"She said, No man, Lord. And Jesus said unto her, Neither do I condemn thee: go, and sin no more."

Apparently this woman truly trusted the Lord Jesus Christ as her Saviour. He forgave her for sinning, but ordered her to go and sin no more, probably in this same sin of adultery and fornication.

Verses On Boldness

- **2 Corinthians 7:4**

"Great *is* my boldness of speech toward you, great *is* my glorying of you: I am filled with comfort, I am exceeding joyful in all our tribulation."

True Christians must have boldness when talking about the Lord Jesus Christ and God's truths.

- **Acts 4:13**

"Now <u>when they saw the boldness of Peter and John</u>, and perceived that they were unlearned and ignorant men, they marvelled; and they took knowledge of them, that they had been with Jesus."

Peter and John were simple men. They did not have much schooling, but their boldness showed that they had been with Jesus.

- **Acts 4:29**

"And now, Lord, behold their threatenings: and <u>grant unto thy servants, that with all **boldness** they may speak thy word</u>,"

They prayed for boldness, even after they were threatened to speak God's Words with boldness. Genuine Christians today must also be bold to speak God's Words.

It must be the proper and faithful Words of God found in the traditional inspired Hebrew Words, the traditional inspired Aramaic Words, and the traditional inspired Greek Words. These Words must very accurately translated into all the languages of the world as the King James Bible has done in the English language.

- **Ephesians 3:12**

"<u>In whom we have boldness</u> and access with confidence by the faith of him."

In the Lord Jesus Christ, genuine Christians can have boldness to face all of life's circumstances.

- **Philippians 1:20**

"According to my earnest expectation and *my* hope, that in nothing I shall be ashamed, but *that* <u>with all boldness, as always, *so* now also Christ shall be magnified in my body, whether *it be* by life, or by death</u>."

Even in prison, Paul wanted to have boldness to magnify the Lord Jesus Christ, whether by his life, or his death.

- **Hebrews 10:19**

"<u>Having</u> therefore, brethren, <u>boldness to enter into the holiest by the blood of Jesus</u>,"

Because of the shed blood of the Lord Jesus Christ, true Christians have boldness to enter the holiest in Heaven.

2 Corinthians 7:4

"Great *is* my boldness of speech toward you, great *is* my glorying of you: I am filled with comfort, I am exceeding joyful in all our tribulation."

Verses On Tribulation
- **Romans 5:3**

"And not only *so*, but <u>we glory in tribulations</u> also: knowing that <u>tribulation worketh patience</u>;"

To succeed in tribulation there must be patience. True Christians must be patient in tribulation because you cannot stop it. It just keeps on going.

- **Romans 12:12**

"Rejoicing in hope; <u>patient in tribulation</u>; continuing instant in prayer;"

This is another verse about being patient in tribulation.

2 Corinthians 7:5

"For, when we were come into Macedonia, our flesh had no rest, but we were troubled on every side; without *were* fightings, within *were* fears."

Paul came to Macedonia, where Corinth was one of its provinces. When he arrived, he was restless, troubled, fearful, and surrounded by fightings.

What will our government do in the days in which true Christians are living today? What will these Christians do when they round them up and put them into FEMA concentration camps? What will happen, when they knock on your door and take you away in a FEMA bus. The driver might say to you, *"You do not have enough food here. We are taking you, with a bus load of others, to a FEMA camp, where we will give you some food."*

I advise every genuine Christian not to get on these FEMA buses, no matter what lies they tell you about food and safety. In these FEMA camps, death will come to all those who do not comply with their outlandish and non-Christian demands. They will falsely interpret the first few verses of Romans 13 by saying that these verses demand obedience to ANYTHING ordered by the FEMA authorities.

2 Corinthians 7:6

"Nevertheless God, that comforteth those that are cast down, comforted us by the coming of Titus;"

This is a wonderful phrase: *"God, that comforteth those that are cast down."* God is the One Who can comfort genuine Christians by His power and might. One of His titles is: *"The God of All Comfort."* That Greek Word for *"comfort"* means *"to console, to encourage, and to strengthen by consolation."*

In this case, the comfort was given by the coming of Titus. Titus was a pastor on the isle of Crete who was one of Paul's closest disciples and followers. If you are a true Christian, are you comforting anyone? Notice, God comforts those who are cast down. That Greek Word for "cast down" means *"not rising far from the ground."*

Verses On Comfort
- **Isaiah 51:12**

"Great is my boldness of speech toward you, great is my glorying of you: <u>I am filled with comfort</u>, I am exceeding joyful in all our tribulation. "I, even I, am he that comforteth you: who art thou, that thou shouldest be afraid of a man that shall die, and of the son of man which shall be made as grass;"

Lots of times mothers are comforters to their children. We have four sons and a daughter, five children and their mother comforted them as need be. The comfort is for Israel, a promise, Isaiah 66:13.

- **2 Corinthians 1:4**

"Who <u>comforteth us</u> in all our tribulation, that we may be able <u>to comfort</u> them which are in any trouble, <u>by the comfort</u> wherewith we ourselves <u>are comforted of God</u>."

Some form of the word *"comfort"* is used by Paul four times. God comforts all genuine Christians so that they might comfort others, by the comfort that God gives to them. It is a wonderful thing, to have comfort, by the power of the Holy Spirit that indwells all the true Christians.

Verses On Cast Down
- **Job 22:29**

"<u>When men are cast down</u>, then thou shalt say, <u>There is lifting up</u>; and he shall save the humble person."

God is able to lift up those who are cast down.
- **Psalms 37:24**
"Though he fall, he shall not be utterly cast down: for the LORD upholdeth *him with* his hand."

God upholds, even though His genuine Christians are cast down.
- **Psalms 42:6**
"O my God, my soul is cast down within me: therefore will I remember thee from the land of Jordan, and of the Hermonites, from the hill Mizar."

David had a remembrance of the Lord, even when his soul was cast down.
- **2 Corinthians 4:9**
"Persecuted, but not forsaken; cast down, but not destroyed;"

He was cast down many times but not destroyed.

2 Corinthians 7:7

"And not by his coming only, but by the consolation wherewith he was comforted in you, when he told us your earnest desire, your mourning, your fervent mind toward me; so that I rejoiced the more."

Paul was comforted by the coming of Titus, but also by the genuine Christians at Corinth who had earnest desire, mourning and fervent mind toward Paul. That made Paul rejoice more.

Verses On Fervent
- **Acts 18:25**
"This man was instructed in the way of the Lord; and being fervent in the spirit, he spake and taught diligently the things of the Lord, knowing only the baptism of John."

Appolos was a fervent teacher of the Words of God.
- **Romans 12:11**
"Not slothful in business; fervent in spirit; serving the Lord;"

True Christians who work in businesses should be fervent in spirit as though they are serving the Lord Himself.
- **1 Peter 4:8**
"And above all things have fervent charity among yourselves: for charity shall cover the multitude of sins."

The charity or love of the genuine Christians should be fervent, not mediocre.

2 Corinthians 7:8

"For though I made you sorry with a letter, I do not repent, though I did repent: for I perceive that the same epistle hath made you sorry, though *it were* but for a season."

In referring to his letter in 1 Corinthians, Paul realized that the letter made the Corinthians sorry. He did not repent about the letter because the church deserved it. But in time, he did repent. He was glad the church was made sorry only for a season.

The man who had committed incest was kicked out of the church until he repented and got right with the Lord.

Verses On Repent
- **Numbers 23:19**

"God *is* not a man, that he should lie; neither the son of man, that he should repent: hath he said, and shall he not do *it*? or hath he spoken, and shall he not make it good?"

What God says, he will make good. He never lies. He never changes.

- **Job 42:6**

"Wherefore I abhor *myself,* and repent in dust and ashes."

Job realized he had made a mistake and he repented or changed his mind about it.

- **Jeremiah 18:8**

"If that nation, against whom I have pronounced, turn from their evil, I will repent of the evil that I thought to do unto them."

If a nation turns from their evil, God will repent or change His mind regarding punishing them.

- **Jeremiah 18:10**

"If it do evil in my sight, that it obey not my voice, then I will repent of the good, wherewith I said I would benefit them."

When a nation does evil, God will repent or change His mind regarding the good He was going to do them.

2 Corinthians 7:9

"Now I rejoice, not that ye were made sorry, but that ye sorrowed to repentance: for ye were made sorry after a godly manner, that ye might receive damage by us in nothing."

Paul was not rejoicing that this church was made sorry because of his strong letter to them, but he was glad that they sorrowed to repentance. They changed their ways because of his letter. In a godly manner. Twice, Paul said that the church sorrowed to repentance. They were sorry after a godly manner. That Greek Word for *"repentance"* means *"a change of mind."*

Verses On Repentance

- **Mark 2:17**

"When Jesus heard *it*, he saith unto them, They that are whole have no need of the physician, but they that are sick: I came not to call the righteous, but sinners to repentance."

If a people think they are whole and well, they do not think they need a physician? That is why repentance is necessary.

- **Luke 24:47**

"And that repentance and remission of sins should be preached in his name among all nations, beginning at Jerusalem."

Repentance by a person needed and genuine faith in the Lord Jesus Christ are needed for true salvation.

- **Acts 5:31**

"Him hath God exalted with his right hand *to be* a Prince and a Saviour, for to give repentance to Israel, and forgiveness of sins."

Before Israel, or anyone, can have true salvation, they obtain the forgiveness of their sins by genuine faith in the Lord Jesus Christ.

- **Acts 11:18**

"When they heard these things, they held their peace, and glorified God, saying, Then hath God also to the Gentiles granted repentance unto life."

God granted to the Gentiles repentance unto eternal life.

- **Acts 20:21**

"Testifying both to the Jews, and also to the Greeks, <u>repentance toward God, and faith toward our Lord Jesus Christ</u>."

Both Jews and Greeks must have a repentant change of mind toward God the Father and true faith in the Lord Jesus Christ to receive eternal life.

- **2 Timothy 2:25**

"In meekness instructing those that oppose themselves; if <u>God peradventure will give them repentance to the acknowledging of the truth</u>;"

Repentance is needed to acknowledge the truth of the Bible and God's offer of salvation. Many people reject God Words of truth.

- **2 Peter 3:9**

"<u>The Lord</u> is not slack concerning his promise, as some men count slackness; but <u>is longsuffering to us-ward, not willing that any should perish, but that all should come to repentance</u>."

This is contrary to the hyper-Calvinists' heresy. The hyper-Calvinist heresy says God does not allow all people to come to repentance and change of mind regarding Christ and promise of salvation. They say that is foolishness. The hyper-Calvinists teach that God only wants the elect (a certain little group of people He picked out a long time ago) to be saved.

They falsely teach that the rest of us not in this "elect" group will be lost and sent to Hell. They falsely teach that the Lord Jesus Christ did not die for their sins, only for this tiny "elect" group. That is the foolishness and the heresy of the a hyper-Calvinist message that is growing in Presbyterian churches as well as various other churches all over the world. It is growing and growing and growing. The Bible is crystal clear that the Lord Jesus Christ died for the sins of the entire world!

2 Corinthians 7:10

"For godly sorrow worketh repentance to salvation not to be repented of: but the sorrow of the world worketh death."

Paul mentions two kinds of sorrow are mentioned in this verse. One is godly sorrow and the other is the sorrow of the world. Godly sorrow works repentance leading to salvation. When people have godly sorrow, they are able to come to the Lord Jesus Christ and be come genuine Christians, but the sorrow of the world works spiritual death.

Verses On Sorrow
- **John 16:6**
"But because I have said these things unto you, <u>sorrow hath filled your heart</u>."

The Lord Jesus told his disciples that He was going to be crucified on the cross. He told them he was going to die at the cross of Calvary; and after three days and three nights He would be bodily raised up. Because I told these things, sorrow filled your heart.

- **John 16:20**
"Verily, verily, I say unto you, That ye shall weep and lament, but the world shall rejoice: and <u>ye shall be sorrowful, but your sorrow shall be turned into joy</u>."

The Lord Jesus Christ told His apostles "*your sorrow shall be turned into joy*" after His bodily resurrection.

- **2 Corinthians 2:7**
"So that contrariwise <u>ye *ought* rather to forgive *him*, and comfort *him*</u>, lest perhaps such a one should be swallowed up with overmuch sorrow."

This man committed a great sin. He was dismissed from the church, but they were to comfort him because he sorrowed greatly. They let him back into the church once he repented and changed his mind concerning his sin.

- **1 Thessalonians 4:13**
"But I would not have you to be ignorant, brethren, <u>concerning them which are asleep, that ye sorrow not, even as others which have no hope</u>."

Those true Christians who died were in Heaven. Though there is sorrow for them, it is different than for those who have no hope and are in Hell. There is godly sorrow when a genuine Christian dies. We miss them.

2 Corinthians 7:11

"For behold this selfsame thing, that ye sorrowed after a godly sort, what carefulness it wrought in you, yea, *what* clearing of yourselves, yea, *what* indignation, yea, *what* fear, yea, *what* vehement desire, yea, *what* zeal, yea, *what* revenge! In all *things* ye have approved yourselves to be clear in this matter."

Because they had godly sorrow, they had carefulness, zeal, and these other things mentioned in this verse. These genuine Christians were made better, not worse by the death of this true Christian who has gone Home to Heaven. The loss of this Christian friend worked for the good of those true Christians who were left behind, not for their ill.

2 Corinthians 7:12

"Wherefore, though I wrote unto you, I *did it* not for his cause that had done the wrong, nor for his cause that suffered wrong, but that our care for you in the sight of God might appear unto you."

Paul explained why he wrote his first letter to this group of genuine Christians. It was so they could see that his sincere care for them in the Lord might appear unto them. Pastors must care for their people and all true Christians should care for each other as well.

Verses On Caring For Others
- Luke 10:34

"And went to *him*, and bound up his wounds, pouring in oil and wine, and set him on his own beast, and brought him to an inn, and took care of him."

This good Samaritan took care of this man who was beaten and left for dead. Genuine Christians should care for one another as well. The good Samaritan was half Greek and half Jew, and yet he is the one who stopped. He took care of this man who was beaten up and almost dead. The priest did not care. The Levite did not care. But this man, half Greek and half Jew, took care of him.

- **Luke 10:35**
"And on the morrow when he departed, he took out two pence, and gave *them* to the host, and said unto him, Take care of him; and whatsoever thou spendest more, when I come again, I will repay thee."

This man was cared for completely, in body and in spirit.

- **1 Corinthians 12:25**
"'That there should be no schism in the body; but *that* the members should have the same care one for another."

Genuine Christian church members should have the same care one toward one another.

- **2 Corinthians 8:16**
"But thanks *be* to God, which put the same earnest care into the heart of Titus for you."

Titus, the pastor of the church at Crete, was sent to the Corinthians to care for them.

- **2 Corinthians 11:28**
"Beside those things that are without, that which cometh upon me daily, the care of all the churches."

Paul had the care of the churches at Colosse, Ephesus, Colossi, Philippi, Thessalonica, and all the other churches he founded. Some of the members of those churches were sick, sorrowful, grumpy, and complaining. It was not an easy task.

- **Philippians 2:20**
"For I have no man likeminded, who will naturally care for your state."

Timothy was a good care-giver for Onesimus a runaway slave.

- **1 Peter 5:7**
"Casting all your care upon him; for he careth for you."

The Lord Jesus Christ is One on Whom true Christians can cast their cares, for He cares for them.

2 Corinthians 7:13

"Therefore we were comforted in your comfort: yea, and exceedingly the more joyed we for the joy of Titus, because his spirit was refreshed by you all."

Paul was comforted by the comfort of the genuine Christians at Corinth. He was also joyful for the joy of Titus whose spirit was refreshed by the Corinthians.

Verses On Comfort
- **2 Corinthians 1:3**
"Blessed *be* God, even the Father of our Lord Jesus Christ, the Father of mercies, and <u>the God of all comfort</u>;"
One of the appropriate names of the God of the Bible is *"the God of all comfort."* He is a comforting God.
- **2 Corinthians 1:4**
"<u>Who comforteth us in all our tribulation</u>, that we may be <u>able to comfort</u> them which are in any trouble, <u>by the comfort</u> wherewith we ourselves are <u>comforted of God</u>."
Comfort is used four times in this verse. If we have comfort, we can comfort others.
- **2 Corinthians 7:6**
"Nevertheless <u>God, that comforteth those that are cast down, comforted us by the coming of Titus</u>;"
God comforted Paul through Titus who was the pastor of the church of Crete.
- **1 Thessalonians 2:11**
"As ye know how <u>we exhorted and comforted and charged every one of you</u>, as a father doth his children,"
We have four sons and a daughter. When there is a need, we as parents have sought to comfort our children as best as we knew how.

Verses On Joy
- **Galatians 5:22**
"But <u>the fruit of the Spirit is love, joy</u>, peace, longsuffering, gentleness, goodness, faith,"
There are nine different fruits of the Holy Spirit. The second one is joy. If we have the fruit of the Spirit, we have God's joy.
- **1 Thessalonians 1:6**
"And ye became followers of us, and of the Lord, having received the word in much affliction, <u>with joy of the Holy Ghost</u>."
There was a lot of trouble at the church of Thessalonica. They received the Word in much affliction, but with the joy of the Holy Spirit. Affliction does not have to sadden the heart of true Christians. They can be joyful in the power of God the Holy Spirit Who indwells and leads them.

- **1 Peter 1:8**
  "Whom having not seen, ye love; in whom, though now ye see *him* not, yet believing, ye rejoice with joy unspeakable and full of glory:"

In the Lord Jesus Christ, true Christians can rejoice with unspeakable joy.

- **1 John 1:4**
  "And these things write we unto you, that your joy may be full."

One of the purposes of the writings of the Apostle John was to make genuine Christians full of joy.

- **3 John 1:4**
  "I have no greater joy than to hear that my children walk in truth."

That is a great joy for any pastor to have ones he shepherds in Christ to walk in the truth of the Scriptures. It is one thing to have the truth; it is another thing to walk, follow, and abide in the truth.

2 Corinthians 7:14

"For if I have boasted any thing to him of you, I am not ashamed; but as we spake all things to you in truth, even so our boasting, which I *made* before Titus, is found a truth."

Paul was not ashamed of what he told others about the church at Corinth. He told the truth to Titus and to others as well. Every genuine Christian should always tell the truth as Paul did here.

Verses On Ashamed

- **Psalms 119:80**
  "Let my heart be sound in thy statutes; that I be not ashamed."

God's Words should be known and practiced soundly. True Christians should never be ashamed of them.

- **Romans 1:16**
  "For I am not ashamed of the Gospel of Christ: for it is the power of God unto salvation to every one that believeth; to the Jew first, and also to the Greek."

No genuine Christian should ever be ashamed of the good news about the Lord Jesus Christ's death on the cross. On the cross He carried the sins of world in His body as an atonement for them if they would but truly trust In Him as their Saviour.

- **2 Timothy 1:16**

"The Lord give mercy unto the house of Onesiphorus; for he oft refreshed me, and was not ashamed of my chain:"

Second Timothy was written by Paul during his second and final Roman imprisonment before his execution. Many people were ashamed of Paul's chains, but not Onesimus. He visited Paul faithfully. He was not ashamed of his chains.

- **Hebrews 2:11**

"For both he that sanctifieth and they who are sanctified *are* all of one: for which cause he is not ashamed to call them brethren,"

The Lord Jesus Christ is not ashamed, and God the Father is not ashamed, to call those who are genuine Christians, brethren. If we are genuine Christians, we are brothers, sisters in the Lord and the Saviour is not ashamed to call them brethren.

2 Corinthians 7:15

"And his inward affection is more abundant toward you, whilst he remembereth the obedience of you all, how with fear and trembling ye received him."

Titus's inward affection was abundant toward the true Christians at Corinth as he remembered their obedience and how they received Titus as a faithful servant of the Lord.

Verses On Obedience

- **Romans 16:19**

"For your obedience is come abroad unto all *men*. I am glad therefore on your behalf: but yet I would have you wise unto that which is good, and simple concerning evil."

The genuine Christians at Rome were obedient to the Lord. This was known by all men.

- **2 Corinthians 10:5**

"Casting down imaginations, and every high thing that exalteth itself against the knowledge of God, and bringing into captivity every thought to the obedience of Christ;"

Not just every word, but every thought of all true Christians should be brought into obedience unto the Lord Jesus Christ.

2 Corinthians 7:16

"I rejoice therefore that I have confidence in you in all *things*."

Paul can now say that he has confidence in the genuine Christians at Corinth in all things. They changed their ways and repented for what they had done which was wrong.

Verses On Confidence

- **Proverbs 25:19**

  "Confidence in an unfaithful man in time of trouble *is like* a broken tooth, and a foot out of joint."

This is caution about having confidence in unfaithful people, especially in time of trouble. Have confidence in faithful people only.

- **Isaiah 30:15**

  "For thus saith the Lord GOD, the Holy One of Israel; In returning and rest shall ye be saved; in quietness and in confidence shall be your strength: and ye would not."

Israel should have had confidence in the Lord, but they would not.

- **2 Corinthians 2:3**

  "And I wrote this same unto you, lest, when I came, I should have sorrow from them of whom I ought to rejoice; having confidence in you all, that my joy is *the joy* of you all."

Paul finally had confidence in the genuine Christians at Corinth, as he wrote 2 Corinthians, but he had little as he wrote 1 Corinthians.

- **2 Corinthians 8:22**

  "And we have sent with them our brother, whom we have oftentimes proved diligent in many things, but now much more diligent, upon the great confidence which *I have* in you."

Paul said another time that he had great confidence in the Corinthian church because they amended their ways.

- **Galatians 5:10**

  "I have confidence in you through the Lord, that ye will be none otherwise minded: but he that troubleth you shall bear his judgment, whosoever he be."

Paul had confidence in the true Christians at Galatia that they would do as they had promised.

2 Corinthians Chapter Eight

2 Corinthians 8:1

"Moreover, brethren, we do you to wit of the grace of God bestowed on the churches of Macedonia;"

God's grace was bestowed on the churches of Macedonia. Corinth was one of the churches in the province of Macedonia. Paul wanted The church at Corinth to be thankful God's grace.

Verses Mentioning Macedonia

- **Acts 16:9-10**

"And a vision appeared to Paul in the night; <u>There stood a man of Macedonia, and prayed him, saying, Come over into Macedonia, and help us</u>. And after he had seen the vision, immediately we endeavoured to go into Macedonia, assuredly gathering that the Lord had called us for to preach the Gospel unto them."

When Paul saw in this vision a man from Macedonia asking him to "*come over*" and "*help us*," he went there as a missionary to the area, the province, of Macedonia.

- **Acts 16:12**

"And from thence to <u>Philippi, which is the chief city of that part of Macedonia</u>, *and* a colony: and we were in that city abiding certain days."

Paul went to Philippi and met the Philippian jailer whom he led to the Lord Jesus Christ.

- **Acts 19:21**

"After these things were ended, Paul purposed in the spirit, when <u>he had passed through Macedonia and Achaia, to go to Jerusalem</u>, saying, After I have been there, I must also see Rome."

Paul went through Macedonia and Achaia, to go back to Jerusalem.

- **Acts 19:22**

"So he sent into Macedonia two of them that ministered unto him, Timotheus and Erastus; but he himself stayed in Asia for a season."

Paul was interested in the Macedonian Christians and the churches there. He sent these two Christian leaders to help them.

Acts 20:1

"And after the uproar was ceased, Paul called unto him the disciples, and embraced them, and departed for to go into Macedonia."

Paul went back to Macedonia, over and over and over again.

- **Acts 20:3**

"And there abode three months. And when the Jews laid wait for him, as he was about to sail into Syria, he purposed to return through Macedonia."

Paul went through that territory again.

- **Romans 15:26**

"For it hath pleased them of Macedonia and Achaia to make a certain contribution for the poor saints which are at Jerusalem."

They were a giving group of churches in Macedonia. They gave to the poor genuine Christians at Jerusalem.

- **1 Corinthians 16:5**

"Now I will come unto you, when I shall pass through Macedonia: for I do pass through Macedonia."

Paul tells them that he will be coming to their territory soon.

- **2 Corinthians 2:13**

"I had no rest in my spirit, because I found not Titus my brother: but taking my leave of them, I went from thence into Macedonia."

Paul went back to that Macedonia when he could not find Titus.

- **2 Corinthians 7:5**

"For, when we were come into Macedonia, our flesh had no rest, but we were troubled on every side; without were fightings, within were fears."

So, it was not always a pleasant time in Macedonia with fears and fightings.

- **2 Corinthians 9:2**

"For I know the forwardness of your mind, for which I boast of you to them of Macedonia, that Achaia was ready a year ago; and your zeal hath provoked very many."

Paul spoke kindly to those in Corinth about those in Macedonia.

- **2 Corinthians 9:4**
"Lest haply if they of Macedonia come with me, and find you unprepared, we (that we say not, ye) should be ashamed in this same confident boasting."
He did not want people to be ashamed of anything when the Macedonians came with him.
- **2 Corinthians 11:9**
"And when I was present with you, and wanted, I was chargeable to no man: for that which was lacking to me the brethren which came from Macedonia supplied: and in all *things* I have kept myself from being burdensome unto you, and *so* will I keep *myself*."
The people of Macedonia supplied what Paul needed for his ministry.
- **Philippians 4:15**
"Now ye Philippians know also, that in the beginning of the Gospel, when I departed from Macedonia, no church communicated with me as concerning giving and receiving, but ye only."
No other church gave Paul funds except the Philippian church did when he left Macedonia.
- **1 Thessalonians 1:7**
"So that ye were ensamples to all that believe in Macedonia and Achaia."
Thessalonian genuine Christians were good examples to all those in Macedonia.
- **1 Thessalonians 1:8**
"For from you sounded out the word of the Lord not only in Macedonia and Achaia, but also in every place your faith to God-ward is spread abroad; so that we need not to speak any thing."
They were a good testimony, the Thessalonica Christians from Macedonia. Their faith was spread abroad.
- **1 Timothy 1:3**
"As I besought thee to abide still at Ephesus, when I went into Macedonia, that thou mightest charge some that they teach no other doctrine,"

2 Corinthians 8:2

"How that in a great trial of affliction the abundance of their joy and their deep poverty abounded unto the riches of their liberality."

This group of people in the Macedonian churches, had four things noted here: (1) great trial of affliction; (2) deep poverty; (3) abundance of joy; and (4) riches of liberality. As in our day, so in the days when 2 Corinthians was written. It was and is not easy for Bible-believing and Bible-preaching churches to survive with a struggle. However, then and now Christian joy never ceased and will never cease.

Verses On Joy

- **Psalms 16:11**

"Thou wilt shew me the path of life: in thy presence is fulness of joy; at thy right hand there are pleasures for evermore."
This Psalm was written by David after the murder of Uriah, the Hittite, and after his adultery, with Uriah's wife. He repented of these sins, and returned to God's fulness of joy.

- **Psalms 51:12**

"Restore unto me the joy of thy salvation; and uphold me *with thy* free spirit."
Sometimes the joy of God's salvation must be restored to true Christians today as well as in David's day.

- **Habakkuk 3:17-18**

"Although the fig tree shall not blossom, neither *shall* fruit *be* in the vines; the labour of the olive shall fail, and the fields shall yield no meat; the flock shall be cut off from the fold, and *there shall be* no herd in the stalls: Yet I will rejoice in the LORD, I will joy in the God of my salvation."
No matter how many things might to wrong with genuine Christians today.

- **Luke 2:10-11**

"And the angel said unto them, Fear not: for, behold, I bring you good tidings of great joy, which shall be to all people. For unto you is born this day in the city of David a Saviour, which is Christ the Lord."
God brought great joy to all people by the announcement of the virgin birth of His only begotten Son, the Lord Jesus Christ.

- **John 15:11**
"These things have I spoken unto you, that my joy might remain in you, and <u>that your joy might be full</u>."

God wants every true Christian to have His fulness of joy.

- **John 16:22**
"And ye now therefore have sorrow: but I will see you again, and your heart shall rejoice, and <u>your joy no man taketh from you</u>."

The Lord Jesus Christ told His disciples that no man could take away their joy.

- **Acts 13:52**
"And <u>the disciples were filled with joy</u>, and with the Holy Ghost."

Joy was there, even though the disciples were expelled from this city.

- **Romans 15:13**
"<u>Now the God of hope fill you with all joy and peace in believing</u>, that ye may abound in hope, through the power of the Holy Ghost."

- **Galatians 5:22-23**
"But the fruit of the Spirit is love, joy, peace, longsuffering, gentleness, goodness, faith, meekness, temperance: against such there is no law."

If the fruit of the Holy Spirit is present in the lives of genuine Christians, they can have His joy.

- **Philippians 1:4-5**
"Always in every prayer of mine for you all <u>making request with joy</u>, For your fellowship in the Gospel from the first day until now;"

Paul was joyous, even while in the midst of all his persecutions.

- **1 Peter 1:8**
"Whom having not seen, ye love; in whom, though now ye see *him* not, yet believing, <u>ye rejoice with joy unspeakable and full of glory</u>:"

If true Christians are rightly related to God the Holy Spirit, they can experience His *"joy unspeakable and full of glory."*

- **1 John 1:4**
"And these things write we unto you, <u>that your joy may be full</u>."

John's purpose in writing was that the joy of his friends might be full.

- **3 John 1:4**
"I have no greater joy than to hear that my children walk in truth."

The Apostle John had great joy when those to whom he wrote walked in truth rather than doctrinal error.

2 Corinthians 8:3

"For to *their* power, I bear record, yea, and beyond *their* power *they were* willing of themselves;"

Again, Paul speaks of the churches in Macedonia, the province where Corinth is located. He commends the genuine Christians there for their willingness regarding their gifts for the Lord's uses.

Verses On Willingness

- **Exodus 35:5**
"Take ye from among you an offering unto the LORD: whosoever *is* of a willing heart, let him bring it, an offering of the LORD; gold, and silver, and brass,"

God wanted those with a willing heart to bring offerings to Him.

- **Exodus 35:21-22**
"And they came, every one whose heart stirred him up, and every one whom his spirit made willing, *and* they brought the LORD's offering to the work of the tabernacle of the congregation, and for all his service, and for the holy garments. And they came, both men and women, as many as were willing hearted, *and* brought bracelets, and earrings, and rings, and tablets, all jewels of gold: and every man that offered, *offered* an offering of gold unto the LORD."

The people of Israel with willing hearts brought needed gifts to build the tabernacle.

- **Exodus 35:29**
"The children of Israel brought a willing offering unto the LORD, every man and woman, whose heart made them willing to bring for all manner of work, which the LORD had commanded to be made by the hand of Moses."

The tabernacle was provided for its needed materials from people who were willing to offer them.

- **1 Chronicles 29:5**

"The gold for *things* of gold, and the silver for *things* of silver, and for all manner of work *to be made* by the hands of artificers. And who then is willing to consecrate his service this day unto the Lord?"

God wanted His people to give their wiling service to Him.

- **Matthew 26:41**

"Watch and pray, that ye enter not into temptation: the spirit indeed *is* willing, but the flesh *is* weak."

The apostles had a willing spirit to watch with the Lord in Gethsemane, but their flesh was weak.

- **2 Corinthians 5:8**

"We are confident, *I say*, and willing rather to be absent from the body, and to be present with the Lord."

Paul was willing to be absent from the body, present with the Lord.

- **2 Corinthians 9:7**

"Every man according as he purposeth in his heart, *so let him give*; not grudgingly, or of necessity: for God loveth a cheerful giver."

A willing and cheerful giver is what God wants.

2 Corinthians 8:4

"Praying us with much intreaty that we would receive the gift, and *take upon us* the fellowship of the ministering to the saints."

Paul was going to take the gifts that the Macedonia genuine Christians had given and minister to the true Christians there in Jerusalem.

Verses On Helping True Christians

- **Romans 12:13**

"Distributing to the necessity of saints; given to hospitality."

Genuine Christians should help other believers.

- **Romans 15:26**

"For it hath pleased them of Macedonia and Achaia to make a certain contribution for the poor saints which are at Jerusalem."

The saints in the Bible are genuine Christians, not those called "saints" in Roman Catholicism.

- **2 Corinthians 9:1**

"For as touching the <u>ministering to the saints</u>, it is superfluous for me to write to you:"

This was to genuine Christians.

- **2 Corinthians 9:12**

"For the administration of this service not only <u>supplieth the want of the saints</u>, but is abundant also by many thanksgivings unto God;"

Again, it is true Christians helping one another. Here are the believers who are in need.

2 Corinthians 8:5

"And *this they did*, not as we hoped, but first gave their own selves to the Lord, and unto us by the will of God."

These genuine Christians first gave their own selves to the Lord for His ministry. A lot of people can give money but they do not give themselves to the Lord.

Verses On Ministering

- **Exodus 28:41**

"And thou shalt put them upon Aaron thy brother, and his sons with him; and shalt anoint them, and consecrate them, and <u>sanctify them, that they may minister unto me in the priest's office</u>."

Aaron and his sons sought to minister unto the Lord.

- **Exodus 30:30**

"And thou shalt anoint Aaron and his sons, and consecrate them, that *they* may minister unto me in the priest's office."

They gave themselves for ministry to the Lord, himself.

- **Exodus 32:29**

"For Moses had said, Consecrate yourselves today to the LORD, even every man upon his son, and upon his brother; that he may bestow upon you a blessing this day."

In other words, give yourself over to help the Lord.

2 Corinthians 8:6

"Insomuch that we desired Titus, that as he had begun, so he would also finish in you the same grace also."

Titus was a faithful pastor on the isle of Crete. Now Paul wants Titus to help the church at Corinth in the grace of giving, so that they might give to the needs of the believers all around the area.

Verses On Titus

- **2 Corinthians 7:6**

"Nevertheless God, that comforteth those that are cast down, comforted us by the coming of Titus;"

Titus was a comforting pastor who comforted various Christians. He comforted Paul when he came to Corinth.

- **2 Corinthians 8:16**

"But thanks *be* to God, which put the same earnest care into the heart of Titus for you."

Titus was a pastor who had earnest care for the genuine Christians at Corinth.

- **2 Corinthians 8:23**

"Whether *any do enquire* of Titus, *he is* my partner and fellowhelper concerning you: or our brethren *be enquired of, they are* the messengers of the churches, and the glory of Christ."

Titus was a very close helper and partner of Paul.

- **Galatians 2:1**

"Then fourteen years after I went up again to Jerusalem with Barnabas, and took Titus with *me* also."

When Paul went to Jerusalem, he took Titus with him.

- **Titus 1:4**

"To Titus, *mine* own son after the common faith: Grace, mercy, *and* peace, from God the Father and the Lord Jesus Christ our Saviour."

Paul led Titus to the Lord Jesus Chris so he was Paul's spiritual son.

2 Corinthians 8:7

"**Therefore, as ye abound in every *thing*, *in* faith, and utterance, and knowledge, and *in* all diligence, and *in* your love to us, *see* that ye abound in this grace also.**"

Paul wanted the genuine Christians in Corinth to abound in the grace of giving as well as in these five other things that he mentions in this verse. The second thing, in utterance. They knew how to speak.

Verses On Utterance Of Speaking
- **1 Corinthians 1:5**
"That in every thing ye are enriched by him, in all utterance, and *in* all knowledge;"

These true Christians at Corinth knew how to talk to people about their faith in the Lord Jesus Christ.

- **Ephesians 6:19**
"And for me, that utterance may be given unto me, that I may open my mouth boldly, to make known the mystery of the Gospel,"

Paul wanted prayer that he might be bold in preaching the Gospel of Christ.

- **Colossians 4:3**
"Withal praying also for us, that God would open unto us a door of utterance, to speak the mystery of Christ, for which I am also in bonds:"

Paul was writing from prison in Rome asking the true Christians in Colosse to pray that God would open a door for him to speak about the Lord Jesus Christ.

A Verse On Knowledge
- **2 Peter 3:18**
"But grow in grace, and *in* the knowledge of our Lord and Saviour Jesus Christ. To him *be* glory both now and for ever. Amen."

The only place that you can get that knowledge of the Saviour is in the Bible. That is why I encourage all true Christians to read the Bible (in English, from the KJB) from Genesis to Revelation every year. This can be done by reading 85 verses per day.

Verses On Diligence
- **Proverbs 4:23**

"Keep thy heart with all diligence; for out of it *are* the issues of life."

The heart, not simply the head, must be kept with all diligence.

- **2 Peter 1:10**

"Wherefore the rather, brethren, give diligence to make your calling and election sure: for if ye do these things, ye shall never fall:"

So, they abounded in diligence.

Verse On Love
- **John 13:34-35**

"A new commandment I give unto you, That ye love one another; as I have loved you, that ye also love one another."

Though it is Impossible to love as Christ loved all of us, that is the goal and aim of all true Christians. Love as I have loved you.

2 Corinthians 8:8

"I speak not by commandment, but by occasion of the forwardness of others, and to prove the sincerity of your love."

Paul said that he was not talking about the grace of giving as by some commander ordering you to do it. Apparently they were asking him about this. They were curious about the sincerity of their love.

Verses On Sincerity
- **Joshua 24:14**

"Now therefore fear the LORD, and serve him in sincerity and in truth: and put away the gods which your fathers served on the other side of the flood, and in Egypt; and serve ye the LORD."

The service of the Lord by true Christians should be in sincerity and truth.

- **1 Corinthians 5:8**

"Therefore let us keep the feast, not with old leaven, neither with the leaven of malice and wickedness; but with the unleavened *bread* of sincerity and truth."

Both of these two words, sincerity and truth, are important. A genuine Christian should be sincere, but it should all be based upon truth.

- **2 Corinthians 1:12**

  "For our rejoicing is this, the testimony of our conscience, that in simplicity and godly sincerity, not with fleshly wisdom, but by the grace of God, we have had our conversation in the world, and more abundantly to you-ward."

The rejoicing of true Christians should be with godly sincerity rather than in the flesh.

- **Ephesians 6:24**

  "Grace *be* with all them that love our Lord Jesus Christ in sincerity. Amen."

Grace is requested for those who love the Lord Jesus Christ in sincerity.

2 Corinthians 8:9

"For ye know the grace of our Lord Jesus Christ, that, though he was rich, yet for your sakes he became poor, that ye through his poverty might be rich."

The grace of our Lord Jesus Christ was and is a tremendous fact to ponder. Though He was rich in Heaven, He became poor by enduring the painful and ignominious death on the cross to offer the riches of forgiveness of sins and Heaven to all who will sincerely trust Him as their Saviour.

Verses Contrasting Poverty And Riches

- **Matthew 8:20**

  "And Jesus saith unto him, The foxes have holes, and the birds of the air *have* nests; but the Son of man hath not where to lay his head."

The Lord Jesus Christ was rich in Heaven. He created the whole world but on earth, He did not have any home for his head.

- **John 1:3**

  "All things were made by him; and without him was not any thing made that was made."

He was the rich Creator, but He was made the Son of Man in His incarnation.

- **John 1:10**

  "He was in the world, and the world was made by him, and the world knew him not."

Rich and powerful, but He became poor through the incarnation.

- **Philippians 2:5-11**

"Let this mind be in you, which was also in Christ Jesus: Who, being <u>in the form of God, thought it not robbery to be equal with God</u>: But made himself of no reputation, and <u>took upon him the form of a servant</u>, and was made in the likeness of men: And being found in fashion as a man, he humbled himself, and <u>became obedient unto death, even the death of the cross</u>. Wherefore <u>God also hath highly exalted him, and given him a name which is above every </u>name: That at the name of Jesus every knee should bow, of *things* in heaven, and *things* in earth, and *things* under the earth; And *that* every tongue should confess that Jesus Christ *is* Lord, to the glory of God the Father."

This entire narrative illustrates from His richness and power to His being obedient unto death.

- **Colossians 1:15-16**

"<u>Who is the image of the invisible God, the firstborn of every creature</u>: For by him were all things created, that are in heaven, and that are in earth, visible and invisible, whether *they be* thrones, or dominions, or principalities, or powers: <u>all things were created by him, and for him</u>:"

The Lord Jesus Christ was the Creator of all things, yet was rejected of men.

- **Romans 8:17**

"And if children, then <u>heirs; heirs of God, and joint-heirs with Christ</u>; if so be that we suffer with *him*, that we may be also glorified together."

Genuine Christians are made rich by being made heirs of God and joint heirs with Christ through true faith in the Saviour.

- **1 Corinthians 3:21-23**

"Therefore let no man glory in men. For <u>all things are yours</u>; Whether Paul, or Apollos, or Cephas, or the world, or life, or death, or things present, or things to come; all are yours; <u>And ye are Christ's; and Christ</u> *is* <u>God's</u>."

All things belong to true Christians through the Lord Jesus Christ and God has made them rich in Christ.

- **2 Corinthians 6:10**

"As sorrowful, yet alway rejoicing; as poor, yet making many rich; as having nothing, and *yet* possessing all things."

Here are great contrasts for true Christians: sorrowful yet rejoicing and having nothing, but possessing all things.

- **Colossians 1:13**
"Who hath delivered us from the power of darkness, and hath translated us into the kingdom of his dear Son:"

This darkness is changed to light and riches when people become true Christians through genuine faith in the Lord Jesus Christ

- **James 2:5**
"Hearken, my beloved brethren, Hath not God chosen the poor of this world rich in faith, and heirs of the kingdom which he hath promised to them that love him?"

The Lord Jesus, who was rich in Heaven, became poor, by coming to earth and leaving the perfections of Heaven. They are now rich in faith.

2 Corinthians 8:10

"And herein I give my advice: for this is expedient for you, who have begun before, not only to do, but also to be forward a year ago."

Paul advised this church to begin where they were a year ago and continue going on by perseverance and faith in the Lord Jesus Christ and doing the will of God day by day.

2 Corinthians 8:11

"Now therefore perform the doing of it; that as there was a readiness to will, so there may be a performance also out of that which ye have."

Paul told the church to perform God's will. They had a readiness to do it, but he urged them to have a performance in actually doing what they knew was God's will.

- **Jeremiah 33:14**
"Behold, the days come, saith the LORD, that I will perform that good thing which I have promised unto the house of Israel and to the house of Judah."

God performs what he promises. We should perform what we promise as well.

2 Corinthians 8:12

"For **if there be first a willing mind, *it is* accepted according to that a man hath,** *and* **not according to that he hath not.**"

God wants His true Christians to have a willing mind to do whatever God wants of them in accord to what they have to give. He does not expect them to do what they are unable to do. A willing mind is what the Lord wants in all of His true Chistians.

2 Corinthians 8:13

"**For I *mean* not that other men be eased, and ye burdened:**"

Paul is talking about giving. He does not want to have some people eased and others burdened. He was a tent maker and worked for a living instead of having the churches to supply his needs although that was possible. He did not want to be a financial burden upon others.

- **Exodus 30:15**

"The rich shall not give more, and the poor shall not give less than half a shekel, when *they* give an offering unto the LORD, to make an atonement for your souls."

- **Mark 12:41-44**

"And Jesus sat over against the treasury, and beheld how the people cast money into the treasury: and many that were rich cast in much. And there came a certain poor widow, and she threw in two mites, which make a farthing. And he called *unto him* his disciples, and saith unto them, Verily I say unto you, That this poor widow hath cast more in, than all they which have cast into the treasury: For all *they* did cast in of their abundance; but she of her want did cast in all that she had, *even* all her living."

It is interesting. The Lord Jesus Christ respects the little that people have more than the much that the rich have.

- **Galatians 6:2**

"Bear ye one another's burdens, and so fulfil the law of Christ."

True Christians should help other Christians in their need.

2 Corinthians 8:14

"But by an equality, *that* now at this time your abundance *may be a supply* for their want, that their abundance also may be *a supply* for your want: that there may be equality."

Each genuine Christian church which has an abundance can help other true Christian churches which have needs as the did in the churches at Corinth, Jerusalem or at other locations.

Verses On Want

- **Psalms 23:1**

"The LORD *is* my shepherd; I shall not want."

If the Lord Jesus Christ is your Shepherd, He will supply your needs.

- **Psalms 34:9**

"O fear the LORD, ye his saints: for *there is* no want to them that fear him."

God supplies the needs for those who honor Him and fear Him. The Lord Jesus Christ gave a command to these people around Him, including His apostles and disciples.

- **Luke 12:15**

"And he said unto them, Take heed, and beware of covetousness: for a man's life consisteth not in the abundance of the things which he possesseth."

Every genuine Christian should beware of covetousness or wanting more possessions or power than they have. God will supply their wants and needs.

- **Philippians 4:11**

"Not that I speak in respect of want: for I have learned, in whatsoever state I am, *therewith* to be content."

Paul was in prison in Rome when he wrote this. He had plenty of wants but God supplied them all. He learned that "*in whatsoever state I am, therewith to be content.*" That is a learning process. State of poverty, content. State of riches, content. State of mediocrity, contentment. State of health, contentment. State of sickness, contentment. I have learned. Paul, in prison, God taught him many things and Paul was a good learner. God has to teach us many things, too, but if we are not willing to learn from him, it is wasted. We have to be a good learner.

2 Corinthians 8:15

"As it is written, He that *had gathered* much had nothing over; and he that *had gathered* little had no lack."

Notice this word, "*As it is written,*" As I have said many times, this is a Greek perfect tense. A such it refers to something that happened in the past and continues into the present time, and on into the future. This phrase, ("*it is written*") guarantees the Bible preservation of every Word in the Hebrew and Aramaic Old Testament and every Word in the Greek New Testament. The quotation Paul made is from Exodus 16:18

- **Exodus 16:18**

"And when they did mete *it* with an homer, he that gathered much had nothing over, and he that gathered little had no lack; they gathered every man according to his eating."

This was in the time of manna, when manna was sent from heaven for forty years, to feed the people of Israel, in the wilderness. The quotation, Paul could not quote if God had not preserved that Hebrew text which was written in the past and preserved to Paul's day and right down to our day.

2 Corinthians 8:16

"But thanks *be* to God, which put the same earnest care into the heart of Titus for you."

Paul is speaking of earnest care that Titus had for the genuine Christians at Corinth. Such care should be manifested today between true Christians.

Verses On Caring

- **Psalms 142:4**

"I looked on *my* right hand, and beheld, but *there was* no man that would know me: refuge failed me; no man cared for my soul."

Most people care for their bodies, but few care also for their souls. The Lord Jesus Christ came into this world to seek and to save that which was lost, dying for the sins of every single person in this world. Genuine Christians should care for people who are lost. They are lost souls.

- **Mark 4:38**

"And he was in the hinder part of the ship, asleep on a pillow: and they awake him, and say unto him, <u>Master, carest thou not that we perish?</u>"

It was during a storm. The Lord Jesus Christ in the ship asleep during the storm. The apostles woke Him up and asked Him: "*Master, carest thou not that we perish?*" He did care for them and He just spoke the word and the storm was stilled. He was Deity and God the Son, perfect God and perfect Man. The Lord Jesus Christ cares for the apostles and cares for everyone today as well. He cares for those who are genuine Christians, that they may love Him and serve Him. He also cares for the lost, Hell- bound non-Christians who are lost and in sin destined for Hell. He wants them to come to Him, and trust Him as their Saviour.

- **Luke 10:34**

"And went to *him*, and bound up his wounds, pouring in oil and wine, and set him on his own beast, and <u>brought him to an inn, and took care of him</u>."

This Samaritan cared for this man in six ways.

    (#1) He went to this wounded man;
    (#2) He cared for him with earnest care.
    (#3) He poured in oil and wine helping to ease his pain.
    (#4) He set him on his own beast.
    (#5) He brought him to an inn.
    (#6) He took care of him.

This man, who was a Samaritan, had a genuine, earnest care for this poor man, who was beaten up by thieves on that road.

- **Luke 10:35**

"And on the morrow when he departed, he took out two pence, and gave *them* to the host, and said unto him, <u>Take care of him; and whatsoever thou spendest more, when I come again, I will repay thee</u>."

That is earnest care, not only taking care of the man's present needs, but also for the future. The Samaritan paid for everything.

- **John 10:13**

"<u>The hireling fleeth</u>, because he is an hireling, <u>and careth not for the sheep</u>."

The hired servant was not the real shepherd. He "*careth not for the sheep.*" The Lord Jesus Christ cares for His sheep and beats off the wolves that come after the sheep.

- **1 Corinthians 12:25**
"That there should be no schism in the body; but *that* the members should have the same care one for another."
All genuine Christians in Biblical churches should have genuine care for one another.
- **2 Corinthians 7:12**
"Wherefore, though I wrote unto you, I *did it* not for his cause that had done the wrong, nor for his cause that suffered wrong, but that our care for you in the sight of God might appear unto you."
Paul wrote the church at Corinth a very strong letter to try to correct that church and show them that he had earnest care for the church at Corinth.
- **Philippians 2:20**
"For I have no man likeminded, who will naturally care for your state."
Paul is referring to Pastor Timothy who was one of his fellow helpers who could take good care of the church at Philippi.
- **1 Timothy 3:5**
"(For if a man know not how to rule his own house, how shall he take care of the church of God?)"
That is one of the qualifications of Biblical pastors. They must be able to take good care of their own houses and children. Praise the Lord, Mrs. Waite and I have five godly children. The Scriptures are true. If a pastor does not know how to take care of his own children, how is he going to take care of the house of God? If he cannot keep his children in line to behave in church and elsewhere, he has no business being a pastor.
- **1 Peter 5:7**
"Casting all your care upon him; for he careth for you."
The Lord Jesus Christ cares for all His true Christians. Because of this, they can cast all their cares upon Him for His help. He cares for them more than any person could ever care. He cared enough to die for sins of the whole world.

Verses On The Heart
- Psalms 119:11
"Thy word have I hid in mine heart, that I might not sin against thee."
To have God's Words in the head is one thing, in the hands is another thing, but in the heart is the place where God wants His Words to prevent sin.

- **Psalms 139:23**

"<u>Search me, O God, and know my heart</u>: try me, and know my thoughts:"

The hearts and thoughts of true Christians must want to be searched by God.

- **Psalms 139:24**

"And <u>see if *there be any* wicked way in me, and lead me in the way everlasting</u>."

After the hearts are searched, genuine Christians should want God to lead them in the way everlasting.

- **Proverbs 3:5**

"<u>Trust in the LORD with all thine heart</u>; and lean not unto thine own understanding."

God wants trust in Him with all the hearts of His true Christians.

- **Proverbs 4:23**

"<u>Keep thy heart with all diligence</u>; for out of it *are* the issues of life."

The heart is the simplest part of a person, but it must be guarded.

- **Matthew 6:20-21**

"But lay up for yourselves treasures in heaven, where neither moth nor rust doth corrupt, and where thieves do not break through nor steal: For <u>where your treasure is, there will your heart be also</u>."

If your treasures are on earth, your heart will be on earth. If your treasures are in Heaven, your heart will be in Heaven.

- **Matthew 12:34-35**

"O generation of vipers, how can ye, being evil, speak good things? for <u>out of the abundance of the heart the mouth speaketh. A good man out of the good treasure of the heart bringeth forth good things: and an evil man out of the evil treasure bringeth forth evil things</u>."

Good genuine Christians bring good things out of their mouth. Non Christians's mouths bring forth many evil things.

2 Corinthians 8:17

"**For indeed he accepted the exhortation; but being more forward, of his own accord he went unto you.**"

Pastor Titus accepted Paul's exhortation and did what Paul suggested. Some people accept exhortations and many do not.

Verses On Exhortation
- **2 Timothy 4:2**

"Preach the word; be instant in season, out of season; reprove, rebuke, <u>exhort with all longsuffering and doctrine</u>."
Exhortation is important, but it must be with longsuffering and with doctrine.
- **Hebrews 3:13**

"But <u>exhort one another daily</u>, while it is called To day; lest any of you be hardened through the deceitfulness of sin."
Genuine Christians are to exhort and encourage daily as they have opportunity.
- **Jude 1:3**

"Beloved, when I gave all diligence to write unto you of the common salvation, it was needful for me to write unto you, and <u>exhort *you* that ye should earnestly contend for the faith</u> which was once delivered unto the saints."
True Christians are to earnestly contend for or battle for the faith and teachings taught in the Bible. This is God's command.

2 Corinthians 8:18

"And we have sent with him the brother, whose praise *is* in the Gospel throughout all the churches;"

Paul sent another true Christian with Titus, to take a gift to the poor saints of Jerusalem and other people whose praise is in the Gospel of the Lord Jesus Christ.

Though "*Gospel*" in Greek means "*good news*" about the Saviour, there is some bad news that people have to know about. (1) The bad news is they must believe that they are sinners who are lost and bound for Hell, without the Lord Jesus Christ. (2) they must realize and believe is that the Lord Jesus Christ died for and paid for their sins on the cross of Calvary. (3) They must genuinely believe, trust, and receive the Lord Jesus Christ as their Saviour Who died in their place on the cross.

Verses On The Gospel
- **Acts 16:10**

"And after he had seen the vision, immediately we endeavoured to go into Macedonia, assuredly gathering that <u>the Lord had called us for to preach the Gospel unto them</u>."
These disciples were called to preach the Gospel to those in Macedonia.

- **Romans 1:15**
  "So, as much as in me is, <u>I am ready to preach the Gospel to you that are at Rome also</u>."

Paul was ready to preach the Gospel to those in Rome as well as other places.

- **Romans 1:16**
  "For <u>I am not ashamed of the Gospel of Christ: for it is the power of God unto salvation to every one that believeth</u>; to the Jew first, and also to the Greek."

Paul was not ashamed of the Gospel for it is God's power unto salvation for those who truly believe it.

- **Romans 10:15**
  "And <u>how shall they preach, except they be sent?</u> as it is written, How beautiful are the feet of them that preach the Gospel of peace, and bring glad tidings of good things!"

A Bible-believing preacher should be called by the Lord Jesus Christ and be sent.

- **Romans 15:19**
  "Through mighty signs and wonders, by the power of the Spirit of God; so that from Jerusalem, and round about unto Illyricum, <u>I have fully preached the Gospel of Christ</u>."

Paul fully and truly preached the Gospel of Christ to those in Rome.

- **1 Corinthians 1:17**
  "For <u>Christ sent me not to baptize, but to preach the Gospel: not with wisdom of words</u>, lest the cross of Christ should be made of none effect."

Paul preached the Gospel with God's power, not with the wisdom or words.

- **1 Corinthians 9:16**
  "For though I preach the Gospel, I have nothing to glory of: for <u>necessity is laid upon me; yea, woe is unto me, if I preach not the Gospel!</u>"

Necessity was laid upon Paul. He would have "*woe*" if he did not preach the true, Biblical Gospel.

- **2 Corinthians 2:12**
  "Furthermore, <u>when I came to Troas to *preach* Christ's Gospel</u>, and a door was opened unto me of the Lord,"

A door was opened by the Lord when Paul went to Troas to preach Christ's Gospel.

2 Corinthians 8:19
"And not *that* only, but who was also chosen of the churches to travel with us with this grace, which is administered by us to the glory of the same Lord, and *declaration* of your ready mind:"

Titus and his helper were chosen by the churches to take this offering for the poor Christians in Jerusalem. This was a gift to the glory of the Lord Jesus Christ. Their trip with this offering showed the ready mind of Titus and his helper.

- **1 Peter 5:2**

"Feed the flock of God which is among you, taking the oversight *thereof*, not by constraint, but <u>willingly; not for filthy lucre, but of a ready mind</u>;"

This verse from Peter spoke of a "*ready mind*" also. A ready mind is a mind that is ready to preach the Gospel of the Lord Jesus Christ.

2 Corinthians 8:20
"Avoiding this, that no man should blame us in this abundance which is administered by us:"

Paul did not want to be thought of as being a thief. That is why he took Titus and others with him, with the money for the poor saints of Jerusalem, so he would not be criticized or blamed for having this abundant offering.

Verses On Blameless Or Without Blame
- **1 Corinthians 1:8**

"Who shall also confirm you unto the end, <u>that ye may be blameless in the day of our Lord Jesus Christ</u>."

Those generous Christians, which are meant to be blameless in his sight. This money was gifts from the churches. These men did not steal it.

- **Ephesians 1:4**

"According as he hath chosen us in him before the foundation of the world, <u>that we should be holy and without blame before him in love</u>:"

Every genuine Christian believer should be without blame before the Lord in love.

- **Philippians 2:15**
  "That ye may be blameless and harmless, the sons of God, without rebuke, in the midst of a crooked and perverse nation, among whom ye shine as lights in the world;"

God wants His true Christians to be blameless and harmless in the midst of a crocked and perverse environment.

- **1 Thessalonians 5:23**
  "And the very God of peace sanctify you wholly; and *I pray God* your whole spirit and soul and body be preserved blameless unto the coming of our Lord Jesus Christ."

God wants the genuine Christians' spirit, soul and body to be blameless.

- **2 Peter 3:14**
  "Wherefore, beloved, seeing that ye look for such things, be diligent that ye may be found of him in peace, without spot, and blameless."

True Christians should be blameless in the sight of people, as well as in the sight of the Lord.

2 Corinthians 8:21

"Providing for honest things, not only in the sight of the Lord, but also in the sight of men."

When Paul and his helpers take the money to the poor saints in Jerusalem, they want to be sure that there is no thievery going on. They wanted honesty, "*not only in the sight of the Lord, but also in the sight of men*" so that it was an honest gift.

Verses On Honesty

- **Luke 8:15**
  "But that on the good ground are they, which in an honest and good heart, having heard the word, keep *it*, and bring forth fruit with patience."

These are people who planted their seed on good ground with an honest and good heart.

- **Acts 6:3**
  "Wherefore, brethren, look ye out among you seven men of honest report, full of the Holy Ghost and wisdom, whom we may appoint over this business."

Deacons must be of honest report in order to qualify Scripturally. This is important, in addition to all the other standards.

- **Romans 12:17**
"Recompense to no man evil for evil. Provide things honest in the sight of all men."
There should be no thievery or stealing.
- **Romans 13:13**
"Let us walk honestly, as in the day; not in rioting and drunkenness, not in chambering and wantonness, not in strife and envying."
Day by day genuine Christians should walk an honest walk.
- **Philippians 4:8**
"Finally, brethren, whatsoever things are true, whatsoever things *are* honest, whatsoever things *are* just, whatsoever things *are* pure, whatsoever things *are* lovely, whatsoever things *are* of good report; if *there be* any virtue, and if *there be* any praise, think on these things."
Think on these things. One of them to think about is things that are honest.
- **1 Thessalonians 4:12**
"That ye may walk honestly toward them that are without, and *that* ye may have lack of nothing."
True Christians should live honestly especially toward those who are not Christians.
- **1 Peter 2:12**
"Having your conversation honest among the Gentiles: that, whereas they speak against you as evildoers, they may by *your* good works, which they shall behold, glorify God in the day of visitation."
Conversation means your way of life. It should be honest among the heathen or non-Christians that are round about you.

2 Corinthians 8:22

"And we have sent with them our brother, whom we have oftentimes proved diligent in many things, but now much more diligent, upon the great confidence which *I have* in you."

Paul is talking about Titus who is diligent. Paul has confidence in him.

Verses On Diligence
- **Deuteronomy 6:17**

"Ye shall diligently keep the commandments of the LORD your God, and his testimonies, and his statutes, which he hath commanded thee."

Genuine Christians today must diligently keep God's Words as the Israelites should have done in the Old Testament.

- **Psalms 119:4**

"Thou hast commanded *us* to keep thy precepts diligently."

God's Words must be kept diligently.

- **Proverbs 22:29**

"Seest thou a man diligent in his business? he shall stand before kings; he shall not stand before mean *men*."

If a true Christian is diligent in his business, God will prosper him.

- **Luke 15:8**

"Either what woman having ten pieces of silver, if she lose one piece, doth not light a candle, and sweep the house, and seek diligently till she find *it*?"

This woman lost some valuable silver, so she sought it diligently until she found it.

- **Hebrews 11:6**

"But without faith *it is* impossible to please *him*: for he that cometh to God must believe that he is, and *that* he is a rewarder of them that diligently seek him."

God is a rewarder of those who diligently seek Him.

Verses On Confidence
- **Proverbs 14:26**

"In the fear of the LORD *is* strong confidence: and his children shall have a place of refuge."

True Christians today can have strong confidence in the Lord.

- **Proverbs 25:19**

"Confidence in an unfaithful man in time of trouble *is like* a broken tooth, and a foot out of joint."

This is bad confidence. Do not have confidence in unfaithful people.

- **2 Corinthians 7:16**

"I rejoice therefore that I have confidence in you in all *things*."

At this time, Paul had confidence in the genuine Christians at Corinth.

2 Corinthians 8:23

"Whether *any do enquire* of Titus, *he is* my partner and fellowhelper concerning you: or our brethren *be enquired of, they are* the messengers of the churches, *and* the glory of Christ."

Titus was Paul's partner and helper. Paul made Titus a pastor at the church on the island of Crete.

2 Corinthians 8:24

"Wherefore shew ye to them, and before the churches, the proof of your love, and of our boasting on your behalf."

The genuine Christians at Corinth were to show the brethren the proof of their love for the other brethren and of the Words of God.

Verses On Proof

- **2 Corinthians 2:9**

"For to this end also did I write, that I might know the proof of you, whether ye be obedient in all things."

In this case, Paul wanted to know proof of the obedience of the true Christians at Corinth.

- **2 Timothy 4:5**

"But watch thou in all things, endure afflictions, do the work of an evangelist, make full proof of thy ministry."

After Paul is gone, Timothy was to watch and make full proof of his ministry at Ephesus. He should preach the Words of God faithfully and consistently in each service.

2 Corinthians Chapter Nine

2 Corinthians 9:1

"For as touching the ministering to the saints, it is superfluous for me to write to you:"

These genuine Corinthians were serving and helping the saints. In the New Testament, the word, *"saints,"* refers to those who are genuine Christians, and not to those who have been canonized by the Church of Rome. That is paganism from the word go. Those that are genuine Christians can minister to other true Christians who are called *"saints."*

Verses On Ministering

- **Matthew 27:55**

"And many women were there beholding afar off, which followed Jesus from Galilee, ministering unto him:"

These women ministered to and helped the Lord Jesus Christ. They took care of him.

- **2 Corinthians 8:4**

"Praying us with much intreaty that we would receive the gift, and *take upon us* the fellowship of the ministering to the saints."

Genuine Christians have needs and true Christians can help them when possible.

- **Hebrews 1:14**

"Are they not all ministering spirits, sent forth to minister for them who shall be heirs of salvation?"

The angels are ministering spirits to help genuine Christians. This is a very valuable help to true Christians.

2 Corinthians 9:2

"For I know the forwardness of your mind, for which I boast of you to them of Macedonia, that Achaia was ready a year ago; and your zeal hath provoked very many."

The zeal of the true Christians at Corinth provoked many to serve the Lord Jesus Christ and help other genuine Christians.

Verses On Zeal

- **Romans 10:2**

"For I bear them record that <u>they have a zeal of God</u>, but not according to knowledge."

This is a terrible situation when people have a strong zeal, but are not using that zeal in line with proper Biblical knowledge. These people have a false zeal. True Christians must have zeal according to Biblical knowledge. The only place you can find that kind of knowledge is in the Scriptures, the Words of God, from Genesis through Revelation.

- **2 Corinthians 7:11**

"For behold this selfsame thing, that ye sorrowed after a godly sort, what carefulness it wrought in you, yea, *what* clearing of yourselves, yea, *what* indignation, yea, *what* fear, yea, *what* vehement desire, yea, <u>*what* zeal</u>, yea, *what* revenge! In all *things* ye have approved yourselves to be clear in this matter."

They had zeal at Corinth and I trust it was a proper zeal after they repented for their actions concerning the incestuous man. At first there was an improper zeal to cover up this incest. In Corinth there was a zeal to cover up an incestuous, filthy, wicked man who had his own father's wife. Here, they apparently had gotten over that, they repented of that sin and they had a proper zeal and approval of the Lord.

- **Philippians 3:6**

"<u>Concerning zeal, persecuting the church</u>; touching the righteousness which is in the law, blameless."

Before he became a genuine Christian, Paul used to have the wrong kind of zeal. He persecuted the true Christians by putting them into prison, making them suffer, and causing many to die.

- **Hebrews 10:24**
"And let us consider one another to provoke unto love and to good works:"

We are not to be provoking in a bad sense just to provoke others. But we are to provoke in the sense of improving and helping people to do that which is right.

2 Corinthians 9:3

"Yet have I sent the brethren, lest our boasting of you should be in vain in this behalf; that, as I said, ye may be ready:"

Paul is talking about being ready to give to the saints at Jerusalem, the offering they promised to give them earlier. He wanted to make sure they fulfilled that promise.

Verses On Vain

- **Psalms 127:1**
"Except the LORD build the house, <u>they labour in vain</u> that build it: except the LORD keep the city, <u>the watchman waketh but in vain</u>."

The work of the house builders and watchmen is vain and useless unless it is done in the proper way and manner.

- **1 Corinthians 15:58**
"Therefore, my beloved brethren, be ye stedfast, unmoveable, always abounding in the work of the Lord, forasmuch as ye know <u>that your labour is not in vain in the Lord</u>."

When genuine Christians' labor is in the Lord, their labor is not in vain.

- **Galatians 4:11**
"I am afraid of you, lest I have <u>bestowed upon you labour in vain</u>."

Paul told those genuine Christians at Galatia that they were not under the law of Moses. When the Galatians tried to go back under the law of Moses, Paul thought he had bestowed his labor in vain.

- **Philippians 2:16**
"Holding forth the word of life; that I may rejoice in the day of Christ, <u>that I have not run in vain, neither laboured in vain</u>."

Paul was writing to the true Christians at Philippi when he was in prison in Rome. He hoped the Philippian Christians that he had led to the Lord were serving the Lord Jesus Christ so that he had not run or labored in vain.

- **1 Thessalonians 3:5**

  "For this cause, when I could no longer forbear, I sent to know your faith, lest by some means the tempter have tempted you, and our labour be in vain."

Three different times, Paul says that he hopes his labor is not in vain. He wrote that to the Thessalonians, the Philippians and to other true Christians. It's a terrible thing, to think that you have labored in vain. Paul did not want this to happen.

2 Corinthians 9:4

"Lest haply if they of Macedonia come with me, and find you unprepared, we (that we say not, ye) should be ashamed in this same confident boasting."

If the genuine Christians in Macedonia would come with him, they would want to know if they had some gifts for the poor saints of Jerusalem. He hopes they might not be ashamed of their not giving to these Jerusalem true Christians.

Verses On Being Ashamed

- **Mark 8:38**

  "Whosoever therefore shall be ashamed of me and of my words in this adulterous and sinful generation; of him also shall the Son of man be ashamed, when he cometh in the glory of his Father with the holy angels."

The Lord Jesus Christ said that genuine Christians should not be ashamed of Him or He would be ashamed of them.

- **Romans 1:16**

  "For I am not ashamed of the Gospel of Christ: for it is the power of God unto salvation to every one that believeth; to the Jew first, and also to the Greek."

Paul was not ashamed of the Gospel of Christ, nor should true Christians be ashamed either.

- **Romans 10:11**

  "For the scripture saith, Whosoever believeth on him shall not be ashamed."

No true Christian should be ashamed of truly believing in the Lord Jesus Christ their Saviour.

- **Philippians 1:20**
"According to my earnest expectation and *my* hope, that <u>in nothing I shall be ashamed</u>, but *that* with all boldness, as always, *so* now also <u>Christ shall be magnified in my body, whether</u> *it be* <u>by life, or by death</u>."

Paul did not want to be ashamed of His Saviour, but wanted Him to be magnified in his body, "*whether by life, or by death.*" That is a very strong statement. He was prepared for death.

I was almost ready to die some twenty-nine or thirty years ago of Hodgkin's disease, cancer. My days were numbered. I was prepared to die. My wife knows I was prepared to die and everybody else knew it also. The Lord stepped in. I went down to another area of the world and had some intravenous Laetrile, called Vitamin B17. It seemed to help. They found by inspection of my mouth that there was poison in my teeth. These metal fillings in my the teeth were causing the cancer. So they removed all those poisonous metal fillings in my teeth and put in others. This straightened the whole thing out. I, as Paul was prepared for death on that occasion.

- **2 Timothy 1:8**
"<u>Be not thou therefore ashamed of the testimony of our Lord, nor of me his prisoner</u>: but be thou partaker of the afflictions of the Gospel according to the power of God;"

2 Timothy was the last letter that Paul wrote before he was executed by the Roman government. Paul urged Pastor Timothy not to be ashamed of the testimony of the Lord or of Paul His prisoner.

- **2 Timothy 2:15**
"Study to shew thyself approved unto God, <u>a workman that needeth not to be ashamed, rightly dividing the word of truth</u>."

By studying God's Words, and dividing them rightly, there should be no need for being ashamed of it.

2 Corinthians 9:5

"Therefore I thought it necessary to exhort the brethren, that they would go before unto you, and make up beforehand your bounty, whereof ye had notice before, that the same might be ready, as *a matter of* **bounty, and not as** *of* **covetousness."**

Paul exhorted the brethren from Macedonia to get their money ready to give to the poor saints at Jerusalem.

Verses On Exhorting

- **Acts 11:23**

"Who, when he came, and had seen the grace of God, was glad, and <u>exhorted them all, that with purpose of heart they would cleave unto the</u> Lord."

Paul exhorted the genuine Christians. Exhort. Paul was an exhorter.

- **Acts 14:22**

"Confirming the souls of the disciples, *and* <u>exhorting them to continue in the faith</u>, and that we must through much tribulation enter into the kingdom of God."

Continuing in the faith or doctrines taught in the Bible is very important. It is a sad thing when genuine Christians stop holding to the faith and stop growing in the Lord Jesus Christ.

- **1 Thessalonians 2:11**

"As ye know how <u>we exhorted and comforted and charged every one of you, as a father *doth* his children</u>,"

To the true Christians at Thessalonica, Paul was like a father exhorting his children. If they are out of line, a father must speak very strongly to his children as well as comforting them.

- **1 Timothy 4:13**

"Till I come, <u>give attendance to reading, to exhortation, to doctrine.</u>"

Paul told Timothy, pastor of the church at Ephesus, to reading, doctrine, and exhortation.

- **2 Timothy 4:2**

"Preach the word; be instant in season, out of season; reprove, rebuke, <u>exhort with all longsuffering and doctrine</u>."

Timothy was to exhort his church at Ephesus with longsuffering and doctrine.

- **Titus 1:9**

"Holding fast the faithful word as he hath been taught, that he may be able <u>by sound doctrine both to exhort and to convince the gainsayers.</u>"

Paul told Pastor Titus that he was, by sound doctrine, to exhort and to convince the gainsayers. To convince is not an easy task.

- **Jude 1:3**

"Beloved, when I gave all diligence to write unto you of the common salvation, <u>it was needful for me to</u> write unto you, and <u>exhort *you* that ye should earnestly contend for the faith</u> which was once delivered unto the saints."

Jude exhorted his listeners to contend and fight earnestly for the faith that was delivered for the saints. This means to battle strongly for the doctrines in the New Testament and even the Old Testament which was given to the true Christians to use and believe. Whenever you contend for anything, people might accuse you of being contentious, angry. Genuine Christians should contend for Biblical faith and doctrines whatever people might think of them.

2 Corinthians 9:6

"But this I *say*, He which soweth sparingly shall reap also sparingly; and he which soweth bountifully shall reap also bountifully."

It is plain to understand. If you sow a lot, you will reap a lot. If you sow just a little, you will reap just a little.

Verses On Sowing

- **Matthew 6:26**

"<u>Behold the fowls of the air: for they sow not, neither do they reap</u>, nor gather into barns; yet your heavenly Father feedeth them. Are ye not much better than they?"

God takes care of the fowls of the air without their sowing anything.

- **Matthew 13:3**

"And he spake many things unto them in parables, saying, Behold, <u>a sower went forth to sow</u>;"

The Lord Jesus Christ often used parables to teach the people. On this occasion, He told about sowing on four different types of soil.

- **Galatians 6:7**

"Be not deceived; God is not mocked: for whatsoever a man soweth, that shall he also reap."

- **Galatians 6:8**

"For <u>he that soweth to his flesh</u> shall of the flesh reap corruption; but <u>he that soweth to the Spirit</u> shall of the Spirit reap life everlasting."

For true Christians to sow to their flesh, they reap corruption. When they sow to the Spirit, reap life everlasting.

2 Corinthians 9:7

"Every man according as he purposeth in his heart, *so let him give*; not grudgingly, or of necessity: for God loveth a cheerful giver."

This verse defines what Biblical giving should be like.
1. It should be purposed in the heart.
2. It should include every person. (In Greek, "*man*" includes every human).
3. It should not be given grudgingly.
4. It should not be given of necessity.
5. It should be given cheerfully.

Verses On Purpose

- **Daniel 1:8**

"But <u>Daniel purposed in his heart</u> that he would not defile himself with the portion of the king's meat, nor with the wine which he drank: therefore he requested of the prince of the eunuchs that he might not defile himself."

He just ate vegetables and he survived, stronger and better than any of the magicians of Egypt. God used Daniel's heart-purpose.

- **2 Timothy 1:9**

"<u>Who hath saved</u> us, and called *us* with an holy calling, not according to our works, but <u>according to his own purpose and grace</u>, which was given us in Christ Jesus before the world began,"

It talks about the Lord who saved us. God's purpose in saving sinners, his purpose in saving those who are genuine Christians.

- **2 Timothy 3:10**

"But <u>thou hast fully known my</u> doctrine, manner of life, <u>purpose</u>, faith, longsuffering, charity, patience,"

One of the things that God knew about Paul was his purpose. Paul's purpose was to evangelize the lost, and to establish Biblically sound local churches.

- **1 John 3:8**

"He that committeth sin is of the devil; for the devil sinneth from the beginning. For <u>this purpose the Son of God was manifested, that he might destroy the works of the devil</u>."

One of the purposes of the Lord Jesus Christ was to destroy the works of the Devil.

Verses On Necessity
- **Luke 23:17**

"(For <u>of necessity he must release one unto them at the feast</u>.)"

At the Passover feast, of necessity, one man must be released from prison and from death. Would it be Barabbas, a murderer, or would it be the Lord Jesus Christ? Pilate really wanted to release the Lord Jesus Christ, but the crowd, motivated by the Pharisees said, give us Barabbas. What about the Lord Jesus Christ? The crowd shouted out "Let Him be crucified!! Another word for necessity is grudgingly.

- **Philemon 1:14**

"But without thy mind would I do nothing; that <u>thy benefit should not be as it were of necessity, but willingly</u>."

Paul is writing to Philemon, the slave-owner of Onesimus who had escaped from Onesimus, his owner. Paul did not want to release Onesimus back to Philemon of necessity, but willingly.

Verses On Cheer
- **Proverbs 15:13**

"<u>A merry heart maketh a cheerful countenance</u>: but by sorrow of the heart the spirit is broken."

A merry heart makes a cheerful countenance.

- **Ecclesiastes 11:9**

"Rejoice, O young man, in thy youth; and <u>let thy heart cheer thee in the days of thy youth, and walk in the ways of thine heart</u>, and in the sight of thine eyes: but know thou, that for all these *things* God will bring thee into judgment."

The heart can cheer genuine Christians.

- **Matthew 9:2**

"And, behold, they brought to him a man sick of the palsy, lying on a bed: and Jesus seeing their faith said unto the sick of the palsy; <u>Son, be of good cheer; thy sins be forgiven thee</u>."

The Lord Jesus Christ told the man healed of palsy to be of good cheer because his sins were forgiven.

- **John 16:33**

"These things I have spoken unto you, that in me ye might have peace. In the world ye shall have tribulation: but <u>be of good cheer; I have overcome the world</u>."

There should be good cheer for the genuine Christians because the Lord Jesus Christ has overcome the world.

- **Romans 12:8**
"Or <u>he that exhorteth, on exhortation</u>: he that giveth, *let him do it* with simplicity; he that ruleth, with diligence; he that sheweth mercy, with cheerfulness."

So there should be cheerfulness in giving. It should not be grudgingly or out of necessity.

Verses On Giving And Offering

- **Exodus 36:3**
"And <u>they received of Moses all the offering</u>, which the children of Israel had brought for the work of the service of the sanctuary, to make it *withal*. And they brought yet unto him <u>free offerings</u> every morning."

God's work is made possible by the giving and offerings of His people.

- **Exodus 36:5**
"And they spake unto Moses, saying, <u>The people bring much more than enough</u> for the service of the work, which the LORD commanded to make."

The people gave much more than enough for the needs the LORD had commanded.

- **Exodus 36:6**
"And Moses gave commandment, and they caused it to be proclaimed throughout the camp, saying, <u>Let neither man nor woman make any more work for the offering</u> of the sanctuary. So the people were restrained from bringing."

No more offerings or gifts were needed for it is sufficient for all the work to make it and too much.

Our church has a box in the back where those who wish can place their offerings. We took this practice from Scripture in 2 Kings 12:9-11,

- **2 Kings 12:9**
"But Jehoiada the priest took a chest, and bored a hole in the lid of it, and set it beside the altar, on the right side as one cometh into the house of the LORD: and <u>the priests that kept the door put therein all the money</u> *that was* <u>brought into the house of the LORD</u>."

The chest was used for offerings in the Old Testament.

- **2 Kings 12:10**
"And it was *so*, <u>when they saw that</u> *there was* <u>much money in the chest, that the king's scribe and the high priest came up, and they put up in bags</u>, and told the money that was found in the house of the LORD."

- **2 Kings 12:11**
"And they gave the money, being told, into the hands of them that did the work, that had the oversight of the house of the LORD: and they laid it out to the carpenters and builders, that wrought upon the house of the LORD,"
So, that is the way the Lord did it with the nation of Israel and the tabernacle and various other things. This is what our church decided to do here instead of passing the offering plates around the church.

2 Corinthians 9:8

"And God *is* able to make all grace abound toward you; that ye, always having all sufficiency in all *things*, may abound to every good work:"

The genuine Christians at Corinth are about to give gifts to the poor saints at Jerusalem. Paul says that "*God is able to make all grace abound toward you*" in this act of giving their funds.

God's grace is able to abound in their hearts and lives to enrich them and to encourage them in the things of the Lord. By doing this, they will have "*all sufficiency in all things.*" God will supply all their needs.

- **2 Corinthians 3:5**
"Not that we are sufficient of ourselves to think any thing as of ourselves; but our sufficiency *is* of God;"
No true Christian man, woman, or child should ever think they are sufficient in themselves. Their sufficiency is from God from which they can do every good work.

2 Corinthians 9:9

"(As it is written, He hath dispersed abroad; he hath given to the poor: his righteousness remaineth for ever."

In this verse, you have Bible preservation of the Words in the Hebrew, Aramaic and Greek Words. The Greek Word for "*it is written*" GEGRAPTAI is in the Greek perfect tense. This means that the Words that were written in the past will be preserved to the present and on into the future. This is Bible preservation.

2 Corinthians 9:10

"Now he that ministereth seed to the sower both minister bread for *your* food, and multiply your seed sown, and increase the fruits of your righteousness;)"

As these genuine Christians they are giving to the poor saints of Jerusalem, Paul's prayer to the church of Corinth, that God would minister to their needs, as seed to the sower.

Verses On Fruit

- **Matthew 3:8**

"Bring forth therefore fruits meet for repentance:"
Fruits should be brought forth fitting for a repentant heart.

- **Matthew 7:16**

"Ye shall know them by their fruits. Do men gather grapes of thorns, or figs of thistles?"
True Christians are fruit inspectors for those who profess to be genuine Christians. The fruit of their lives will reveal who they are.

- **Matthew 7:20**

"Wherefore by their fruits ye shall know them."
This is similar to Matthew 7:16. The result of true faith should produce the fruit of righteousness and Christian testimony.

- **Philippians 1:11**

"Being filled with the fruits of righteousness, which are by Jesus Christ, unto the glory and praise of God."
Filled with fruits, that which produces, henceforth, the righteousness of God, through genuine faith in Christ. Notice, the fruits of righteousness which are by Jesus Christ. The only fruits we can have are by the Saviour, the Lord Jesus. We must know him, his fruit by him, "unto the glory and praise of God."
Another verse on fruits,

- **James 3:17**

"But the wisdom that is from above is first pure, then peaceable, gentle, *and* easy to be intreated, full of mercy and good fruits, without partiality, and without hypocrisy."
Wisdom that is from above is filled with good fruits.

2 Corinthians 9:11

"Being enriched in every thing to all bountifulness, which causeth through us thanksgiving to God."

Genuine Christians are enriched in everything, causing thanksgiving to God.

Verses On Rich

- **1 Corinthians 1:5**

"That <u>in every thing ye are enriched by him</u>, in all utterance, and *in* all knowledge;"

In the Lord Jesus Christ and in His Words, genuine Christians can be enriched by His speaking and knowledge.

- **Luke 12:21**

"So *is* he that layeth up treasure for himself, and is <u>not rich toward God</u>."

People should want to be rich towards God and possessing the riches of Christ, by genuine faith in Him and possessing salvation and forgiveness of sins.

- **2 Corinthians 6:10**

"As sorrowful, yet alway rejoicing; <u>as poor, yet making many rich</u>; as having nothing, and *yet* <u>possessing all things</u>."

Paul had both sorrow and poverty, but with the Lord Jesus Christ, he could make *"many rich"* in eternal treasures.

- **1 Timothy 6:18**

"<u>That they do good, that</u> they be rich in good works, ready to distribute, willing to communicate;"

Every genuine Christian should be rich in good works through obedience to God's Words.

- **James 2:5**

"Hearken, my beloved brethren, <u>Hath not God chosen the poor of this world rich in faith</u>, and heirs of the kingdom which he hath promised to them that love him?"

Mrs. Waite and I went to Africa three times for meetings there. Though those genuine Christians were in poverty, living in huts, they were rich in faith in the Lord Jesus Christ.

- **Revelation 2:9**

"<u>I know thy works, and tribulation, and poverty, (but thou art rich</u>) and I *know* the blasphemy of them which say they are Jews, and are not, but *are* the synagogue of Satan."

This church in Smyrna had poverty, but those true Christians were rich in the Lord Jesus Christ.

- **Revelation 3:17**

"Because <u>thou sayest, I am rich, and increased with goods, and have need of nothing</u>; and knowest not that <u>thou art wretched, and miserable, and poor, and blind, and naked</u>:"

This church said they were rich with many goods, but in reality, they were poor in God's eyes.

- **Revelation 3:18**

"<u>I counsel thee to buy of me gold tried in the fire, that thou mayest be rich</u>; and white raiment, that thou mayest be clothed, and *that* the shame of thy nakedness do not appear; and anoint thine eyes with eyesalve, that thou mayest see."

This church did not want the riches of God, but was rebellious.

Verses On Bountiful

- **Psalms 13:6**

"I will sing unto the LORD, because <u>he hath dealt bountifully with me.</u>"

When God deals bountifully with true Christians, they can sing unto the Lord. Every such person who is in Christ, God has dealt bountifully with them in giving them His salvation.

- **Psalms 116:7-8**

"Return unto thy rest, O my soul; for <u>the LORD hath dealt bountifully with thee</u>. For thou hast delivered my soul from death, mine eyes from tears, *and* my feet from falling."

To every genuine Christ, the Lord Jesus Christ has dealt bountifully. This psalmist was grateful. God delivered this psalmist from death, tears and falling.

- **2 Corinthians 9:6**

"But this I *say*, He which soweth sparingly shall reap also sparingly; and <u>he which soweth bountifully shall reap also bountifully.</u>"

This verse shows that sowing a field bountifully will cause the sower to reap in a bountiful way.

Verses On Thanksgiving

- **Psalms 50:14**

"<u>Offer unto God thanksgiving</u>; and pay thy vows unto the most High:"

Genuine Christians should offer to God the Father their thanksgiving for all that He and His Son, the Lord Jesus Christ, have done for them and given them.

- **Psalms 100:4**
"<u>Enter into his gates with thanksgiving,</u> *and* into his courts with praise: be thankful unto him, *and* bless his name."
True Christians should be thankful for all the Lord has done for them.
- **Philippians 4:6** "Be careful for nothing; but <u>in every thing by prayer and supplication with thanksgiving let your requests be made known unto God.</u>"
Prayer by genuine Christians should be made with thanksgiving to the Lord.
- **Colossians 2:7**
"Rooted and built up in him, and stablished in the faith, as ye have been taught, <u>abounding therein with thanksgiving.</u>"
True Christians should abound with thanksgiving to the Lord Jesus Christ for all He has done for them.
- **Colossians 4:2**
"Continue in prayer, and watch in the same with thanksgiving;"
Prayer should be made by all genuine Christians with thanksgiving to the Lord for all He has done for them.

2 Corinthians 9:12

"For the administration of this service not only supplieth the want of the saints, but is abundant also by many thanksgivings unto God;"

Giving to the poor saints of Jerusalem not only supplied the want or the need of the saints, but is abundant, also, by many thanksgivings unto God.

Verses On Want
- **Psalms 23:1**
"The LORD *is* my shepherd; <u>I shall not want.</u>"
The LORD is the Shepherd of every genuine Christian. Because of this, they shall not have want.
- **Psalms 34:9**
"O fear the LORD, ye his saints: for <u>*there* is no want to them that fear him.</u>"
God has promised that no real want shall come to His true Christians. He will protect them and guide them even in the wants that come into their lives.

- **Luke 15:14**
    "And when he had spent all, there arose a mighty famine in that land; and he began to be in want."
The prodigal son left his father's home and spent all of his father's money that he had given him in riotous living. Then he began to be in want so he went back to his home where his father received him.
- **Philippians 4:11**
    "Not that I speak in respect of want: for I have learned, in whatsoever state I am, *therewith* to be content."
Paul who wrote from a Roman prison had many wants, but he learned to be content through the help of His Saviour.

2 Corinthians 9:13

"Whiles by the experiment of this ministration they glorify God for your professed subjection unto the Gospel of Christ, and for *your* liberal distribution unto them, and unto all *men*;"

By the genuine Christians giving to the poor saints of Jerusalem, they glorified God.

Verses On Glorify
- **Psalms 86:12**
    "I will praise thee, O Lord my God, with all my heart: and I will glorify thy name for evermore."
That means they will give the Name of God glory and praise.
- **Matthew 5:16**
    "Let your light so shine before men, that they may see your good works, and glorify your Father which is in heaven."
When true Christians let their light shine, they glorify their Father in Heaven.
- **John 16:14**
    "He shall glorify me: for he shall receive of mine, and shall shew *it* unto you."
Jesus said that the Holy Spirit of God would glorify the Lord Jesus Christ. He would receive the Words of the New Testament from the Lord Jesus Christ and would give these Words to the Apostles to write them down. That is how the Scriptures were inspired and made.

- **John 17:1**

"These words spake Jesus, and lifted up his eyes to heaven, and said, Father, the hour is come; <u>glorify thy Son, that thy Son also may glorify thee:</u>"

It was the hour, when the Lord Jesus Christ, the sinless, Son of God, was about to bear the sins of the whole world. He wanted the Father to glorify His Son.

- **John 21:19**

"This spake he, <u>signifying by what death he should glorify God</u>. And when he had spoken this, he saith unto him, Follow me."

The Lord Jesus Christ said to Peter three times: *"Lovest thou me?"* He showed Peter how He should glorify God His Father.

- **Romans 15:6**

"<u>That ye may with one mind *and* one mouth glorify God, even the Father</u> of our Lord Jesus Christ."

Genuine Christians should glorify God both with their minds and with their mouths.

- **1 Corinthians 6:20**

"For ye are bought with a price: therefore <u>glorify God in your body, and in your spirit</u>, which are God's."

Because true Christians are bought with a price, they should glorify God in their body and spirit.

2 Corinthians 9:14

"And by their prayer for you, which long after you for the exceeding grace of God in you."

The poor saints at Jerusalem prayed for the genuine Christians at Corinth and longed after them for the grace of God in them.

Verses On The Grace Of God

- **Luke 2:40**

"And <u>the child</u> grew, and waxed strong in spirit, filled with wisdom: and <u>the grace of God was upon him</u>."

The grace of God was on the Lord Jesus Christ, even as a young Child.

- **1 Corinthians 15:10**

"But <u>by the grace of God I am what I am</u>: and his grace which *was bestowed* upon me was not in vain; but I laboured more abundantly than they all: yet not I, but the grace of God which was with me."

So Paul acknowledged that the grace of God helped him minister as an apostle.

- **Ephesians 3:2**
"If ye have heard of the dispensation of the grace of God which is given me to you-ward:"

This dispensation of grace is the dispensation we are living in now. It is the Church Age.

- **John 1:17**
"For the law was given by Moses, *but* grace and truth came by Jesus Christ."

That is the age of Grace. Grace and truth came by the Lord Jesus Christ the Saviour.

- **Titus 2:11-13**
"For the grace of God that bringeth salvation hath appeared to all men, Teaching us that, denying ungodliness and worldly lusts, we should live soberly, righteously, and godly, in this present world; Looking for that blessed hope, and the glorious appearing of the great God and our Saviour Jesus Christ;"

The **provision** for salvation has appeared to all human beings. They must sincerely trust the Lord Jesus Christ Himself by true faith to accept that **provision**. God's grace has appeared to all, not simply to hyper-Calvinists, the elect only, but unto all human beings. God's grace is open to all. The Lord Jesus Christ died for the sins of the whole world. He bids all to trust Him as their Saviour.

- **Matthew 11:28**
"Come unto me, all *ye* that labour and are heavy laden, and I will give you rest."

This verse from the Lord Jesus Christ is an invitation for all people to come to Him and believe on Him to be eternally saved and redeemed.

- **Hebrews 2:9**
"But we see Jesus, who was made a little lower than the angels for the suffering of death, crowned with glory and honour; that he by the grace of God should taste death for every man."

This verse is clear. The Lord Jesus Christ tasted death for every person. Trusting Him by true faith can bring a person to receive everlasting life.

2 Corinthians 9:15

"Thanks *be* unto God for his unspeakable gift." The unspeakable Gift is the Lord Jesus Christ. If a person truly accepts the Lord Jesus Christ as their Saviour, every one of these ten gifts can be theirs.

God's Gift #1
The Gift Of Salvation

- Acts 4:12

"Neither is there salvation in any other: for there is none other name under heaven given among men, whereby we must be saved."

If people truly receive the Lord Jesus Christ as their Saviour, they can receive the gift of **salvation**.

God's Gift #2
The Gift Of Redemption

- Ephesians 1:7

"In whom we have redemption through his blood, the forgiveness of sins, according to the riches of his grace;"

If people truly receive the Lord Jesus Christ as their Saviour, they can receive the gift of **redemption by the blood of Christ**.

God's Gift #3
The Gift Of Forgiveness Of Sins

- Colossians 1:14

"In whom we have redemption through his blood, *even* the forgiveness of sins:"

If people truly receive the Lord Jesus Christ as their Saviour, they can receive the gift of **forgiveness of sins**.

God's Gift #4
The Gift Of Everlasting Life

If people truly receive the Lord Jesus Christ as their Saviour, they can receive the gift of **everlasting life**.

- John 3:16

"For God so loved the world, that he gave his only begotten Son, that whosoever believeth in him should not perish, but **have everlasting life**."

If people truly receive the Lord Jesus Christ as their Saviour, they can receive the gift of **forgiveness of sins**.

God's Gift #5
The Gift Of Peace With God
- **Romans 5:1**
"Therefore being justified by faith, we have **peace with God** through our Lord Jesus Christ:"

If people truly receive the Lord Jesus Christ as their Saviour, they can receive the gift of **peace with God**.

God's Gift #6
The Gift Of The Indwelling Holy Spirit

The sixth result of his gift is that we can have **the indwelling Holy Spirit**,
- **1 Corinthians 6:19**
"What? know ye not that your body is **the temple of the Holy Ghost *which is* in you**, which ye have of God, and ye are not your own?"

If people truly receive the Lord Jesus Christ as their Saviour, they have the **Holy Spirit indwelling them**.

God's Gift #7
The Gift Of Never Perishing

The seventh result of God's unspeakable gift, you have eternal security and **will never perish**.
- **John 10:27-28**
"My sheep hear my voice, and I know them, and they follow me: And I give unto them eternal life; and **they shall never perish**, neither shall *any* man pluck them out of my hand."

If people truly receive the Lord Jesus Christ as their Saviour, **they shall never perish**.

God's Gift #8
The Gift Of A Resurrected Body

The seventh result of God's unspeakable gift, you have **a resurrected body like Christ's**.
- **Philippians 3:21**
"Who shall change **our vile body, that it may be fashioned like unto his glorious body**, according to the working whereby he is able even to subdue all things unto himself."

The eighth thing we have because of God's unspeakable gift, we can have a resurrected body like Christ's,

God's Gift #9
The Gift Of Being With Christ When We Die

The ninth thing we have through the unspeakable gift, we can be a part of **being with Christ, when we die**.

- Philippians 1:23

"For I am in a strait betwixt two, **having a desire to depart, and to be with Christ**; which is far better:"

The ninth thing we have because of God's unspeakable gift, we can be with Christ when we die.

God's Gift #10
The Gift Of Having A Home In Heaven For Eternity

The tenth thing we have as a result of God's unspeakable gift, is **a Home in Heaven for all of eternity**.

- John 14:2-3

"In my Father's house are many mansions: if *it were* not *so*, I would have told you. **I go to prepare a place for you**. And if I go and prepare a place for you, I will come again, and receive you unto myself; that where I am, *there* ye may be also."

2 Corinthians Chapter Ten

2 Corinthians 10:1

"Now I Paul myself beseech you by the meekness and gentleness of Christ, who in presence *am* base among you, but being absent am bold toward you:"

Paul is talking to the genuine Christians at Corinth by the means of meekness and gentleness of the Lord Jesus Christ.

Verses On Meekness

- **1 Corinthians 4:21**

"What will ye? shall I come unto you with a rod, or in love, and in the spirit of meekness?"

That man that sinned, who had taken his own father's wife and committed incest was very evil. The church was evil for not using discipline on him.

- **Galatians 5:23**

"Meekness, temperance: against such there is no law."

Meekness is one of the fruits of the Spirit.

- **Galatians 6:1**

"Brethren, if a man be overtaken in a fault, ye which are spiritual, restore such an one in the spirit of meekness; considering thyself, lest thou also be tempted."

Those who are controlled by the Spirit of God, should be the only ones to go to one to try and restore such a Christian in the spirit of meekness.

- **Ephesians 4:1-2**

"I therefore, the prisoner of the Lord, beseech you that ye walk worthy of the vocation wherewith ye are called, With all lowliness and meekness, with longsuffering, forbearing one another in love;"

Meekness is a part of the traits that Paul asked the people at the church at Ephesus to walk in. That is true of any believers, anywhere in the world.

- **1 Peter 3:15**

"But sanctify the Lord God in your hearts: and *be* ready always to <u>*give an answer*</u> to every man that asketh you a reason of the hope that is in you <u>with meekness and fear</u>:"

Answer them you about the hope that is in you with meekness and with fear.

Verses On Gentleness

- **Psalms 18:35**

"Thou hast also given me the shield of thy salvation: and thy right hand hath holden me up, and <u>thy gentleness hath made me great</u>."

God's gentleness can make any true Christian great.

- **Galatians 5:22**

"But <u>the fruit of the Spirit is love, joy, peace, longsuffering, gentleness</u>, goodness, faith,"

When true Christians are controlled by the Spirit of God, they can be gentle.

Verses On Bold

- **Proverbs 28:1**

"The wicked flee when no man pursueth: but <u>the righteous are bold as a lion</u>."

Genuine Christians should be bold as a lion when witnessing for the Saviour.

- **Philippians 1:14**

"And many of the brethren in the Lord, waxing confident by my bonds, <u>are much more bold to speak the word without fear</u>."

Because Paul was in a Roman prison, true Christians were much more bold to speak the Gospel without fear.

- **1 Thessalonians 2:2**

"But even after that we had suffered before, and were shamefully entreated, as ye know, at Philippi, <u>we were bold in our God to speak unto you the Gospel of God</u> with much contention."

Bold to speak the Gospel with much contention. The Gospel always brings contention.

2 Corinthians 10:2

"But I beseech *you*, that I may not be bold when I am present with that confidence, wherewith I think to be bold against some, which think of us as if we walked according to the flesh."

Paul hoped that he will not be bold when he is present with them, but he wants confidence in what he says to them.

Verses On Confidence

- **Proverbs 14:26**

"In the fear of the LORD *is* strong confidence: and his children shall have a place of refuge."

If a true Christian walks in God's will, he will have strong confidence.

- **Proverbs 25:19**

"Confidence in an unfaithful man in time of trouble *is like* a broken tooth, and a foot out of joint."

Confidence, in this case, is wrong confidence. Do not have this kind of confidence.

- **Ephesians 3:12**

"In whom we have boldness and access with confidence by the faith of him."

Genuine Christians have confidence and access to the Lord Jesus Christ.

- **Philippians 3:3**

"For we are the circumcision, which worship God in the spirit, and rejoice in Christ Jesus, and have no confidence in the flesh."

Paul had no confidence in his flesh, nor should true Christians today. They should walk in the power of God the Holy Spirit Who indwells them.

2 Corinthians 10:3

"For though we walk in the flesh, we do not war after the flesh:"

Genuine Christians still have their sinful flesh even after they become true Christians, but they should not war after their flesh, but by the Holy Spirit Who indwells them. The non-Christian has just one nature–the flesh.

Verses On The Flesh

- **Romans 7:18**

"For I know that <u>in me (that is, in my flesh,) dwelleth no good thing</u>: for to will is present with me; but *how* to perform that which is good I find not."

In the flesh of every human being there is no good thing in God's eyes, despite what people say about their flesh.

- **Romans 8:1**

"*There is* therefore now no condemnation to them which are <u>in Christ Jesus, who walk not after the flesh, but after the Spirit</u>."

For genuine Christians who walk after the Spirit rather than the flesh, there is no condemnation.

- **Romans 8:4-5**

"That the righteousness of the law might be fulfilled in us, <u>who walk not after the flesh, but after the Spirit</u>. For they that are after the flesh do mind the things of the flesh; but they that are after the Spirit the things of the Spirit."

The righteousness of the Law of Moses is fulfilled in the true Christians who walk after the Spirit. The flesh and the Spirit are warring against each other in all genuine Christians.

- **Romans 8:8-9**

"So then <u>they that are in the flesh cannot please God</u>. But ye are not in the flesh, but in the Spirit, if so be that the Spirit of God dwell in you. Now <u>if any man have not the Spirit of Christ, he is none of his</u>."

This describes every non-Christian in the world. Though many deny this, God's Word clearly teaches it. A person who is in Christ has the Spirit of God. If you do not have the Spirit of Christ, the Spirit of the Lord Jesus Christ, the Holy Spirit, you are not His. You do not belong to Him. It is very clear in Romans 8:9. So be if that the Spirit of God dwell in you, you are in the Spirit, not in the flesh.

- **Romans 13:14**

"But put ye on the Lord Jesus Christ, and <u>make not provision for the flesh, to *fulfil* the lusts *thereof*</u>."

No provision for the flesh means not to fulfill its lusts by any genuine Christian. It does not mean to make no provision to eat food, take a rest at night, drink water, or other things like this; it means no provision for evil things. Do not give the flesh opportunity whether it is in the thought life, what in what their eyes see, what their ears hear, and so on.

- **1 Corinthians 1:29**
"That no flesh should glory in his presence."
God does not want any flesh (whether that of true Christians, or that of non-Christians) to glory in His presence.
- **1 Corinthians 15:50**
"Now this I say, brethren, that flesh and blood cannot inherit the kingdom of God; neither doth corruption inherit incorruption."
Flesh and blood cannot inherit the kingdom of God. No one can go to Heaven with their flesh and blood bodies. They must have new bodies like Christ's resurrected body.
- **2 Corinthians 7:1**
"Having therefore these promises, dearly beloved, let us cleanse ourselves from all filthiness of the flesh and spirit, perfecting holiness in the fear of God."
Genuine Christians should cleanse themselves from the filthiness of both their flesh and their spirit.
- **Galatians 5:13**
"For, brethren, ye have been called unto liberty; only use not liberty for an occasion to the flesh, but by love serve one another."
Liberty from the law of Moses should not use that freedom to serve the flesh. They should serve one another.

2 Corinthians 10:4

"(For the weapons of our warfare *are* not carnal, but mighty through God to the pulling down of strong holds;)"

There are three kinds of weapons of war for the true Christians:
1. They are not carnal or fleshly.
2. They are mighty through God.
3. They can pull down strongholds.
4. They can cast down imaginations
5. They can cast down every high thing.
6. They can bring into captivity every thought

Verses On Weapons Of War
- **2 Samuel 1:27**

"How are the mighty fallen, and the weapons of war perished!"

David and Saul were in battle. The mighty have fallen and the weapons of war perished. That is what Israel said when their enemies were defeated.

- **Ecclesiastes 9:18**

"Wisdom *is* better than weapons of war: but one sinner destroyeth much good."

Genuine Christians should use God's weapons through the Holy Spirit and God's Words with His wisdom.

- **John 18:3**

"Judas then, having received a band *of men* and officers from the chief priests and Pharisees, cometh thither with lanterns and torches and weapons."

This is what the traitor, Judas Iscariot, did. He brought men and weapons to take the Lord Jesus Christ. He identified Jesus by a kiss—the kiss of betrayal.

- **1 Corinthians 9:7**

"Who goeth a warfare any time at his own charges? who planteth a vineyard, and eateth not of the fruit thereof? or who feedeth a flock, and eateth not of the milk of the flock?"

When you signed up, if you were in the military, you were paid by them, whether by Army, Navy, Air Force, Marine Corp. or others.

- **1 Timothy 1:18**

"This charge I commit unto thee, son Timothy, according to the prophecies which went before on thee, that thou by them mightest war a good warfare;"

The prophecies, Scriptures, or Words of God, that went before Paul, by these Pastor Timothy should war a good warfare for the things of the Lord.

Verses On Throwing Down Strongholds
- **Micah 5:11-12**

"And I will cut off the cities of thy land, and throw down all thy strong holds: And I will cut off witchcrafts out of thine hand; and thou shalt have no *more* soothsayers:"

God promised to fight for Micah and throw down strong holds. He would also be against witchcrafts and soothsayers.

2 Corinthians 10:5

"Casting down imaginations, and every high thing that exalteth itself against the knowledge of God, and bringing into captivity every thought to the obedience of Christ;"

Throw down any imaginations that are not true and any high thing and every thought that is not in line with truth and God's Words. Many books and philosophies of men should be cast down. Disagree with it, whether it is evolution or whatever it may be. People might look at you as if you are crazy. Well, let them look. God says all people are sinners. The world says everybody is good. The world says there is no such thing as Heaven, cast it down. The world says the Lord Jesus Christ was not perfect God, as well as perfect Man. Cast that false doctrine down. He was and he is perfect God and perfect Man. If they say we are saved by good works, not by trusting the Lord Jesus Christ as their Saviour, cast that out.

- **Proverbs 6:18**

"An heart that deviseth wicked imaginations, feet that be swift in running to mischief,"

True Christians should cast our these imaginations.

- **Lamentations 3:61**

"Thou hast heard their reproach, O LORD, *and* all their imaginations against me;"

It is the thought life and imaginations of godless people that God hears and hates.

- **Romans 1:21**

"Because that, when they knew God, they glorified *him* not as God, neither were thankful; but became vain in their imaginations, and their foolish heart was darkened."

They had vain imaginations and darkened hearts.

- **Romans 7:23**

"But I see another law in my members, warring against the law of my mind, and bringing me into captivity to the law of sin which is in my members."

Paul's warring heart brought him into captivity to sin.

- **Job 42:2**
"I know that thou canst do every *thing*, and *that* <u>no thought can be withholden from thee.</u>"

God knows the thoughts of every person in the world, whether true Christians or non-Christians. The Lord Jesus knew the thoughts of his disciples. He has omniscience and knows every thought of every person in the world.

- **Psalms 139:2**
"Thou knowest my downsitting and mine uprising, <u>thou understandest my thought afar off.</u>"

Even before the thoughts get into our brains, God knows what they are in His omniscience.

- **Proverbs 24:9**
"<u>The thought of foolishness *is* sin</u>: and the scorner *is* an abomination to men."

Do not even think about any foolish thing. Even the thought of them is sin in the eyes of God.

- **Luke 9:46-47**
"Then <u>there arose a reasoning among them, which of them should be greatest.</u> And Jesus, perceiving the thought of their heart, took a child, and set him by him,"

As to who would be the greatest, the Lord Jesus Christ took a child and set him by Himself. That was the Saviour's answer.

- **Acts 8:19-20**
"Saying, <u>Give me also this power, that on whomsoever I lay hands, he may receive the Holy Ghost.</u> But Peter said unto him, Thy money perish with thee, because thou hast thought that the gift of God may be purchased with money."

This Simon the sorcerer wanted to perform the miracles that he saw the apostles performing with his own eyes. His request was not granted. Peter knew his thoughts and knew his heart. The request was not granted.

- **Acts 8:22**
"Repent therefore of this thy wickedness, and <u>pray God, if perhaps the thought of thine heart may be forgiven thee.</u>"

Thoughts, if they are bad thoughts, need to be forgiven as well as other sins.

2 Corinthians 10:6
"And having in a readiness to revenge all disobedience, when your obedience is fulfilled."

Genuine Christians must be ready to revenge and stand against all disobedience to the Words of God, whether it is in our own hearts, the hearts of our loved ones, hearts of our friends, or the hearts of our neighbors.

2 Corinthians 10:7
"Do ye look on things after the outward appearance? If any man trust to himself that he is Christ's, let him of himself think this again, that, as he *is* Christ's, even so *are* we Christ's."

Notice, outward appearance. Many people, that is all they look at. It is all they have. It is all they believe in. That is outward appearance but he says, that is not what we are to do.

If a true Christian belongs to the Lord Jesus Christ, this cannot be seen by outward appearance, but the Lord knows those that belong to Him by personal faith in His Son.

Verses On Appearance
- 1 Samuel 16:7

"But the LORD said unto Samuel, Look not on his countenance, or on the height of his stature; because I have refused him: for *the LORD seeth* not as man seeth; for man looketh on the outward appearance, but the LORD looketh on the heart."

Human beings look at the outward appearance of people, but God looks on hearts.
- John 7:24

"Judge not according to the appearance, but judge righteous judgment."

The Scriptures are clear, true Christians. We are not to judge according to appearances, but they are to judge, righteous judgment.
- 2 Corinthians 5:12

"For we commend not ourselves again unto you, but give you occasion to glory on our behalf, that ye may have somewhat to *answer* them which glory in appearance, and not in heart."

There are people who glory in appearance rather in the inner matters of the heart. This is wrong.

- **1 Thessalonians 5:22**
"Abstain from all appearance of evil."
Genuine Christians must be very careful about this. Sometimes they give the appearance of evil, even though they do not mean to. They have to be very careful.

2 Corinthians 10:8

"For though I should boast somewhat more of our authority, which the Lord hath given us for edification, and not for your destruction, I should not be ashamed:"

Paul did not have authority over the churches by himself but God gave him that authority. He wanted to edify and build them up. He did not want to tear them down, though his first letter to the church at Corinth was very strong against the incestuous man and how the church did not handle it rightly.

2 Corinthians 10:9

"That I may not seem as if I would terrify you by letters."

Paul wanted to edify the church and build them up in the Words of God. He did not want to tear them down. His first letter to them had bee very strong because he wanted to straighten the church out in dealing with the man who committed incest. The church finally did the proper thing and removed this man from the membership until he repented of this sin. After his repentance, he was received back into church membership. That was a good result of his terrible sin.

2 Corinthians 10:10

"For *his* letters, say they, *are* weighty and powerful; but *his* bodily presence *is* weak, and *his* speech contemptible."

Because Paul's first letter to the genuine Christians at Corinth was strong against the incestuous man and against the church for not dismissing him from membership immediately, the church was angry with him. They did not like him. They agreed that his letters were weighty and powerful. They liked what he wrote, "*but his bodily presence is weak, and his speech contemptible.*" They did not like him when he was there.

Verses On Weak
- **Matthew 26:41**
"Watch and pray, that ye enter not into temptation: the spirit indeed is willing, but the flesh is weak."

The disciples fell asleep, when the Lord Jesus Christ prayed in the garden of Gethsemane before His crucifixion. They could not stay awake though they wanted to watch and pray with the Lord Jesus Christ.

- **Romans 8:3**
"For what the law could not do, in that it was weak through the flesh, God sending his own Son in the likeness of sinful flesh, and for sin, condemned sin in the flesh:"

The law of Moses depended on weak flesh to obey it.

- **Romans 15:1**
"We then that are strong ought to bear the infirmities of the weak, and not to please ourselves."

True Christians who are strong should help the weak ones.

- **1 Corinthians 1:27**
"But God hath chosen the foolish things of the world to confound the wise; and God hath chosen the weak things of the world to confound the things which are mighty;"

God chooses the weak things to confound the things that are mighty.

- **1 Corinthians 9:22**
"To the weak became I as weak, that I might gain the weak: I am made all things to all *men*, that I might by all means save some."

For Paul to help the weak people, he became like he was weak in order to understand them and help them.

- **2 Corinthians 12:10**
"Therefore I take pleasure in infirmities, in reproaches, in necessities, in persecutions, in distresses for Christ's sake: for when I am weak, then am I strong."

When Paul is weak, he relies on the strength of the Lord Jesus Christ to make him strong in the Lord.

The genuine Christians at Corinth said Paul's bodily presence was weak and that his speech was contemptible. They did not like what he said or the way he talked. Maybe that was his thorn in his flesh. The Bible does not say what that thorn in the flesh was. It could be his speech, his weakness. It could be his failing eyesight.

2 Corinthians 10:11

"Let such an one think this, that, such as we are in word by letters when we are absent, such *will we be* also in deed when we are present."

Paul is going to match his words with his deeds. When he is with them, he's going to be just as strong as he is in his letters as he will be when he is present with them. He's going to match his words with his deeds. The words of true Christians should match their deeds as well.

Verses On Words And Deeds
- **Romans 15:18**

"For I will not dare to speak of any of those things which Christ hath not wrought by me, to make the Gentiles obedient, by word and deed,"

The Gentiles, and everyone else, should be obedient to God's Words by their words and by their deeds.

- **Colossians 3:17**

"And whatsoever ye do in word or deed, *do* all in the name of the Lord Jesus, giving thanks to God and the Father by him."

Obedient Christians should do all their words and their deeds in the Name of the Lord Jesus Christ.

- **1 John 3:18**

"My little children, let us not love in word, neither in tongue; but in deed and in truth."

True Christians should love one another in deed and truth.

2 Corinthians 10:12

"For we dare not make ourselves of the number, or compare ourselves with some that commend themselves: but they measuring themselves by themselves, and comparing themselves among themselves, are not wise."

Paul did not want the true Christians to compare themselves among themselves by measuring themselves by themselves. They are not wise who do this. They are foolish, if they compare or measure themselves by one another. They must be measured and compared to the Words of God in the Bible, not to people.

Verses On Measuring
- **Psalms 39:4**

"LORD, make me to know mine end, and the measure of my days, what it *is*; *that* I may know how frail I *am*."

Genuine Christians do not know when they are going to die. Sometimes in the Scriptures, God tells certain ones that they were going to die at a certain time, but we today do not know the measure of our days. We have to live for the Lord Jesus Christ no matter how old we are.

- **Mark 4:24**

"And he said unto them, Take heed what ye hear: with what measure ye mete, it shall be measured to you: and unto you that hear shall more be given."

Measures by people come back on them. They are measured by others. Genuine Christians should compare themselves by the Words of God, not by other Christians.

2 Corinthians 10:13

"But we will not boast of things without *our* measure, but according to the measure of the rule which God hath distributed to us, a measure to reach even unto you."

Paul did not want to boast of things without his measure. He did not want to go beyond what God distributed to him by His gift.

Verses On Gift
- **1 Corinthians 7:7**

"For I would that all men were even as I myself. But every man hath his proper gift of God, one after this manner, and another after that."

Every true Christian has been given God's gift of salvation as well as various other gifts.

- **Ephesians 3:7**

"Whereof I was made a minister, according to the gift of the grace of God given unto me by the effectual working of his power."

Paul was made a genuine Christian by God as he was on his way to imprison and slay many Chistians in Damascus. He had no desire to be a Christian at the time. All he wanted to do at the time was to put Christians in prison, or to kill them. He was a Pharisee of the Pharisees at the time. The Lord Jesus Christ asked him: *"Saul, Saul, why persecuteth thou me?"*

Paul was blinded for several days. On that day, the light was even brighter than the sun. This was noonday special sunshine, the brightest possible light. Finally, Paul sincerely trusted the Lord Jesus Christ as His Saviour and began to preach Him as the Saviour. He was saved by God's grace.

- **1 Peter 4:10**
"As every man hath received the gift, *even so* minister the same one to another, as good stewards of the manifold grace of God."

All true Christians should be a good steward and share with others the gift God gave them.

2 Corinthians 10:14

"For we stretch not ourselves beyond *our measure*, as though we reached not unto you: for we are come as far as to you also in *preaching* the Gospel of Christ:"

Paul was coming to them to preach the Gospel of the Lord Jesus Christ, according to the Gospel of God's grace as taught in the Bible. It was not the social Gospel or any other Gospel of works preached by modernistic churches, ungodly churches, many other Protestant churches, and other churches preach today.

What is involved in the Gospel of the Lord Jesus Christ? I believe there are three major parts to this good news Gospel:

1. Every person in the world must realize that God considers them to be sinners who are condemned to be cast into the Lake of Fire in Hell for all eternity to come.

2. The Lord Jesus Christ's death on the Cross of Calvary was an offering, sacrifice, and an atonement for the sins of every person in the world, making provision for everlasting life and Heaven.

3. Each person in the world must sincerely believe on, trust and receive the Lord Jesus Christ as their Saviour and thus receive God's forgiveness and eternal life as stated in John 3:16:

"For God so loved the world, that he gave his only begotten Son, that whosoever believeth in him should not perish, but have everlasting life."

Verses On Preaching
- **Acts 10:36**

"The word which *God* sent unto the children of Israel, **preaching peace by Jesus Christ: (he is Lord of all:)**"
That is the effect of the Gospel of the Lord Jesus Christ. It brings peace with God the Father, God the Son, and God the Holy Spirit.

- **Acts 11:20**

"And some of them were men of Cyprus and Cyrene, which, when they were come to Antioch, spake unto the Grecians, preaching the Lord Jesus."
These men preached about the Lord Jesus Christ, rather than what apostate preachers today preach.

- **Acts 15:35**

"Paul also and Barnabas continued in Antioch, teaching and preaching the word of the Lord, with many others also."
Preaching and teaching the Word of the Lord is what preachers should do today.

- **Romans 16:25**

"Now to him that is of power to stablish you according to my Gospel, and the preaching of Jesus Christ, according to the revelation of the mystery, which was kept secret since the world began,"
Preaching the good news about the Lord Jesus Christ Who can give eternal life to those who trust Him.

- **1 Corinthians 1:18**

"For the preaching of the cross is to them that perish foolishness; but unto us which are saved it is the power of God."
Preaching of the Cross of our Saviour is foolishness to the world, but it is the power God to genuine Christians.

- **1 Corinthians 1:21**

"For after that in the wisdom of God the world by wisdom knew not God, it pleased God by the foolishness of preaching to save them that believe."
The so-called *"foolishness of preaching"* the Lord Jesus Christ is what brings salvation to those who truly believe.

- **1 Corinthians 2:4**

"And my speech and my preaching *was* not with enticing words of man's wisdom, but in demonstration of the Spirit and of power:"
The enticing words of man's wisdom will not lead people to become true Christians. It must be using the Bible's Words in the power of God the Holy Spirit.

2 Corinthians 10:15

"Not boasting of things without *our* measure, *that is*, of other men's labours; but having hope, when your faith is increased, that we shall be enlarged by you according to our rule abundantly,"

Paul was not boasting about things about which he did not know anything. He hoped that when the faith of the genuine Christians at Corinth is increased, he would be blessed by them abundantly.

2 Corinthians 10:16

"To preach the Gospel in the *regions* beyond you, *and* not to boast in another man's line of things made ready to our hand."

Paul wanted to preach the Gospel in the regions beyond Corinth. He did not want to stay in one place. He wanted to be a traveling missionary.

By our use of the international Internet, our church has ministry in the regions beyond us even as Paul did. Sixty-five to seventy foreign countries download our messages, every single month. Every one of our fifty states have people who download our messages through the Internet from the regions beyond. If and when the Internet goes down, we can send our messages on DVD's and send it to those who ask for them.

After convincing me to do this, Pastor Daniel Waite, our son, who is the Assistant Pastor of our church, connected us to the Internet. He is skilled in all these technical matters and knew exactly how to do this. We began with two cameras in the back and two cameras in the front of our church to record the services in words and pictures. We have added a few more cameras lately.

Pastor Daniel preaches the Word on Sundays when I am in other meetings and each week on Friday afternoons he teaches many different classes on many important and needed Bible subjects.

Verses On Ministry In Regions Beyond
- **Acts 8:1**

"And Saul was consenting unto his death. And at that time there was a great persecution against the church which was at Jerusalem; and <u>they were all scattered abroad throughout the regions of Judaea and Samaria, except the apostles</u>."

Before Saul (Paul) became a true Christian, the Christians were scattered throughout many regions.

- **2 Corinthians 11:10**

"As the truth of Christ is in me, no man shall stop me of this <u>boasting in the regions of Achaia</u>."

Paul traveled to different regions of Achaia preaching the Gospel of Christ.

- **Galatians 1:21**

"Afterwards I came into the regions of Syria and Cilicia;"

Paul was a missionary to all the different regions of the then known world.

2 Corinthians 10:17

"But he that glorieth, let him glory in the Lord."

If any genuine Christians glory, let them primarily glory about the Lord Jesus Christ and all the things He has done for them.

- **Jeremiah 9:23-24**

"Thus saith the LORD, Let not the wise *man* glory in his wisdom, neither let the mighty *man* glory in his might, let not the rich *man* glory in his riches: But let him that glorieth glory in this, that he understandeth and knoweth me, that I *am* the LORD which exercise lovingkindness, judgment, and righteousness, in the earth: for in these *things* I delight, saith the LORD."

Paul is quoting parts of Jeremiah 9:23-24. Bible preservation is seen here. He could not have quoted from Jeremiah here if that Old Testament book had not been verbally preserved by the Lord's power. The entire Bible has been preserved by God in the languages of Hebrew and Aramaic in the Old Testament, and Greek in the New Testament. Bible preservation is an important and vital doctrine of the Bible.

- **1 Corinthians 1:31**
"That, according as it is written, He that glorieth, let him glory in the Lord."

As "*it is written*" is a translation for the Greek Word GEGRAPTAI. Gregraptai is the verb GRAPHO in the perfect tense. The perfect tense means something that happened the past whose results are continued into the present time and on into the future. This is the chief Greek Word that proves Bible preservation of all of the original Hebrew, Aramaic, and Greek Words of the entire Bible from Genesis through Revelation.

2 Corinthians 10:18

"For not he that commendeth himself is approved, but whom the Lord commendeth."

Commending themselves is not profitable. It is much better when genuine Christians are commended by the Lord Jesus Christ. True Christians and those listening by the Internet and by other means, all over the world, should be asking themselves this question: "Is the Lord Jesus Christ commending what I do, what I say, where I go, what I think in my heart, and what I think in my mind?" These are very important questions for genuine Christians to ask themselves.

Words Of Commendation

- **Proverbs 12:8**
"A man shall be commended according to his wisdom: but he that is of a perverse heart shall be despised."

God commends according to wisdom, but despises a perverse heart.

- **Matthew 25:21**
"His lord said unto him, Well done, *thou* good and faithful servant: thou hast been faithful over a few things, I will make thee ruler over many things: enter thou into the joy of thy lord."

May every genuine Christian hear this "well done" from the lips of their Saviour when they are in Heaven with Him.

- **Luke 16:8**
"And the lord commended the unjust steward, because he had done wisely: for the children of this world are in their generation wiser than the children of light."

Though unjust, the Lord commended this man for the wise thinking he had done in this instance.

- **Acts 20:32**

"And now, <u>brethren, I commend you to God, and to the word of his grace, which is able to build you up, and to give you an inheritance</u> among all them which are sanctified."

True Christians should be commended to God their Father and to the Words of His grace found in the Bible.

- **2 Corinthians 3:1**

"<u>Do we begin again to commend ourselves</u>? or <u>need we</u>, as some *others*, epistles of commendation to you, or *<u>letters</u> of <u>commendation from you</u>*?"

Paul did not want to commend himself or need letters of commendation from others.

Verses On Approved

- **Acts 2:22**

"Ye men of Israel, hear these words; <u>Jesus of Nazareth, a man approved of God among you by miracles and wonders and signs</u>, which God did by him in the midst of you, as ye yourselves also know:"

The Lord Jesus Christ was approved by God the Father by miracles, wonders, and signs.

- **Romans 16:10**

"Salute <u>Apelles approved in Christ</u>. Salute them which are of Aristobulus' *household*."

Apelles was approved by being *"in"* the Lord Jesus Christ.

- **1 Corinthians 11:19**

"For there must be also heresies among you, <u>that they which are approved may be made manifest among you</u>."

In the midst of heresies in Paul's day, and in our day, those true Christians who are following the Bible are approved by God and made manifest to those observing them

- **2 Timothy 2:15**

"<u>Study to shew thyself approved unto God</u>, a workman that needeth not to be ashamed, rightly dividing the word of truth."

Every true Christian should do diligent study of the Words of God and rightly dividing these Words, never being ashamed of them.

2 Corinthians Chapter Eleven

2 Corinthians 11:1

"Would to God ye could bear with me a little in *my* folly: and indeed bear with me."

Paul is going to expose Satanic ministers in his day. Because of this, people of his day called him a fool. In this message, I am going to try to expose Satanic ministers in our days. I'll give twelve different marks of Satan's ministers.

2 Corinthians 11:2

"For I am jealous over you with godly jealousy: for I have espoused you to one husband, that I may present *you as* a chaste virgin to Christ."

Paul was jealous over those he had led to the Lord Jesus Christ. He wanted them to be as chaste and pure virgins to the Saviour.

As far as God considers people, there are only two groups of people in the world: (1) Those who are in Satan's family by not truly believing in and receiving the Lord Jesus Christ as their Saviour; and (2)Those who are in God's family by truly believing in and receiving the Lord Jesus Christ as their Saviour.

Paul wants those he has led to Christ to be as pure as chaste virgins, walking after the Holy Spirit and not after their flesh.

Verses On Godly Women

- Titus 2:5

"*To be* discreet, chaste, keepers at home, good, obedient to their own husbands, that the word of God be not blasphemed."

These Christian women should have many godly attributes.

- 1 Peter 3:2

"While they behold your chaste conversation *coupled* with fear."

People should be able to see these Christian women's chaste manner of life.

2 Corinthians 11:3

"But I fear, lest by any means, as the serpent beguiled Eve through his subtilty, so your minds should be corrupted from the simplicity that is in Christ."

The first three marks of Satan and his ministers are (1) beguiling; (2) subtilty; and (3) corrupting. Satan as the serpent beguiled Eve through his subtilty and cleverness.

1. Satan And His Followers Beguile

One of the methods that Satan uses is beguilement. This is a clever trick that works on many people.

Verses On Beguile

- **Genesis 3:13**

"And the LORD God said unto the woman, What is this that thou hast done? And the woman said, The serpent beguiled me, and I did eat."

"*Beguiled me*" means "*fooled me.*" The very first sin, in the Garden of Eden, was because of the beguiling of Satan. Every one of Satan's ministers, who are unsaved ministers, whether they are Protestants, Catholics, or of any false religion beguile those to whom they minister. They pull the wool over their eyes and they do not understand or believe the Scriptures. I was led to Christ as my Saviour by my high school janitor rather than by any of the apostate preachers in my Ohio home town. One of these Methodist preachers tried to beguile me and make me doubt my conversion to the Lord Jesus Christ.

- **Genesis 29:25**

"And it came to pass, that in the morning, behold, it was Leah: and he said to Laban, What is this thou hast done unto me? did not I serve with thee for Rachel? wherefore then hast thou beguiled me?"

Laban beguiled Jacob and gave him Leah as his wife instead of Rachel as he had promised.

- **Joshua 9:22**

"And Joshua called for them, and he spake unto them, saying, Wherefore have ye beguiled us, saying, We are very far from you; when ye dwell among us?"

Joshua was to kill and enslave those people that dwelled close by them. These people beguiled Joshua by saying they lived far away from them.

- **Colossians 2:4**
  "And this I say, <u>lest any man should beguile you with enticing words</u>."

That is how Satan and his followers keep many people following them. They use enticing, nice, beautiful, clever, beguiling but lying words.

2. Satan And His Followers Are Subtle

This technique has the effect of being very quiet or secretive in their operations.

- **Genesis 3:1**
  "<u>Now the serpent was more subtil than any beast of the field</u> which the LORD God had made. And he said unto the woman, Yea, hath God said, Ye shall not eat of every tree of the garden?"

Yes, God did say that, but he also said, "***But of the fruit of the tree which is in the midst of the garden, God hath said, Ye shall not eat of it***, [*neither shall ye touch it,*] ***lest ye die***" (Genesis 3:2). God did say this about the tree in the center of the garden, but he did not say the words, [*"neither shall ye touch it."*] Satan's ministers misquote and leave out many of the Bible's Words by using these new modern Bible versions. This is subtlety and doctrinal error.

- **Genesis 27:35**
  "And he said, <u>Thy brother came with subtilty</u>, and hath taken away thy blessing."

This is subtilty because Esau did not deserve that blessing.

- **Matthew 26:4**
  "And consulted <u>that they might take Jesus by subtilty, and kill *him*</u>."

The chief priests, scribes and elders wanted to take the Lord Jesus Christ by subtlety and trickery that they might kill Him.

3. Satan And His Followers Corrupt The Minds

The mind can be corrupted. That is why it is so dangerous for our true Christian children to go to a secular school of any kind-- whether grade school, elementary school, high school, college or university or theological seminary. It is very dangerous, because in these schools, Satan and his followers are there to corrupt the minds of those who attend these schools.

It is sad, but often true, that so-called "Christian" schools are quite often not very different from the "secular" schools. That is why it is a better plan to use home-schooling for young people. Sad to say, in many areas, home schooling is being very difficult to use for our children. The mind is Satan's target of attack, to change, and to put doubts in the minds of our children.

I remember one of our families used to be faithful listeners to our radio programs. Then they moved to different state. They had a son whom they sent to college. All of a sudden, their son began to hate the Lord Jesus Christ and God the Father. Soon, he left our church completely. Often, when someone selects the wrong schools, their lives are corrupted.

2 Corinthians 11:4

"For if he that cometh preacheth another Jesus, whom we have not preached, or *if* ye receive another spirit, which ye have not received, or another Gospel, which ye have not accepted, ye might well bear with *him*."

Here are three more marks of Satan's ministers and preachers. (4) They preach another Jesus. (5) they preach another spirit. (6) They preach other Gospel.

4. Satan And His Followers Preach Another Jesus

All the Satanic un-genuine Christian apostate preachers, whether they are Protestant, Roman Catholic, other denominations or all the other false religions of the world preach "*another Jesus.*" Here are some the teachings about the Lord Jesus Christ which are denied by these Satanic followers:

1. They deny the Deity of the Lord Jesus Christ.
2. They deny the Virgin Birth of the Lord Jesus Christ.
3. They deny the bodily resurrection of the Lord Jesus Christ.
4. They deny that the Lord Jesus Christ is the Creator of all things in the universe.
5. They deny that salvation is only possible if the person believes on and receives the Lord Jesus Christ as their Saviour.
6. They deny the Lord Jesus Christ's returning to earth in two phases (1) His rapture of true Christians to Heaven and (2) His return to earth to set up His 1,000-year reign of peace upon earth.

5. Satan And His Followers Preach Another Spirit

1. They do not believe and teach that God the Holy Spirit is a member of the Trinity Who, with God the Father and God the Son, created all things.
2. They do not believe that God the Holy Spirit indwells every genuine Christian the moment they truly accept the Lord Jesus Christ as their Saviour.
3. They do not believe that they themselves and all other non-genuine Christians do not have God the Holy Spirit indwellng them, but have the evil spirit of Satan the Devil indwelling them.

Verses On Non-Christians Status

- **John 8:44**

"Ye are of *your* father the devil, and the lusts of your father ye will do. He was a murderer from the beginning, and abode not in the truth, because there is no truth in him. When he speaketh a lie, he speaketh of his own: for he is a liar, and the father of it."

All these Satanic followers and ministers have the Devil as their father and do his lusts.

- **Ephesians 2:2**

"Wherein in time past ye walked according to the course of this world, according to the prince of the power of the air, the spirit that now worketh in the children of disobedience:"

These non-Christians walk after the spirit of Satan, the Devil.

6. Satan And His Followers Preach And Follow Another Gospel

1. Satan and his followers preach another unbiblical Gospel.
2. Satan and his followers preach men are saved by their good works rather than trusting the work of the Lord Jesus Christ on Calvary's cross.
3. Satan and his followers preach and follow another Gospel that everyone from the beginning of time has eternal life and will not be sent to Hell's everlasting fire.
4. Satan and his followers do not preach the Biblical Gospel that all people are sinners and bound for Hell unless they truly believe on and receive the Lord Jesus Christ as their Saviour who died for their sins.

- 1 John 5:12

"He that hath the Son hath life; *and* he that hath not the Son of God hath not life."

That is the true and Biblical Gospel.

2 Corinthians 11:5

"For I suppose I was not a whit behind the very chiefest apostles."

Paul talks about his apostleship. He had equal status to all the rest of the apostles. He took the place of Judas Iscariot the traitor.

- 1 Corinthians 15:9

"For I am the least of the apostles, that am not meet to be called an apostle, because I persecuted the church of God."

The Lord Jesus Christ picked Paul as an apostle. Peter and the others picked Matthias.

- 1 Corinthians 15:10

"But by the grace of God I am what I am: and his grace which *was bestowed* upon me was not in vain; but I laboured more abundantly than they all: yet not I, but the grace of God which was with me."

Paul was saved by the Lord Jesus Christ and made an apostle.

2 Corinthians 11:6

"But though I *be* rude in speech, yet not in knowledge; but we have been throughly made manifest among you in all things."

It is possible that Paul's being *"rude in speech"* might be his *"thorn in the flesh."* We are not sure what it was. But Paul was not rude or defective in knowledge. He knew the Word of God thoroughly. He was taught by Gamaliel.

Verses On Gamaliel

- Acts 5:34

"Then stood there up one in the council, a Pharisee, named Gamaliel, a doctor of the law, had in reputation among all the people, and commanded to put the apostles forth a little space;"

Gamaliel was skilled in the Law of Moses.

- **Acts 22:3**
"I am verily a man *which am* a Jew, born in Tarsus, a *city* in Cilicia, yet brought up in this city at the feet of Gamaliel, *and* taught according to the perfect manner of the law of the fathers, and was zealous toward God, as ye all are this day."
Paul knew well the Old Testament Law of Moses. He was not rude in knowledge by any means.

2 Corinthians 11:7

"Have I committed an offence in abasing myself that ye might be exalted, because I have preached to you the Gospel of God freely?"

Paul preached to them without receiving any offerings from them. He did not want to make trouble for them is how he might have phrased it. Evangelists, ministers, and missionaries should receive, from the congregations, but he had not received anything from this church at this time. He gave the Gospel of God freely.

Verses On Giving To God's Servants

- **Luke 10:7**
"And in the same house remain, eating and drinking such things as they give: for the labourer is worthy of his hire. Go not from house to house.

Those who minister for the Lord are worthy to receive gifts for their labor.

- **1 Corinthians 9:11-13**
"If we have sown unto you spiritual things, *is it* a great thing if we shall reap your carnal things? If others be partakers of *this* power over you, *are* not we rather? Nevertheless we have not used this power; but suffer all things, lest we should hinder the Gospel of Christ. Do ye not know that they which minister about holy things live *of the things* of the temple? and they which wait at the altar are partakers with the altar?

Spiritual labor for the Lord deserves funds from those who receive that labor. "Even so hath the Lord ordained that they which preach the Gospel should live of the Gospel." These verses are very clear that Christian ministries should support their Pastors or leaders.

2 Corinthians 11:8

"I robbed other churches, taking wages *of them*, to do you service."

Paul took money from other churches in order to help and serve the church at Corinth. Paul was a tent-maker to earn his money. He worked very hard day and night so he could help some of these churches.

2 Corinthians 11:9

"And when I was present with you, and wanted, I was chargeable to no man: for that which was lacking to me the brethren which came from Macedonia supplied: and in all *things* I have kept myself from being burdensome unto you, and *so* will I keep *myself.*"

When Paul had a need, the brethren from Macedonia supplied the need so that the genuine Christians at Corinth did not have to help him.

2 Corinthians 11:10

"As the truth of Christ is in me, no man shall stop me of this boasting in the regions of Achaia."

Paul was truthful in his boasting for the help given him from the regions of Achaia. He was not violating anything in receiving gifts from those he served.

2 Corinthians 11:11

"Wherefore? because I love you not? God knoweth."

It is not because Paul did not love the Corinthian Christian believers. Paul did not want to receive wages from the true Christians at Corinth. God knew that Paul still loved the true Christians at Corinth. When he wrote First Corinthians, Paul had to correct them because of this member's incest with his father's wife and because the church thought there was nothing wrong with this incestuous sin. Paul wrote a very firm letter to them and corrected them strongly in First Corinthians. There were many other things that he said in that letter, but he still loved them. In Second Corinthians, it was a little bit different. They had corrected themselves in the meantime. The man repented and he was brought back into the church.

2 Corinthians 11:12

"But what I do, that I will do, that I may cut off occasion from them which desire occasion; that wherein they glory, they may be found even as we."

Paul wanted to cut off those that have occasion. He will continue to talk about the marks of these Satanic false teachers.

2 Corinthians 11:13

"For such *are* false apostles, deceitful workers, transforming themselves into the apostles of Christ."

The first six marks of these Satanic teachers were discussed in previous verses. They were (1)beguiling, (2) subtle, (3) corrupt, (4) they had another Jesus, (5) they spoke about another spirit, and (6) preached another Gospel.

7. Satan And His Followers Are False Apostles

These false apostles claim they are apostles of the Lord Jesus Christ but they are not. They are apostles of Satan. They are not Christ's apostles. They are false and phony. This is true whether they are Protestants, Catholics, Jews, Muslims, or any other of the false religions of the world.

8. Satan And His Followers Are Deceitful Workers

Notice the eighth of the marks of Satan's ministers. They are deceitful workers. They say one thing and they do something entirely different.

- **Jeremiah 17:9**
"The heart *is* deceitful above all *things*, and desperately wicked: who can know it?"

These Satanic ministers and pastors are deceitful. You might say, how could this wonderful man who looks so nice, dresses so nice and speaks so well, be deceitful? His smile that you see is part of his deceit. He is a wolf in sheep's clothing. If you were able to look at his heart, you could see that he is a ravening wolf.

- **Jeremiah 48:10**
"Cursed *be* he that doeth the work of the LORD deceitfully, and cursed *be* he that keepeth back his sword from blood."

God's work must not be done deceitfully.

- **Mark 7:21-23**
"For from within, out of the heart of men, proceed evil thoughts, adulteries, fornications, murders, Thefts, covetousness, wickedness, <u>deceit</u>, lasciviousness, an evil eye, blasphemy, pride, foolishness: All these evil things come from within, and defile the man."

Deceit comes from the old nature, the flesh. These Satanic ministers have this mark of deceitfulness, that comes from their wicked, devilish heart. All those who are not genuine Christians are Satan's shepherds and in the devil's family.

- **Romans 1:29**
"Being filled with all unrighteousness, fornication, wickedness, covetousness, maliciousness; full of envy, murder, debate, <u>deceit,</u> malignity; whisperers,"

Deceit is one of the twenty-two things listed in Romans 1:29-31, which is possessed by the flesh of every human being, including Satan's ministers.

2 Corinthians 11:14

"And no marvel; for Satan himself is transformed into an angel of light."

9. Satan And His Followers Pretend To Be Angels Of Light

This is the ninth characteristic of Satan's ministers. Though they are not *"light,"* but darkness, they have a way of pretending to be transformed into fake, phony and pretend angels of light in order to fool people.

10. Satan And His Followers Are Roaring Devouring Lions

- **1 Peter 5:8**
"Be sober, be vigilant; because <u>your adversary the devil, as a roaring lion, walketh about, seeking whom he may devour</u>:"

If Satan and his followers are, in reality, "roaring lions," genuine Christians should stay far away from them. If Satan and his followers come as fake angels of light, true Christians should also stay far away from them.

Satan Is Darkness And Evil
- **Ephesians 6:12**

"For we wrestle not against flesh and blood, but against principalities, against powers, <u>against the rulers of the darkness of this world</u>, against spiritual wickedness in high places."

Satan is the ruler of the darkness of this world. It is Satanic darkness. Satan's ministers parade themselves as light, but, in fact, they are dark, black, sinful, wicked, and corrupt.

- **Colossians 1:13**

"<u>Who hath delivered us from the power of darkness</u>, and hath translated *us* into the kingdom of his dear Son:"

This verse mentions that the Lord Jesus Christ has given genuine Christians deliverance from the power of Satan's darkness and translated them into the kingdom of his dear Son.

2 Corinthians 11:15

"Therefore *it is* no great thing if his ministers also be transformed as the ministers of righteousness; whose end shall be according to their works."

11. Satan And His Followers Are Transformed As Ministers Of Righteousness

Satan and his followers are as unrighteous and sinful in God's eyes as the lowest and foulest criminals. Yet, in order to fool people, they transform themselves into what they are not–ministers of righteousness.

12. Satan And His Followers Are Like Whited Sepulchres With Dead Bones

- **Matthew 23:27**

"Woe unto you, scribes and Pharisees, hypocrites! for ye are like unto whited sepulchres, which indeed appear beautiful outward, but are within full of dead *men's* bones, and of all uncleanness."

The white paint on the outside makes these sepulchres look very good, but inside are the smelly dead bodies. This is a picture of Satan and his ministers who follow him. They look white, but are dead and spiritually foul and smelling.

Sepulchres are for burying dead people. "Whited" means they are painted white. They look wonderful, dazzling white, but in the sepulchres, there is darkness and blackness and death and the Lord Jesus Christ said that these Pharisees and scribes are just like whited sepulchres. Outwardly they appear righteous unto men but within they are full of hypocrisy and iniquity.

They pretend to be ministers of righteousness but they are corrupt. They will have the same destiny as Satan–The Lake of Fire in Hell. If they are serving their master, Satan, they are going to be in exactly the same place where Satan goes. Hell is *"prepared for the devil and his angels."*

- **Matthew 25:41**

"Then shall he say also unto them on the left hand, <u>Depart from me, ye cursed, into everlasting fire, prepared for the devil and his angels</u>:"

For people who reject the Lord Jesus Christ as their Saviour, they are going to that same place.

- **Revelation 20:10**

"And the devil that deceived them was cast into the lake of fire and brimstone, where the beast and the false prophet *are*, and shall be tormented day and night for ever and ever."

2 Corinthians 11:16

"I say again, Let no man think me a fool; if otherwise, yet as a fool receive me, that I may boast myself a little."

People might think Paul is a fool for exposing Satan, but he is going to expose him anyway just like I am going to expose him in my preaching and writing. This is involved in obeying God's command to *"preach the Word..."*

2 Corinthians 11:17

"That which I speak, I speak *it* not after the Lord, but as it were foolishly, in this confidence of boasting."

Genuine Pastors and preachers are supposed to expose the Devil, his followers, and his ministers. Some people may think this is foolish, but it is commanded by God's Words. Because of this, I will continue to continue to do it.

2 Corinthians 11:18

"Seeing that many glory after the flesh, I will glory also."

Paul wanted to give his testimony as to how he lived before and how he was saved by the Lord Jesus Christ. Paul gloried in the way God saved him, helped him and guided him.

- **Acts 9:1-6**

"And <u>Saul, yet breathing out threatenings and slaughter against the disciples of the Lord, went unto the high priest, And desired of him letters to Damascus to the synagogues, that if he found any of this way, whether they were men or women, he might bring them bound unto Jerusalem</u>. And as he journeyed, he came near Damascus: and <u>suddenly there shined round about him a light from heaven</u>: This was noon day, high noon, a light from heaven. <u>And he fell to the earth, and heard a voice saying unto him, Saul, Saul, why persecutest thou me? And he said, Who art thou, Lord? And the Lord said, I am Jesus whom thou persecutest: *it is* hard for thee to kick against the pricks. And he trembling and astonished said, Lord, what wilt thou have me to do? And the Lord *said* unto him, Arise, and go into the city, and it shall be told thee what thou must do.</u>"

Paul obeyed what the Lord Jesus Christ told him to do. He trusted the Lord Jesus Christ as His Saviour. He then obeyed the Lord and went into the city.

- **Philippians 3:4-6**

"<u>Though I might also have confidence in the flesh. If any other man thinketh that he hath whereof he might trust in the flesh, I more</u>: Circumcised the eighth day, of the stock of Israel, *of* the tribe of Benjamin, <u>an Hebrew of the Hebrews; as touching the law, a Pharisee; Concerning zeal, persecuting the church</u>; touching the righteousness which is in the law, blameless."

Everybody in this world has flesh. Non-Christians have only the flesh. Genuine Christians have both the flesh and the indwelling Holy Spirit. Though Paul had a good education and could have trusted in his flesh, he did not.

2 Corinthians 11:19

"For ye suffer fools gladly, seeing ye *yourselves* are wise."

Paul says the true Christians at Corinth are wise. They know how to understand and put up with fools.

Verses On Fools

- **Proverbs 14:9**

"Fools make a mock at sin: but among the righteous *there is* favour."

Fools do not even believe there is such a thing as sin. In fact, they make a mockery of sin.

- **Luke 11:40**

"*Ye fools, did not he that made that which is without make that which is within also?*"

God created human beings with both their inside and their outside.

- **Luke 24:25**

"Then he said unto them, O fools, and slow of heart to believe all that the prophets have spoken:"

The resurrected Saviour appeared to a man and his wife on the road to Emmaus. Being omniscient and knowing their thoughts, he asked them why they did not believe all that the Old Testament prophets had spoken about the Lord Jesus Christ's death for the sins of all people and His bodily resurrection.

- **Ephesians 5:15**

"See then that ye walk circumspectly, not as fools, but as wise,"

Circumspectly means looking around in all directions. The only thing that will make us wise is the Scriptures, the Words of God. Genuine Christians should read it, study it, know it, believe it and live by it.

2 Corinthians 11:20

"For ye suffer, if a man bring you into bondage, if a man devour *you*, if a man take *of you*, if a man exalt himself, if a man smite you on the face."

These are different ways that people suffer and are harmed. The first way is if a man brings you into bondage, if he puts you into slavery, you are certainly going to suffer. Paul was a slave. He was imprisoned at times. He knew that being a prisoner would bring you suffering. A second way a man can harm you is to devour you. He can wear you down until it makes you feel incompetent.

Or, the third way, if a man takes of you, if he steals from you. That is a man that is a thief and you are going to suffer. People steal and plunder. Our government does that with its high taxation. That is a suffering.

If a man exalts himself. That is a word meaning *"to be lifted up in pride, exalting himself against you."* That brings suffering to you.

If a man smites you on your face by slapping or with his fist that also causes suffering.

2 Corinthians 11:21

"I speak as concerning reproach, as though we had been weak. Howbeit whereinsoever any is bold, (I speak foolishly,) I am bold also."

Paul was bold even when reproached as being weak in his positions and walk.

Verses On Reproach

- **1 Timothy 4:10**

  "For therefore <u>we both labour and suffer reproach</u>, because we trust in the living God, who is the Saviour of all men, specially of those that believe."

Paul labored and was reproached because he trusted the Saviour of all who truly believe in Him.

- **Hebrews 13:13**

  "<u>Let us go forth</u> therefore unto him without the camp, <u>bearing his reproach</u>."

There are things that genuine Christians must bear; including the reproach of the Lord Jesus Christ. Many people hate Him, and they hate true Christians as well.

2 Corinthians 11:22

"Are they Hebrews? so *am* I. Are they Israelites? so *am* I. Are they the seed of Abraham? so *am* I."

Those who are persecuting Paul in these verses were Hebrews just as Paul was. They were his own countrymen.

Verses On Paul's Background
- Philippians 3:4-6

"Though I might also have confidence in the flesh. If any other man thinketh that he hath whereof he might trust in the flesh, I more: Circumcised the eighth day, of the stock of Israel, of the tribe of Benjamin, an Hebrew of the Hebrews; as touching the law, a Pharisee; Concerning zeal, persecuting the church; touching the righteousness which is in the law, blameless."

Though Paul was thoroughly living as a religious Jew before he became a true Christian, now all has been changed. He serves his Saviour.

2 Corinthians 11:23

"Are they ministers of Christ? (I speak as a fool) I *am* more; in labours more abundant, in stripes above measure, in prisons more frequent, in deaths oft."

Here are the first four of many hardships Paul mentions that he endured.

Paul's Many Punishments And Pain
- 1 Corinthians 4:12

"And labour, working with our own hands: being reviled, we bless; being persecuted, we suffer it:"

Paul worked with his hands as a tent-maker. When he as reviled, he put up with it.

- Acts 16:23

"And when they had laid many stripes upon them, they cast them into prison, charging the jailor to keep them safely:"

These stripes were laid on Paul and Silas with a whip. The whip would cut into their flesh.

- **2 Corinthians 6:5**
"<u>In stripes, in imprisonments, in tumults, in labours, in watchings, in fastings</u>;"

Paul listed more suffering he underwent. Notice, he says "in prison", as well. That was the third time, he mentioned it. His enemies did not like the Lord Jesus so they put him in jail. That was a terrible hardship.

We mentioned this earlier,
- **Acts 16:23**
"And <u>when they had laid many stripes upon them, they cast them into prison</u>, charging the jailor to keep them safely:"

Many more stripes were laid upon Paul and he was cast into prison.
- **Acts 16:24**
"Who, having received such a charge, thrust them into the inner prison, and made their feet fast in the stocks."

Paul and Silas were locked up in the inner prison and their feet put into stocks.
- **1 Corinthians 4:9**
"For I think that God hath set forth us the apostles last, as it were <u>appointed to death</u>: for we are made a spectacle unto the world, and to angels, and to men."

The Jews and Romans wanted to kill Paul and all the apostles, who were genuine Christians.
- **2 Corinthians 1:9**
"But <u>we had the sentence of death in ourselves</u>, that we should not trust in ourselves, but in God which raiseth the dead:"

Paul and others had the sentence of death in them. They had to trust, not in themselves, but in God.

2 Corinthians 11:24

"Of the Jews five times received I forty *stripes* save one."

Forty stripes was the limit at that time. The Jews beat the prisoners only thirty-nine stripes so as not to go over. They beat Paul with thirty-nine stripes five times. That makes a total of 195 beatings with the lash. The lash had stones or metal at the end of the lash. That caused blood to come out of Paul's back. This was a terrible, terrible punishment.

Verses On Many Beatings Of Paul And Others
- **Deuteronomy 25:2**

"And it shall be, <u>if the wicked man be worthy to *be* beaten, that the judge shall cause him to lie down, and to be beaten before his face</u>, according to his fault, by a certain number."

Paul was not a wicked man but the Jews thought he was because he was a true Christian. The Jews hated the Lord Jesus Christ.

- **Deuteronomy 25:3**

"<u>Forty stripes he may give him, *and* not exceed</u>: lest, *if* he should exceed, and beat him above these with many stripes, then thy brother should seem vile unto thee."

No more than forty stripes were to be given. The judge was looking at them, counting, one, two, three up to thirty-nine.

- **Mark 13:9**

"But take heed to yourselves: for they shall deliver you up to councils; and in the synagogues <u>ye shall be beaten: and ye shall be brought before rulers and kings for my sake, for a testimony against them</u>."

The Lord Jesus Christ predicted that the apostles would be beaten.

- **Acts 5:40**

"And to him they agreed: and <u>when they had called the apostles, and beaten *them*, they commanded that they should not speak in the name of Jesus, and let them go</u>."

The rulers beat the apostles and ordered them not to speak any more in the Name of the Lord Jesus Christ. The apostles disobeyed that order. They obeyed God rather than man.

- **Acts 16:37**

"But Paul said unto them, <u>They have beaten us openly uncondemned, being Romans</u>, and have cast *us* into prison; and now do they thrust us out privily? nay verily; but <u>let them come themselves and fetch us out</u>."

The Romans disobeyed Roman law in beating them and putting them in prison uncondemned. Paul objected and made them do things properly.

2 Corinthians 11:25

"Thrice was I beaten with rods, once was I stoned, thrice I suffered shipwreck, a night and a day I have been in the deep;"

Paul lists more of his hardships and persecutions:
    1. He was beaten with rods.

2. He was stoned three times.

3. He had shipwreck for a night and a day in the ocean.

Verses Paul's Further Persecutions

- **Acts 14:19**

"And there came thither *certain* Jews from Antioch and Iconium, who persuaded the people, and, having stoned Paul, drew *him* out of the city, supposing he had been dead."

Further verses show that Paul was dead, went to Heaven, and returned to serve the Lord further. The Lord took him Home to Heaven to show him some of its glories.

- **Acts 27:41**

"And falling into a place where two seas met, they ran the ship aground; and the forepart stuck fast, and remained unmoveable, but the hinder part was broken with the violence of the waves."

Paul had another shipwreck on his way to be tried at Rome as a prisoner. One of the soldiers' counsel was to kill the prisoners, lest any should swim out and escape. Paul said, do not do it. We are not going to escape. So they did not kill them in that ship wreck.

- **Acts 27:43**

"But the centurion, willing to save Paul, kept them from *their* purpose; and commanded that they which could swim should cast *themselves* first *into the sea*, and get to land:"

The centurion wanted to save Paul. He commanded those who could swim should jump into the water and swim to shore.

- **Acts 27:44**

"And the rest, some on boards, and some on *broken pieces* of the ship. And so it came to pass, that they escaped all safe to land."

So they arrived to land safely. Dr. DeHaan, in one of his Detroit Bible classes that I attended, mentioned that this is the only place in the Bible that "Boards" are mentioned. Of course he was meaning deacon and elder (which he found brought many problems in local churches.)

2 Corinthians 11:26

"*In* journeyings often, *in* perils of waters, *in* perils of robbers, *in* perils by *mine own* countrymen, *in* perils by the heathen, *in* perils in the city, *in* perils in the wilderness, *in* perils in the sea, *in* perils among false brethren;"

A List Of Paul's Nine Other Difficulties
1. Many journeyings
2. Perils of waters
3. Perils of robbers
4. Perils of his own countrymen
5. Perils by the heathen
6. Perils in the city
7. Perils in the wilderness
8. Perils in th sea, and
9. Perils among false brethren.

These nine other difficulties came unto Paul as he faithfully ministered for the Lord Jesus Christ. He was faithful to his Saviour despite this very heavy cost.

2 Corinthians 11:27

"In weariness and painfulness, in watchings often, in hunger and thirst, in fastings often, in cold and nakedness."

A List Of Paul's Eight More Difficulties
1. In weariness
2. In painfulness
3. In watchings often
4. In hunger
5. In thirst
6. In fastings often
7. In cold
8. In nakedness

These eight more difficulties, came upon him while was being faithful in his service to the Lord Jesus Christ. I am certain that many of those many difficulties that Paul experienced would have many (if not all) true Christians alive today to throw up their hands and quit serving the Lord after just a few of these problems descended upon them.

2 Corinthians 11:28

"Beside those things that are without, that which cometh upon me daily, the care of all the churches."

In addition to all the other hardships, Paul had *"the care of all the churches."* He founded many local churches such as Ephesus, Colosse, Philippi, Thessalonica, and all the other local churches that he had under his care. He prayed for them, he talked with them, he visited them, and did many other things to help them and care for them. Churches are not easy to care for. I have been the Pastor of three different churches. I know many things about them, both good and bad.

2 Corinthians 11:29

"Who is weak, and I am not weak? who is offended, and I burn not?"

Paul was one of the apostles. As such, he had to undergo many adversities. He admitted that at times he was weak in some areas because he had many things to undertake in his ministry.

Verses On Weak

- **Psalms 6:2**

"Have mercy upon me, O LORD; for I *am* weak: O LORD, heal me; for my bones are vexed."

David knew that in his flesh, he was weak.

- **Matthew 26:41**

"Watch and pray, that ye enter not into temptation: the spirit indeed *is* willing, but the flesh *is* weak."

All the flesh of human beings is weak. There is nothing about the flesh that is spiritually strong.

- **Romans 15:1**

"We then that are strong ought to bear the infirmities of the weak, and not to please ourselves."

Strong genuine Christians should help to bear the infirmities of the weaker Christians. We do not all agree with each other, as Christians, but we can help to bear the burdens and infirmities of those that are weak.

- **1 Corinthians 1:27**

"But God hath chosen the foolish things of the world to confound the wise; and God hath chosen the weak things of the world to confound the things which are mighty;"

Those who are genuine Christians should help one another as needed.

- **1 Corinthians 4:10**
"We *are* fools for Christ's sake, but ye *are* wise in Christ; <u>we *are* weak, but ye *are* strong</u>; ye *are* honourable, but we *are* despised."

Paul mentions this weakness that he had, maybe because of the thorn in the flesh that Christ gave him.

- **1 Corinthians 9:22**
"To the weak became I as weak, that I might gain the weak: I am made all things to all *men*, that I might by all means save some."

Paul made himself understand the weak so he could lead some to trust the Saviour.

- **2 Corinthians 10:10**
"For *his* letters, say they, *are* weighty and powerful; but <u>*his* bodily presence *is* weak</u>, and *his* speech contemptible."

The Corinthians said his letters are strong but his bodily presence. They had seen him in weakness. Some used that against him. They held him in contempt.

- **2 Corinthians 12:10**
"Therefore I take pleasure in infirmities, in reproaches, in necessities, in persecutions, in distresses for Christ's sake: for <u>when I am weak, then am I strong.</u>"

When Paul was weak, the Lord Jesus Christ gave him what he needed and made him strong.

Some **Verses On Offence And Offending**

- **Psalms 119:165**
"Great peace have they which love thy law: and <u>nothing shall offend them</u>."

Genuine Christians should not be worried or concerned about offenses. Nothing should offend them.

- **Proverbs 18:19**
"<u>A brother offended *is harder to be won* than a strong city</u>: and *their* contentions *are* like the bars of a castle."

Brothers and sisters in Christ who are offended are very hard to win back.

- **Matthew 26:31**
"<u>Then saith Jesus unto them, All ye shall be offended because of me this night</u>: for it is written, I will smite the shepherd, and the sheep of the flock shall be scattered abroad."

The Apostles were offended that night because of the dangers that were present near the Lord Jesus Christ's crucifixion.

- **John 16:1**
"These things have I spoken unto you, that ye should not be offended."

The Lord Jesus Christ did not want his apostles to be offended at all.

2 Corinthians 11:30

"If I must needs glory, I will glory of the things which concern mine infirmities."

Verses On Infirmities

- **Romans 8:26**
"Likewise the Spirit also helpeth our infirmities: for we know not what we should pray for as we ought: but the Spirit itself maketh intercession for us with groanings which cannot be uttered."

Every genuine Christian has the Holy Spirit indwelling them. The Holy Spirit helps their infirmities.

- **2 Corinthians 12:5**
"Of such an one will I glory: yet of myself I will not glory, but in mine infirmities."

Paul wanted to glory in his infirmities and weaknesses, not of himself.

- **2 Corinthians 12:9**
"And he said unto me, My grace is sufficient for thee: for my strength is made perfect in weakness. Most gladly therefore will I rather glory in my infirmities, that the power of Christ may rest upon me."

Paul wanted to glory in his infirmities. He knew that God's grace was sufficient for him.

- **2 Corinthians 12:10**
"Therefore I take pleasure in infirmities, in reproaches, in necessities, in persecutions, in distresses for Christ's sake: for when I am weak, then am I strong."

Though Paul was weak in the flesh, he was strong in the Lord Jesus Christ.

- **Hebrews 4:15**
"For we have not an high priest which cannot be touched with the feeling of our infirmities; but was in all points tempted like as *we are, yet* without sin."

The Lord Jesus Christ understands all the true Christians' infirmities.

2 Corinthians 11:31

"**The God and Father of our Lord Jesus Christ, which is blessed for evermore, knoweth that I lie not.**"

Paul did not lie about any of these tests, any of these hardships. Every single thing he said to the Corinthian Church was true. He called God the Father of our Lord Jesus Christ, Who is Blessed for evermore.

2 Corinthians 11:32

"**In Damascus the governor under Aretas the king kept the city of the Damascenes with a garrison, desirous to apprehend me:**"

That is another hardship that Paul faced. When he was in the large city of Damascus. The commander of the governing garrison, wanted to apprehend him and put him in jail.

2 Corinthians 11:33

"**And through a window in a basket was I let down by the wall, and escaped his hands.**"

To escape capture possible certain death Paul was let down over the city wall in a basket. God delivered him once again. Every true Christian should be thankful to the Lord Who has preserved us thus far from many hardships that Paul had to undergo.

2 Corinthians Chapter Twelve

2 Corinthians 12:1

"It is not expedient for me doubtless to glory. I will come to visions and revelations of the Lord."

Paul did not want to glory or boast. He wanted to come to the visions and revelations of the Lord. Notice this revelation by the Prophet Joel.
- Acts 2:16-20

"But this is that which was spoken by the prophet Joel; And it shall come to pass in the last days, saith God, I will pour out of my Spirit upon all flesh: and your sons and your daughters shall prophesy, and <u>your young men shall see visions</u>, and your old men shall dream dreams: And on my servants and on my handmaidens I will pour out in those days of my Spirit; and they shall prophesy: And I will shew wonders in heaven above, and signs in the earth beneath; blood, and fire, and vapour of smoke: <u>The sun shall be turned into darkness, and the moon into blood</u>, before that great and notable day of the Lord come:"

This prophesy will be fulfilled in the Tribulation time. The sun will be turned into darkness. The color of the moon will be red like blood.

2 Corinthians 12:2

"I knew a man in Christ above fourteen years ago, (whether in the body, I cannot tell; or whether out of the body, I cannot tell: God knoweth;) such an one caught up to the third heaven."

Paul knew the man he is referring to. He was not sure of the circumstances. He does not name this man, but later on, it will become clear that the man was the apostle Paul himself. This is a revelation of Paul's vision when he was taken to Heaven. It was about fourteen years ago. Later on Paul talks about this person again. To see what was happening fourteen years ago, we can look

in the book of Acts in Acts 14 which took place in the city of Lystra.
- **Acts 14:8-12**
"And there sat a certain man at Lystra, impotent in his feet, being a cripple from his mother's womb, who never had walked: The same heard Paul speak: who stedfastly beholding him, and perceiving that he had faith to be healed, Said with a loud voice, Stand upright on thy feet. And he leaped and walked. And when the people saw what Paul had done, they lifted up their voices, saying in the speech of Lycaonia, The gods are come down to us in the likeness of men. And they called Barnabas, Jupiter; and Paul, Mercurius, because he was the chief speaker."

The background of Acts concerned the healing of this crippled man who was lame from his birth.
- **Acts 14:18-21**
"And with these sayings scarce restrained they the people, that they had not done sacrifice unto them. And <u>there came thither certain Jews from Antioch and Iconium, who persuaded the people, and, having stoned Paul, drew *him* out of the city, supposing he had been dead. Howbeit, as the disciples stood round about him, he rose up, and came into the city:</u> and the next day he departed with Barnabas to Derbe. And when they had preached the Gospel to that city, and had taught many, they returned again to Lystra, and *to* Iconium, and Antioch,"

After his stoning, the people supposed Paul was dead. I believe he was really dead, but the Lord revived him. In Paul's epistles he mentioned that he had been to Heaven and seen of its glories. This happened "*about fourteen years ago*" which was the same time as his stoning at Lystra and dragged out of the city.

Verses On Heaven

In verse 2 above, it says that Paul was "*caught up to the third heaven.*" There are three heavens in Scripture. The first heaven is the atmospheric heaven. The second heaven is the starry heaven. The third Heaven is the abode of God and His angels. The Lord Jesus Christ spoke of the Heaven, that Paul was caught up to see.
- **John 14:2**
"<u>In my Father's house are many mansions</u>: if *it were* not *so,* I would have told you. <u>I go to prepare a place for you.</u>"

Jesus went back to Heaven to prepare a place for those who are genuine Christians who have accepted and received Him.

- **John 14:3**
  "And if I go and prepare a place for you, <u>I will come again, and receive you unto myself; that where I am, *there* ye may be also</u>."

The Lord Jesus speaks of this third Heaven in His High Priestly prayer to God the Father.

- **John 17:24**
  "<u>Father, I will that they also, whom thou hast given me, be with me where I am; that they may behold my glory</u>, which thou hast given me: for thou lovedst me before the foundation of the world."

Every true Christian will be where the Lord Jesus Christ is and will behold His glory.

- **Revelation 21:3-4**
  "And I heard a great voice out of heaven saying, <u>Behold, the tabernacle of God *is* with men, and he will dwell with them, and they shall be his people, and God himself shall be with them, *and be* their God. And God shall wipe away all tears from their eyes; and there shall be no more death, neither sorrow, nor crying, neither shall there be any more pain: for the former things are passed away</u>."

This is what the third Heaven is going to be like. Paul saw that when he was taken there. He had a vision of it, a glimpse of Heaven.

- **Revelation 22:3-5**
  "And <u>there shall be no more curse</u>: but the throne of God and of the Lamb shall be in it; and his servants shall serve him: And they shall see his face; and his name *shall be* in their foreheads. And <u>there shall be no night there</u>; and they need no candle, neither light of the sun; for the Lord God giveth them light: <u>and they shall reign for ever and ever</u>."

Heaven is a place, for all eternity future. It is only for genuine Christians who have truly trusted the Lord Jesus Christ as their Saviour. The Bible is clear, however, that all those who have not genuinely trusted and believed on the Lord Jesus Christ will spend eternity future in Hell's Lake of Fire.

2 Corinthians 12:3

"And I knew such a man, (whether in the body, or out of the body, I cannot tell: God knoweth;)"

Paul is speaking of himself and did not know whether he was in his body or out of it. He could not tell if it were a vision or a real experience.

- **2 Corinthians 12:4**

"How that he was caught up into paradise, and heard unspeakable words, which it is not lawful for a man to utter."
One way or the other Paul was caught up into paradise and heard unspeakable Words. He could not repeat what he heard.

- **Luke 16:22-26**

"And it came to pass, that the beggar died, and was carried by the angels into Abraham's bosom: the rich man also died, and was buried; And in hell he lift up his eyes, being in torments, and seeth Abraham afar off, and Lazarus in his bosom. And he cried and said, Father Abraham, have mercy on me, and send Lazarus, that he may dip the tip of his finger in water, and cool my tongue; for I am tormented in this flame. But Abraham said, Son, remember that thou in thy lifetime receivedst thy good things, and likewise Lazarus evil things: but now he is comforted, and thou art tormented. And beside all this, between us and you there is a great gulf fixed: so that they which would pass from hence to you cannot; neither can they pass to us, that *would come* from thence."

This rich man was not trusting the Lord Jesus Christ as his Saviour. He was in Hell.

When the Lord Jesus Christ was dying on the cross of Calvary for the sins of the world, there were two other men dying also, one on his right hand, one on his left hand. They were thieves. At first, they both cursed Him. Then, all of a sudden, one of them changed his mind concerning the Saviour and trusted Him.

- **Luke 23:42-43**

"And he said unto Jesus, Lord, remember me when thou comest into thy kingdom. And Jesus said unto him, Verily I say unto thee, To day shalt thou be with me in paradise."

This thief changed his mind concerning the Lord Jesus Christ and trusted Him.

2 Corinthians 12:4

"**How that he was caught up into paradise, and heard unspeakable words, which it is not lawful for a man to utter.**"

In the Old Testament, "paradise" was the blessed section of Sheol. In the New Testament, paradise is now in Heaven. The Lord Jesus Christ told the thief on the cross that accepted Him as his Saviour: "*thou shalt be with me in paradise.*" The Saviour took him to paradise which was then changed to Heaven.

Verses On The Changed Location Of Paradise
- **Revelation 2:7**

"He that hath an ear, let him hear what the Spirit saith unto the churches; To him that overcometh will I give to eat of the tree of life, which is in the midst of the paradise of God."
Paradise is now in Heaven. Paul went to the Paradise of God. He was caught up to the third Heaven.

2 Corinthians 12:5

"**Of such an one will I glory: yet of myself I will not glory, but in mine infirmities.**"

Paul would not glory in himself except in his infirmities. He will glory in his person that was taken up to the third Heaven and saw all the revelations that he saw. He heard words that were unspeakable. Genuine Christians, with Paul, should also glory in our infirmities as their Saviour aids them and gives them victory in them.

2 Corinthians 12:6

"**For though I would desire to glory, I shall not be a fool; for I will say the truth: but *now* I forbear, lest any man should think of me above that which he seeth me *to be*, or *that* he heareth of me.**"

Paul wanted to say the truth about the revelations he saw in Heaven, but he will forbear for now "*lest any man should think of me above that which he seeth me to be.*" Paul did not want to boast of the things he saw in Heaven.

2 Corinthians 12:7

"And lest I should be exalted above measure through the abundance of the revelations, there was given to me a thorn in the flesh, the messenger of Satan to buffet me, lest I should be exalted above measure."

Lest he should be exalted above measure because of the abundance of the Heavenly revelations, God gave Paul a thorn in the flesh so he would not be exalted above measure. What the thorn in the flesh was, we do not know. People have speculated about it. Some people have thought it was problems with eyes.

- **Galatians 6:11**
"Ye see how large a letter I have written unto you with mine own hand."

It reminds me of Dr. Robert T. Ketcham, the early leader of the General Association of Regular Baptist Churches (GARBC) who had eye trouble. He had to have very large notes to read his sermons. Paul said he wrote with large letters. Maybe his thorn had an effect on his eyes.

- **Galatians 4:15**
"Where is then the blessedness ye spake of, for I bear you record, that, if it had been possible, ye would have plucked out your own eyes, and have given them to me."

Here is another verse indicating he had eye problems.

In Corinth, they said that Paul's speech was contemptible. Maybe his thorn in the flesh had to do with a speech problem. May he could not talk very well. Whatever it was, this thorn in the flesh, was given so Paul would not be exalted above measure. God does not want any of us to lift ourselves up and boast.

2 Corinthians 12:8

"For this thing I besought the Lord thrice, that it might depart from me."

Paul asked the Lord to remove this *"thorn in the flesh"* three different times. Paul did not like that thorn. Nobody likes a thorn in the flesh, whatever it might be.

- **1 John 5:14**
"And this is the confidence that we have in him, that, <u>if we ask any thing according to his will, he heareth us</u>:"
We have the promise of God that if was ask anything according to God's will he will hear us and grant our petition. But if our request is not according to God's will, he hears us but will not grant the request. It was not God's will that Paul's thorn in the flesh should be taken away even though Paul asked that the Lord remove it.

2 Corinthians 12:9

"And he said unto me, My grace is sufficient for thee: for my strength is made perfect in weakness. Most gladly therefore will I rather glory in my infirmities, that the power of Christ may rest upon me."

The Lord Jesus Christ spoke to Paul after his third request and said: "*My grace is sufficient for thee: for my strength is made perfect in weakness.*" Paul accepted God's answer and responded: "*Most gladly therefore will I rather glory in my infirmities, that the power of Christ may rest upon me.*" This is the response that would please the Lord from any true Christian who sincerely makes it under these circumstances. God's grace–giving us something we do not deserve–should be sufficient for every genuine Christian.

If a person is strong, where is God's power to be seen? Where is His might? Others just see the strong person. They do not see the Lord Jesus Christ and His great power.

Verses On Strength

- **Romans 5:6**
"<u>For when we were yet without strength, in due time Christ died for the ungodly</u>."
The Lord Jesus Christ died for the ungodly who were without any strength.

Verses On Weakness

- **1 Corinthians 1:25**
"Because the foolishness of God is wiser than men; and <u>the weakness of God is stronger than men</u>."
God is not weak. But even if it were true, His weakness would be stronger than men's greatest strength.

- **1 Corinthians 2:3**
  "And <u>I was with you in weakness</u>, and in fear, and in much trembling."

When Paul went to the church of Corinth, he was with them in weakness, fear, and trembling as he faced dealing with the incestuous man who had sex with his father's wife. The church was very angry with him. He was with them in weakness. The man finally responded to truth, came back to the Lord, and to the church.

- **Hebrews 11:34**
  "Quenched the violence of fire, escaped the edge of the sword, <u>out of weakness were made strong</u>, waxed valiant in fight, turned to flight the armies of the aliens."

Out of weakness they were made strong. God strengthened them, even in their weakness. God used these people, men of faith, even though they were weak. They were made strong by the Lord.

Verses On Power

- **Acts 1:8**
  "But <u>ye shall receive power, after that the Holy Ghost is come upon you</u>: and ye shall be witnesses unto me both in Jerusalem, and in all Judaea, and in Samaria, and unto the uttermost part of the earth."

Once the Holy Spirit of God would come upon them, the apostles would receive spiritual power.

- **Romans 1:16**
  "For I am not ashamed of <u>the Gospel of Christ: for it is the power of God unto salvation to every one that believeth</u>; to the Jew first, and also to the Greek."

The Gospel is God's power unto salvation to those who truly believe on the Lord Jesus Christ.

The false Gnostic Greek Text and many modern English translations remove "Christ" from this verse. Without the Lord Jesus Christ, there is no power.

- **1 Corinthians 2:5**
  "That <u>your faith should</u> not <u>stand</u> in the wisdom of men, but <u>in the power of God</u>."

Our faith should stand in the power of God, found in the Scriptures, not the voices of men.

- **2 Corinthians 4:7**
"But <u>we have this treasure in earthen vessels</u>, that the excellency of <u>the power may be of God, and not of us</u>."
The treasure is the Holy Spirit indwelling the bodies of true Christians. Their bodies are just earthen vessels--vessels of clay. God made Adam from the dust of the ground and when we die our bodies go back to the dust. *"For dust thou art, and unto dust shalt thou return."*
- **Ephesians 1:19**
"And <u>what *is* the exceeding greatness of his power to us-ward who believe</u>, according to the working of his mighty power."
- **Ephesians 3:7-8**
"Whereof <u>I was made a minister</u>, according to the gift of the grace of God given unto me <u>by the effectual working of his power</u>. Unto me, who am less than the least of all saints, is this grace given, that I should preach among the Gentiles the unsearchable riches of Christ;"
Paul was made a minister of the Lord Jesus Christ only by the working of God's power. It was truly a marvelous working of God's power to save Paul's soul.
- **Ephesians 3:20**
"Now <u>unto him that is able to do</u> exceeding abundantly above all that we ask or think, <u>according to the power that worketh in us</u>,"
The only ones who have God's power working in them are genuine Christians who have the Holy Spirit of God indwelling them. We must then pray to the Lord for making use of this power that is given to us by the Holy Spirit Who indwells every true Christian.
- **Ephesians 6:10**
"Finally, my brethren, <u>be strong in the Lord, and in the power of his might</u>."
True Christians should be *"strong in the Lord, and in the power of his might."*
- **Colossians 1:11**
"<u>Strengthened with all might, according to his glorious power</u>, unto all patience and longsuffering with joyfulness;"
The genuine Christians being indwelt with God the Holy Spirit have God's might and glorious power.

2 Corinthians 12:10

"Therefore I take pleasure in infirmities, in reproaches, in necessities, in persecutions, in distresses for Christ's sake: for when I am weak, then am I strong."

Paul takes pleasure in these five conditions for Christ's sake because when he is weak, Christ makes him strong.

Verses On Infirmities

- **2 Corinthians 11:30**

"If I must needs glory, I will glory of the things which concern mine infirmities."

The Lord Jesus Christ taught Paul this.

- **Hebrews 4:15**

"For we have not an high priest which cannot be touched with the feeling of our infirmities; but was in all points tempted like as *we are,* yet without sin."

The Lord Jesus Christ was perfect God and also perfect Man. As perfect Man, He could feel what we feel, live like we live. He was sinless, he was spotless, but he could feel the infirmities of being here on this wicked earth, touched with the feeling of our infirmities. He was tested in all points, but never failed in anything.

Paul said he took pleasure in his infirmities. What kind of infirmities do you and I have? Genuine Christians ought to take pleasure in these things, since they know the Lord Jesus Christ as their Saviour. His power can overcome these infirmities.

Verses On Reproaches

- **Psalms 44:13**

"Thou makest us a reproach to our neighbours, a scorn and a derision to them that are round about us."

It reminds me of Dr. Jung in Korea. He stands for the King James Bible and is a reproach among those who hate the King James Bible.

- **Psalms 69:7**

"Because for thy sake I have borne reproach; shame hath covered my face."

Shame and reproach that come, as long as it is for Christ's sake and not because of moral failures of the true Christian, is a virtue not a vice.

- **Psalms 102:8**
"<u>Mine enemies reproach me all the day</u>; *and* they that are mad against me are sworn against me."
This happens, for example, from those who cannot stand our position on the King James Bible and other doctrines.

Verses On Necessities
- **2 Corinthians 6:4**
"But in all *things* <u>approving ourselves as the ministers of God</u>, in much patience, in afflictions, <u>in necessities</u>, in distresses,"
As the ministers of God, genuine Christians should approve themselves in so-called necessities. Many Christians have suffered poverty and deprivations because of persecutions.

Verses On Persecutions
- **Mark 10:30**
"But <u>he shall receive an hundredfold now in this time</u>, houses, and brethren, and sisters, and mothers, and children, and lands, <u>with persecutions</u>; and in the world to come eternal life."
Yes, in this life, persecutions will come, if we know the Lord Jesus Christ as our Saviour and are faithful to Him.

- **2 Thessalonians 1:4**
"So that <u>we ourselves glory in you</u> in the churches of God for your patience and faith <u>in all your persecutions</u> and tribulations <u>that ye endure</u>:"
God wants to help genuine Christians so they can endure all their persecutions.

Verses On Distresses
- **Psalms 107:13**
"Then they cried unto the LORD in their trouble, *and* he <u>saved them out of their distresses</u>."
When true Christians cry unto the Lord, he is able to save them out of their distresses.

2 Corinthians 12:11

"I am become a fool in glorying; ye have compelled me: for I ought to have been commended of you: for in nothing am I behind the very chiefest apostles, though I be nothing."

Paul said he was compelled to glory because the genuine Christians at Corinth did not commend him. He was probably referring to his visit to Heaven. The Corinthians did not commend him. They were angry at Paul because he told them about there sin of covering up their member's sin of incest with his father's wife.

- **2 Corinthians 10:18**
  "For not he that commendeth himself is approved, but whom the Lord commendeth."

Paul wanted to look for the Lord's commendation. The Corinthians did not like Paul. They were very much against him.

2 Corinthians 12:12

"Truly the signs of an apostle were wrought among you in all patience, in signs, and wonders, and mighty deeds."

Signs of the apostles. These miracles were apostolic and they ceased when the Bible was completed, as it says in 1 Corinthians 13. When the Bible was completed, they did not have these signs, but the apostles were given these special signs and miracles. The charismatic and Pentecostal movements today are wrong in this. There are Satanic counterfeits of these signs today. All kinds of things are going on today that were meant for apostolic times alone. The Bible was completed in 90 to 100 AD. That is when all those signs from God ceased. They were not from the devil or from the flesh. The flesh and the devil still have these counterfeit signs. Notice Paul says he deals with this in all patience.

Verses On Signs

- **Acts 14:3**
  "Long time therefore abode they speaking boldly in the Lord, which gave testimony unto the word of his grace, and granted signs and wonders to be done by their hands."

These were apostolic times. Signs and wonders did occur in the days of the book of Acts.

- **Romans 15:18-19**

"For I will not dare to speak of any of those things which Christ hath not wrought by me, to make the Gentiles obedient, by word and deed, Through mighty signs and wonders, by the power of the Spirit of God; so that from Jerusalem, and round about unto Illyricum, I have fully preached the Gospel of Christ."

In other words, these special signs and wonders were present in the book of Acts during the apostolic times.

- **Acts 14:3**

"Long time therefore abode they speaking boldly in the Lord, which gave testimony unto the word of his grace, and granted signs and wonders to be done by their hands."

The Lord gave special wonders to be done, in addition to signs.

- **Acts 15:12**

"Then all the multitude kept silence, and gave audience to Barnabas and Paul, declaring what miracles and wonders God had wrought among the Gentiles by them."

Until the Bible was completed God used miracles to authenticate the apostles, Paul and Barnabas. They were able to do special miracles and wonders by the power of God.

- **Romans 15:19**

"Through mighty signs and wonders, by the power of the Spirit of God; so that from Jerusalem, and round about unto Illyricum, I have fully preached the Gospel of Christ."

There were signs and wonders in the apostolic times, but also mighty deeds or miracles, were also wrought by Paul.

- **Acts 15:12**

"Then all the multitude kept silence, and gave audience to Barnabas and Paul, declaring what miracles and wonders God had wrought among the Gentiles by them."

- **Acts 19:11**

"And God wrought special miracles by the hands of Paul:"

God used these apostolic miracles to authenticate their ministry.

- **Galatians 3:5**

"He therefore that ministereth to you the Spirit, and worketh miracles among you, *doeth he it* by the works of the law, or by the hearing of faith?"

Special apostolic miracles by Paul were done by the hearing of faith not by the works of the law.

2 Corinthians 12:13

"For what is it wherein ye were inferior to other churches, except *it be* that I myself was not burdensome to you? forgive me this wrong."

Paul said he wronged the church at Corinth because he did not have them contribute to his ministry. He did not want to be burdensome to them, but he should have taught them to make contributions to him and other workers for the Lord Jesus Christ. This is proper for all true Christian churches then and now.

Verses On Burdensome
- **2 Corinthians 11:9**

"And when I was present with you, and wanted, I was chargeable to no man: for that which was lacking to me the brethren which came from Macedonia supplied: and in all *things* I have kept myself from being burdensome unto you, and so will I keep *myself*."

This is the same thing he did at the church in Corinth. In other words, Paul was not going to take money from them, a poor church. He wanted to raise his own funds rather than be burdensome to them.

- **1 Thessalonians 2:6**

"Nor of men sought we glory, neither of you, nor *yet* of others, when we might have been burdensome, as the apostles of Christ."

Paul could have been burdensome to this local church and could have received funds of them (which is Biblical) but he did not want to be burdensome unto them.

2 Corinthians 12:14

"Behold, the third time I am ready to come to you; and I will not be burdensome to you: for I seek not yours, but you: for the children ought not to lay up for the parents, but the parents for the children."

Notice, he was not going to be burdensome. He was not going to take funds from them. They were a poor church. He did not want to do that, though it was proper. He said, "*I seek not yours, but you:*" This would include their money, property, buildings, or whatever it might be. Paul is not raising funds for ministry. His ministry was *people* not things. But he sought them. He was concerned about their souls. He wanted their obedience to the Lord Jesus Christ. "*The children ought not to lay up for the parents.*" Paul founded the church at Corinth and the genuine Christians they were his children in the faith. He was their parent. The children should not have to provide for the parents, but the parents for the children.

2 Corinthians 12:15

"And I will very gladly spend and be spent for you; though the more abundantly I love you, the less I be loved."

Paul said he wants to give to the church at Corinth. It is sad and unfortunate that the more abundantly he loves them, the less they love him. They are still upset because Paul chastised them for their toleration of a member's sin or incest. They were not going to dismiss this incestuous man, who had sex with his father's wife. They were not going to kick him out of the church. They were fine with that sin, but Paul took them to task, said they were disobedient to the Lord.

Eventually they kicked that man out of the church. He should not be mixed up with the believers of the Lord Jesus Christ.

2 Corinthians 12:16

"But be it so, I did not burden you: nevertheless, being crafty, I caught you with guile."

But be it so ever true. The more he loved them the less he is loved. I did not burden, again, he tells that again. He did not tax them. He did not want gifts from them. He did not make them give and support him, which he could have done. It is proper for churches to support ministers. 1 Corinthians 9 makes it clear. "Nevertheless, being crafty." Now this word 'crafty' means skilled in understanding things about people. He was wise, "I caught you with guile." That word 'guile' is something that has to do with craft and deceit. They were crafty, they were deceitful and they did not want to kick this man out of the church but they did finally. He understood that. He himself was crafty. He caught them in something that was wrong. As far as being with guile,

Verses On Guile

- **1 Peter 2:1**

"Wherefore laying aside all malice, and all guile, and hypocrisies, and envies, and all evil speakings,"
Genuine Christians should lay aside guile. This is deceit and subterfuge.

- 1 Peter 2:22

"Who did no sin, neither was guile found in his mouth:"
The Lord Jesus Christ had no guile in His speech. He never deceived in any way.
- 1 Peter 3:10

"For he that will love life, and see good days, let him refrain his tongue from evil, and his lips that they speak no guile:"
No subterfuge and guile should be spoken if a true Christian loves his life.

2 Corinthians 12:17

"Did I make a gain of you by any of them whom I sent unto you?"

When Paul sent missionaries to them, like Titus, for example, he did not profit from the Church. He did not want to receive any money for himself for sending Titus to help them.

2 Corinthians 12:18

"I desired Titus, and with *him* I sent a brother. Did Titus make a gain of you? walked we not in the same spirit? *walked we* not in the same steps?"

Neither Paul himself nor did Titus, whom he sent to the church, received any money for themselves. Both Paul and Titus agreed on this principle.

Verses On Titus

- 2 Corinthians 7:6

"Nevertheless God, that comforteth those that are cast down, comforted us by the coming of Titus;"
Pastor Titus was a true Christian man who could comfort people. Not all people have the ministry, gift, and technique of comfort. They cannot comfort anyone. Titus had a gift of comforting.
- 2 Corinthians 7:13

"Therefore we were comforted in your comfort: yea, and exceedingly the more joyed we for the joy of Titus, because his spirit was refreshed by you all."
Titus went to the church of Corinth and comforted them. Paul was happy that they were comforted and that Titus was refreshed by them.

- **2 Corinthians 8:16**
"But thanks *be* to God, which put the same earnest care into the heart of Titus for you."

Not only was Paul concerned for the church at Corinth, but Titus had the same earnest care for them as well.

- **2 Corinthians 8:23**
"Whether *any do* enquire of Titus, *he is* my partner and fellowhelper concerning you: or our brethren *be enquired of, they are* the messengers of the churches, *and* the glory of Christ."

Paul is defining who Titus was. He was Paul's trusted partner. Titus was given a commission to be the pastor on the isle of Crete. He preached the same doctrines as Paul.

- **Galatians 2:1**
"Then fourteen years after I went up again to Jerusalem with Barnabas, and took Titus with *me* also."

Paul and Barnabas took Titus with them to Jerusalem.

- **Titus 1:4**
"To Titus, *mine* own son after the common faith: Grace, mercy, *and* peace, from God the Father and the Lord Jesus Christ our Saviour."

Apparently, Paul led Titus to the Lord. He was his son in the faith. Paul had a great admiration for Titus. He sent Titus to Corinth and the Corinthians were comforted by Titus.

2 Corinthians 12:19

"Again, think ye that we excuse ourselves unto you? we speak before God in Christ: but *we do* all things, dearly beloved, for your edifying."

The purpose of Paul is writing to the Corinthian Church was for edifying and building them up in the faith. That is what genuine Christians should be doing to other true Christians. They should edify them through the Bible principles.

Verses On Edifying

- **Romans 14:19**
"Let us therefore follow after the things which make for peace, and things wherewith one may edify another."

You have been charged to try to edify genuine Christians. It is hard to edify if you do not know the Bible. You also need to know things about the Lord Jesus Christ to edify other true Christians.

- **Romans 15:2**
  "Let every one of us please *his* neighbour for *his* good to edification."

Genuine Christians, who are neighbors, need to be built up in the faith and become stronger and stronger in the Lord.

- **1 Corinthians 10:23**
  "All things are lawful for me, but all things are not expedient: all things are lawful for me, but all things edify not."

All things do not build up, so true Christians must be very careful lest they tear people down rather than edifying them.

- **1 Corinthians 14:12**
  "Even so ye, forasmuch as ye are zealous of spiritual *gifts*, seek that ye may excel to the edifying of the church."

Genuine Christians should seek to edify and build up people in their own church.

- **1 Corinthians 14:26**
  "How is it then, brethren, when ye come together, every one of you hath a psalm, hath a doctrine, hath a tongue, hath a revelation, hath an interpretation. Let all things be done unto edifying."

This is when foreign languages or tongues were still a gift in the church before 90 to 100 A.D. This date is historically when this gift disappeared. The Bible was completed then. Even when those gifts were in the church, Paul said, "*let all things be done unto edifying*," and building up in the church.

- **2 Corinthians 13:10**
  "Therefore I write these things being absent, lest being present I should use sharpness, according to the power which the Lord hath given me to edification, and not to destruction."

Paul wanted to use his gift of edification of the genuine Christians.

- **Ephesians 4:12**
  "For the perfecting of the saints, for the work of the ministry, for the edifying of the body of Christ:"

The purpose of all the special gifts mentioned in the Bible is for the edifying and building up of the true Christians in the local church.

- **Ephesians 4:16**

"From whom the whole body fitly joined together and compacted by that which every joint supplieth, according to the effectual working in the measure of every part, <u>maketh increase of the body unto the edifying of itself in love</u>."

The genuine Christians in local churches should help to edify their fellow church members.

- **Ephesians 4:29**

"Let no corrupt communication proceed out of your mouth, but <u>that which is good to the use of edifying</u>, that it may minister grace unto the hearers."

The mouth should be used for edifying.

- **1 Thessalonians 5:11**

"Wherefore comfort yourselves together, and <u>edify one another, even as also ye do</u>."

The true Christians at Thessalonica edified one another.

2 Corinthians 12:20

"For I fear, lest, when I come, I shall not find you such as I would, and *that* I shall be found unto you such as ye would not: lest *there be* debates, envyings, wraths, strifes, backbitings, whisperings, swellings, tumults:"

Paul is afraid that when he comes to visit them, he would not find them as he would want them to be. He hopes there will not be: (1) debates; (2) envyings; (3) wraths; (4) strifes; (5) backbitings; (6) whisperings; (7) swellings; or (8) tumults. These are eight bad things that should not be in any sound genuine Christian Church. We do not know how many of these bad things were in that church, but we would assume that some at least would be there.

Paul is also afraid that if he comes to visit the church as things are they will not be happy for several reasons. Though I do not believe any of these above eight things would be found in Paul, there might be some things that the church would not like.

2 Corinthians 12:21

And lest, when I come again, my God will humble me among you, and *that* I shall bewail many which have sinned already, and have not repented of the uncleanness and fornication and lasciviousness which they have committed.

Paul wants the Lord to humble him when he visits the Church at Corinth. He knows the guilty will bewail many in that church because they have sinned and have not repented of three sins that they have committed: (1) uncleanness; (2) fornication; and (3) lasciviousness. These unrepentant members will make him upset at those in the church that are guilty of all, or many of the eleven sins mentioned in these last two verses.

From these last two verses that Paul wrote concerning the church which was at Corinth is not alone. It seems many of our churches today are becoming as bad as the church at Corinth, or even much morally worse. What will be coming to churches in the decades and centuries to come?

2 Corinthians Chapter Thirteen

2 Corinthians 13:1

"This *is* the third *time* I am coming to you. In the mouth of two or three witnesses shall every word be established."

Paul wrote First Corinthians and Second Corinthians. Now he is coming to them again now. This is the third time he has been with them. He reminds them that in the mouth of two or three witnesses every word might be established.

Verses On Witnesses

- **Numbers 35:30**

"Whoso killeth any person, the murderer shall be put to death by the mouth of witnesses: but one witness shall not testify against any person *to cause him* to die."

One witness cannot cause death to anyone.

- **Deuteronomy 17:6**

"At the mouth of two witnesses, or three witnesses, shall he that is worthy of death be put to death; *but* at the mouth of one witness he shall not be put to death."

The Lord Jesus Christ had witnesses against Him, but at not time did two or three witnesses agree. Yet they crucified Him anyway.

- **Deuteronomy 19:15**

"One witness shall not rise up against a man for any iniquity, or for any sin, in any sin that he sinneth: at the mouth of two witnesses, or at the mouth of three witnesses, shall the matter be established."

No matter what it is, whatever sin it is, you must have two or three witnesses to convict anyone.

- **Matthew 18:16**

"But if he will not hear *thee, then* take with thee one or two more, that in the mouth of two or three witnesses every word may be established."

So this is the rule for establishing truth.

- **Hebrews 10:28**
  "He that despised Moses' law died without mercy under two or three witnesses:"

In the Old Testament, they had to have at least two or three witnesses to prove anything.

2 Corinthians 13:2

"I told you before, and foretell you, as if I were present, the second time; and being absent now I write to them which heretofore have sinned, and to all other, that, if I come again, I will not spare:"

If Paul returns to Corinth again, he will not spare those who have sinned. He is going to be just as non-sparing as he was with this incestuous man who sinned. Paul forewarned them here.

- **Genesis 18:26**
  "And the LORD said, If I find in Sodom fifty righteous within the city, then I will spare all the place for their sakes."

The LORD could not even find ten people in Sodom and Gomorrha that were righteous, so he destroyed the whole city with fire and brimstone.

It is a sad thing, indeed, that our country and our whole world is so amicable to sodomy, homosexuality, and lesbianism. The moral judgment of the Scriptures is that homosexuality is a wicked sin. God judged the cities of Sodom and Gomorrha by fire and brimstone because of that sin. It is in the Bible and I am going to continue to preach the Bible.

- **1 Samuel 15:3**
  "Now go and smite Amalek, and utterly destroy all that they have, and spare them not; but slay both man and woman, infant and suckling, ox and sheep, camel and ass."

God does not spare sinners. A complete and total destruction in the Lake of Fire in hell awaits those that reject his Son. He will not spare them.

2 Corinthians 13:3

"Since ye seek a proof of Christ speaking in me, which to you-ward is not weak, but is mighty in you."

The church at Corinth wanted to see something that proved that Christ had spoken to him. The Lord Jesus Christ spoke to Paul, giving him certain revelations.

Verses On Christ's Revelations To Paul
- **2 Corinthians 12:1**
"It is not expedient for me doubtless to glory. I will come to visions and revelations of the Lord."

The Lord Jesus Christ gave Paul some revelations after he was stoned and left for dead. Paul went up to Heaven for a short time.
- **2 Corinthians 12:7**
"And lest I should be exalted above measure through the abundance of the revelations, there was given to me a thorn in the flesh, the messenger of Satan to buffet me, lest I should be exalted above measure."

Paul mentioned that an abundance of revelations were given to him.
- **Galatians 1:12**
"For I neither received it of man, neither was I taught *it*, but by the revelation of Jesus Christ."

At Paul's conversion on the road to Damascus to imprison Christians, he was taught the Gospel message by revelation of the Lord Jesus Christ.
- **Ephesians 3:3**
"How that by revelation he made known unto me the mystery; (as I wrote afore in few words,"

The Lord Jesus Christ made known to Paul the mystery by revelation.

2 Corinthians 13:4

"For though he was crucified through weakness, yet he liveth by the power of God. For we also are weak in him, but we shall live with him by the power of God toward you."

After the Lord Jesus Christ died on the cross, He was bodily raised from the dead "*by the power of God.*" Genuine Christians who are weak now, will become mighty. They "*shall live with him by the power of God*" for all eternity by resurrection power.

Verses On God's Power
- **Romans 1:4**
"And declared *to be* the Son of God with power, according to the spirit of holiness, by the resurrection from the dead:"

The miraculous power of God that raised the Lord Jesus Christ bodily from the dead testifies that he is the Son of God with power.

- **1 Corinthians 6:14**
"And <u>God hath both raised up the Lord, and will also raise up us by his own power.</u>"
He will raise up all true Christians by His own power.
- **Ephesians 1:19-20**
"And what *is* <u>the exceeding greatness of his power to us-ward who believe, according to the working of his mighty power,</u> Which he wrought in Christ, when he raised him from the dead, and set *him* at his own right hand in the heavenly *places,*"
Genuine Christians are given *"exceeding greatness of His power.*
- **Philippians 3:10**
"That I may know him, <u>and the power of his resurrection,</u> and the fellowship of his sufferings, being made conformable unto his death;"
Paul wanted to know the power of resurrection of the Lord Jesus Christ as well as the fellowship of his sufferings.

2 Corinthians 13:5

"Examine yourselves, whether ye be in the faith; prove your own selves. Know ye not your own selves, how that Jesus Christ is in you, except ye be reprobates?"

Every professing Christian should examine themselves to be certain they are true Christians rather than reprobates who will end up in the Lake of Fire in Hell.

This is a command to examine yourself. There are at least four things to consider regarding your salvation.
1. Do you really want to go to the Bible's Heaven, not a made-up Heaven.
2. You must realize that the Bible teaches that you are, apart from true salvation, a sinner whose destiny is in the Lake of Fire, Hell forever.
3. You must realize that the Lord Jesus Christ died for your sins and the sins of the whole world upon the cross of Calvary.
4. You must wholeheartedly believe the Lord Jesus Christ took your sins in His body on the cross and truly believe in Him and receive Him as your Saviour.

5. *"For God so loved the world, that he gave his only begotten Son, that **whosoever believeth in him should not perish, but have everlasting life**."* (John 3:16)
- **Psalms 26:2**

"Examine me, O LORD, and prove me; try my reins and my heart."

Every human being must examine their hearts to see if they are truly trusting and believing in the Lord Jesus Christ as their Saviour and Lord.

Verses On Reprobate

- **Romans 1:28**

"And even as they did not like to retain God in *their* knowledge, God gave them over to a reprobate mind, to do those things which are not convenient;"

Many people around the world are reprobate concerning the Lord Jesus Christ. They have not received Him as their Saviour, but have totally rejected Him and are forever lost.

- **2 Timothy 3:8**

"Now as Jannes and Jambres withstood Moses, so do these also resist the truth: men of corrupt minds, reprobate concerning the faith."

Many are completely casting off the Words and doctrines that are taught in the Bible. They are reprobate concerning the truth.

- **Titus 1:16**

"They profess that they know God; but in works they deny him, being abominable, and disobedient, and unto every good work reprobate."

These reprobates are completely disapproved of the Lord and destitute of the Truth.

- **1 Corinthians 9:27**

"But I keep under my body, and bring it into subjection: lest that by any means, when I have preached to others, I myself should be a castaway."

2 Corinthians 13:6

"But I trust that ye shall know that we are not reprobates."

You can tell a *"reprobate"* by looking carefully at their fruits and lifestyles.

Verses On Good And Bad Fruits
- **Matthew 7:16**

"<u>Ye shall know them by their fruits</u>. Do men gather grapes of thorns, or figs of thistles?"

Somebody professes to be a Christian, but are they a genuine Christian? You can often tell whether they are true and genuine by their fruits. What do they eat? Where do they sleep? "Where do they go? Do they smoke or drink? Do they swear? These are some of the fruits that can be examined. Since we cannot see their hearts, it will not to give firm truth. But behavior gives you some clues about the possibility of their being genuine Christians or doubtful by the way they live.

- **Matthew 7:17-21**

"Even so every good tree bringeth forth good fruit; but <u>a corrupt tree bringeth forth evil fruit. A good tree cannot bring forth evil fruit, neither *can* a corrupt tree bring forth good fruit</u>. Every tree that bringeth not forth good fruit is hewn down, and cast into the fire. Wherefore <u>by their fruits ye shall know them</u>. Not every one that saith unto me, Lord, Lord, shall enter into the kingdom of heaven; but he that doeth the will of my Father which is in heaven."

Multitudes pretend they are "Christians" and that the Lord Jesus Christ is their real Lord and Saviour. This is not true according to the Bible's clear definition of the true Biblical Christian faith. Every person should objectively examine themselves Biblically to determine whether they are genuinely in the Christian faith taught in the Bible or non Biblical Christian unsaved reprobates.

2 Corinthians 13:7

"Now I pray to God that ye do no evil; not that we should appear approved, but that ye should do that which is honest, though we be as reprobates."

Paul prayed that the Church at Corinth would do no evil, but do that which is honest.

Verses On Evil
- **Matthew 6:13**

"And lead us not into temptation, but <u>deliver us from evil</u>: For thine is the kingdom, and the power, and the glory, for ever. Amen."

Deliver us from evil is a good prayer to make by Genuine Christians. They should ask God to deliver them from evil.

- **John 17:15**
  "I pray not that thou shouldest take them out of the world, but that thou shouldest keep them from the evil."

That is the prayer of the Lord Jesus Christ to His Father. He asked His Father to keep all true Christians from evil.

- **Romans 12:9**
  "*Let* love be without dissimulation. Abhor that which is evil; cleave to that which is good."

Abhor and stay away from evil and evil people, but cleave to that which is good.

- **Galatians 1:4**
  "Who gave himself for our sins, that he might deliver us from this present evil world, according to the will of God and our Father:"

God wants to deliver genuine Christians from this evil world and all of its wicked ways.

- **1 Thessalonians 5:22**
  "Abstain from all appearance of evil."

Here it is not only abstaining from evil, but even what seems to be the appearance of evil though not evil itself.

- **2 Thessalonians 3:3**
  "But the Lord is faithful, who shall stablish you, and keep *you* from evil."

The Lord is faithful to keep true Christians from evil if they will walk closely to Him.

- **2 Timothy 2:9**
  "Wherein I suffer trouble, as an evil doer, *even* unto bonds; but the word of God is not bound."

Though Paul was not an evil doer, he suffered trouble as though he were one. The same thing happens to genuine Christians in our days.

- **1 Peter 3:10**
  "For he that will love life, and see good days, let him refrain his tongue from evil, and his lips that they speak no guile:"

God does not want true Christians to have an evil tongue. The tongue can easily get them in trouble if they do not keep it in control.

- **1 Peter 3:11**
  "Let him eschew evil, and do good; let him seek peace, and ensue it."

Genuine Christians should eschew evil, hating it and departing from it.

- **1 Peter 4:15**

"But <u>let none of you suffer as a murderer, or *as* a thief, or *as* an evildoer</u>, or as a busybody in other men's matters."

True Christians should not suffer as an evil doer as the Apostle Peter said in this verse.

- **3 John 1:11**

"<u>Beloved, follow not that which is evil, but that which is good</u>. He that doeth good is of God: but <u>he that doeth evil hath not seen God</u>."

Genuine Christians are told by the Apostle John not to follow evil but good. He said the one who follows evil has not seen God. This is excellent wisdom for true Christians to follow daily.

- **Romans 12:17**

"<u>Recompense to no man evil for evil</u>. Provide things honest in the sight of all men."

When genuine Christians are given evil treatment, they are not to return evil back to those who give the evil treatment.

- **1 Peter 2:12**

"Having your conversation honest among the Gentiles: that, <u>whereas they speak against you as evildoers, they may by your good works, which they shall behold, glorify God</u> in the day of visitation."

The genuine Christians in the New Testament days, as in the days in which we live, are spoken of as evildoers. May the good works which people may behold, truly glorify God the Father and God the Holy Spirit.

2 Corinthians 13:8

"For we can do nothing against the truth, but for the truth."

Ultimate and vital truth is in the Words of God in the Bible. Some so-called "truth" in our world is false because it goes against the truth found in the Bible.

- **John 1:14**

"And <u>the Word was made flesh, and dwelt among us</u>, (and we beheld his glory, the glory as of the only begotten of the Father,) <u>full of grace and truth</u>."

The Lord Jesus Christ was *"full of grace and truth"*

- **John 1:17**

"For the law was given by Moses, but <u>grace and truth came by Jesus Christ</u>."

Genuine truth came by the Lord Jesus Christ in every area.

- **John 4:24**
"God *is* a Spirit: and they that worship him must worship *him* in spirit and in truth."
Proper worship of the God of the Bible must be in spirit and in the truth of the Bible.
- **John 8:32**
"And ye shall know the truth, and the truth shall make you free."
In English, we have the right Bible in the King James Bible. In that Bible, we have God's truth that He wants genuine Christians to know and follow.
- **John 8:44**
"Ye are of *your* father the devil, and the lusts of your father ye will do. He was a murderer from the beginning, and abode not in the truth, because there is no truth in him. When he speaketh a lie, he speaketh of his own: for he is a liar, and the father of it."
Satan abode not in the truth and there is no truth in him.
- **John 14:6**
"Jesus saith unto him, I am the way, the truth, and the life: no man cometh unto the Father, but by me."
The Lord Jesus Christ is the truth as well as the way and the life.
- **John 16:13**
"Howbeit when he, the Spirit of truth, is come, he will guide you into all truth: for he shall not speak of himself; but whatsoever he shall hear, *that* shall he speak: and he will shew you things to come."
It is important that all true Christians know God's truth found in the Bible. They should know and follow it.
- **John 17:17**
"Sanctify them through thy truth: thy word is truth."
The Lord Jesus Christ prayed to His Father in His High Priestly prayer that the genuine Christians should be sanctified through God's Words, which are truth.
- **1 Corinthians 13:6**
"Rejoiceth not in iniquity, but rejoiceth in the truth;"
This is speaking of true love which rejoices in the truth.
- **Galatians 4:16**
"Am I therefore become your enemy, because I tell you the truth?"
When you tell the truth to people, many will say you are wrong, and become your enemies. Continue telling them God's truth.

- **Ephesians 4:15**
"But speaking the truth in love, may grow up into him in all things, which is the head, *even* Christ:"
True Christians can grow up into Him by speaking the truth in love.
- **Ephesians 4:25**
"Wherefore putting away lying, speak every man truth with his neighbour: for we are members one of another."
Lying should be put away and only truth should be spoken among neighbours.
- **Ephesians 6:14**
"Stand therefore, having your loins girt about with truth, and having on the breastplate of righteousness;"
The Christian soldier should have his loins girt about with the truth of the Words of God.
- **1 Timothy 3:15**
"But if I tarry long, that thou mayest know how thou oughtest to behave thyself in the house of God, which is the church of the living God, the pillar and ground of the truth."
God says that the true Church of genuine Christians is the pillar and ground of the truth.
- **2 Timothy 2:15**
"Study to shew thyself approved unto God, a workman that needeth not to be ashamed, rightly dividing the word of truth."
All true Christians should know to rightly divide the Word of truth. This takes diligent study.
- **2 Timothy 4:4**
"And they shall turn away *their* ears from the truth, and shall be turned unto fables."
Among other things, the new Bible versions have done this. People have been turned to fables rather than Bible truth. Thousands of verses have been either added, subtracted, or changed from the true Hebrew, Aramaic and Greek on which the Bible is founded.
- **3 John 1:4**
"I have no greater joy than to hear that my children walk in truth."
Pastors have great joy as well, when their people walk in the Bible's truths.

2 Corinthians 13:9

"For we are glad, when we are weak, and ye are strong: and this also we wish, *even* your perfection."

Paul would like to see the genuine Christians at Corinth to be perfect, mature, and full grown in the doctrines of the Bible.

Verses On Perfect

- **Matthew 4:21**

"And going on from thence, he saw other two brethren, James *the son* of Zebedee, and John his brother, in a ship with Zebedee their father, mending their nets; and he called them."

"*Perfect*" is the same word, in this context as "*mending*" the nets. They wanted to get them repaired and useful for fishing again.

- **Matthew 21:16**

"And said unto him, Hearest thou what these say? And Jesus saith unto them, Yea; have ye never read, Out of the mouth of babes and sucklings thou hast perfected praise?"

Even out of the young ones, mature praise can proceed.

- **Luke 6:40**

"The disciple is not above his master: but every one that is perfect shall be as his master."

Every one who is mature and fully equipped shall be as his master.

- **1 Corinthians 1:10**

"Now I beseech you, brethren, by the name of our Lord Jesus Christ, that ye all speak the same thing, and *that* there be no divisions among you; but *that* ye be perfectly joined together in the same mind and in the same judgment."

Paul wanted true Christians at Corinth to be joined together in unity in a mature manner.

- **Ephesians 4:12**

"For the perfecting of the saints, for the work of the ministry, for the edifying of the body of Christ:"

Genuine Christians should be perfected and made strong and mature for the edifying of the body of Christ.

- **1 Thessalonians 3:10**

"Night and day praying exceedingly that we might see your face, and might perfect that which is lacking in your faith?"

Paul wanted to perfect and make mature that which these people needed regarding their faith.

- **Hebrews 13:21**
"Make you perfect in every good work to do his will, working in you that which is wellpleasing in his sight, through Jesus Christ; to whom *be* glory for ever and ever. Amen."

God wants true Christians to be perfect, that is, mature and grown up in Christ and in the will of God.

- **1 Peter 5:10**
"But the God of all grace, who hath called us unto his eternal glory by Christ Jesus, after that ye have suffered a while, make you perfect, stablish, strengthen, settle *you*."

After you have suffered a while, make you perfect, that is, make you more mature and grown up.

2 Corinthians 13:10

"Therefore I write these things being absent, lest being present I should use sharpness, according to the power which the Lord hath given me to edification, and not to destruction."

Paul did not want to hurt or destroy anyone. He wanted to build up people, not tear them down.

Verses On Destruction

- **Matthew 7:13**
"Enter ye in at the strait gate: for wide *is* the gate, and broad *is* the way, that leadeth to destruction, and many there be which go in thereat:"

The way to destruction in Hell is broad and many enter into that way.

- **2 Corinthians 10:8**
"For though I should boast somewhat more of our authority, which the Lord hath given us for edification, and not for your destruction, I should not be ashamed:"

Paul wanted to edify and build up the genuine Christians. He did not want to destroy them in any way.

- **2 Thessalonians 1:9**
"Who shall be punished with everlasting destruction from the presence of the Lord, and from the glory of his power;"

Hell is, "everlasting destruction from the presence of the Lord, and from the glory of his power" by definition.

2 Corinthians 13:11

"Finally, brethren, farewell. Be perfect, be of good comfort, be of one mind, live in peace; and the God of love and peace shall be with you."

Here is the four things, vital things, that every church needs. (1) *"be perfect,"* (2) *"be of good comfort,"* (3) *"be of one mind,"* and (4) *"live in peace."*

1. Verses On "Perfect"
(See v. 9 above for Perfect)
2. Verses On Comfort

The second vital thing every church should have is to *"be of good comfort."* It means to console, encourage, and strengthen by consolation. The word translated comfort means *"to comfort one another, it means to console, to encourage, strengthen by consolation."*

- **Acts 9:31**

"Then had the churches rest throughout all Judaea and Galilee and Samaria, and were edified; and walking in the fear of the Lord, and in the comfort of the Holy Ghost, were multiplied."

The Holy Spirit gives comfort to the souls of genuine Christians. This is a vital need for every Biblical church.

- **2 Corinthians 1:3**

"Blessed *be* God, even the Father of our Lord Jesus Christ, the Father of mercies, and the God of all comfort;"

The God of the Bible is the God of all comfort. He is the One Who can comfort true Christians.

- **2 Corinthians 1:4**

"Who comforteth us in all our tribulation, that we may be able to comfort them which are in any trouble, by the comfort wherewith we ourselves are comforted of God."

True Christians can comfort others who are in trouble by the comfort God gives them.

- **2 Corinthians 2:7**

"So that contrariwise ye *ought* rather to forgive *him*, and comfort *him*, lest perhaps such a one should be swallowed up with overmuch sorrow."

This man repented and came back to the Corinthian Church. They had thrown him out. He came back and they comforted him.

- **2 Corinthians 7:6**
"Nevertheless <u>God, that comforteth those that are cast down, comforted us by the coming of Titus</u>;"

Titus came to comfort Paul who was in need of comfort at the time.

- **2 Corinthians 7:7**
"And not by his coming only, but <u>by the consolation wherewith he was comforted in you</u>, when he told us your earnest desire, your mourning, your fervent mind toward me; so that I rejoiced the more."

So the Corinthians had comfort, they comforted Titus, and comforted one another as well.

- **Ephesians 6:22**
"<u>Whom I have sent unto you</u> for the same purpose, that ye might know our affairs, and <u>*that* he might comfort your hearts</u>."

Tychicus was sent these true Christians to comfort the hearts of these genuine Christians.

- **Colossians 2:2**
"<u>That their hearts might be comforted</u>, being knit together in love, and unto all riches of the full assurance of understanding, to the acknowledgement of the mystery of God, and of the Father, and of Christ;"

Again, Tychicus was sent to comfort the hearts of these people.

- **Colossians 4:8**
"<u>Whom I have sent unto you</u> for the same purpose, <u>that he might</u> know your estate, and <u>comfort your hearts</u>;"

People need comfort for their hearts.

- **Colossians 4:11**
"And Jesus, which is called Justus, who are of the circumcision. <u>These only *are my* fellowworkers</u> unto the kingdom of God, <u>which have been a comfort unto me</u>."

Paul thanked his fellow believers who comforted him.

- **1 Thessalonians 3:2**
"<u>And sent Timotheus, our brother, and minister of God</u>, and our fellowlabourer in the Gospel of Christ, to establish you, and <u>to comfort you concerning your faith</u>:"

The Thessalonian Church needed comfort, so Paul sent Timothy to comfort them concerning their faith.

- **1 Thessalonians 3:7**
"Therefore, brethren, we were comforted over you in all our affliction and distress by your faith:"
The faith of the Thessalonian Christians comforted Paul's heart by their faith.
- **1 Thessalonians 4:17-18**
"Then we which are alive *and* remain shall be caught up together with them in the clouds, to meet the Lord in the air: and so shall we ever be with the Lord. Wherefore comfort one another with these words."
There is comfort in the fact that one day the Lord Jesus Christ will come back in the air and take all the genuine Christians Home to Heaven.

3. Be Of One Mind

The third vital need of every church is to "*be of one mind.*" Some of the meanings of that Greek word for "*one mind*" are: "*to be of the same mind, to think the way the others think.*"

To be unified in the doctrines of the faith is one of the things that every true Christian local church should have.

Verses On Be Of One Mind

- **1 Corinthians 1:10**
"Now I beseech you, brethren, by the name of our Lord Jesus Christ, that ye all speak the same thing, and *that* there be no divisions among you; but that ye be perfectly joined together in the same mind and in the same judgment."
That is why our Bible-believing church has a doctrinal statement that our true Christian members agree to.
- **Philippians 1:27**
"Only let your conversation be as it becometh the Gospel of Christ: that whether I come and see you, or else be absent, I may hear of your affairs, that ye stand fast in one spirit, with one mind striving together for the faith of the Gospel;"
These Philippians genuine Christians were with standing fast with one mind for the Gospel.
- **Philippians 2:2**
"Fulfil ye my joy, that ye be likeminded, having the same love, *being* of one accord, of one mind."
This refers to Bible and doctrinal issues. The doctrinal position of our church and the Scriptures. We should be of one accord on these doctrinal matters.

- **Philippians 4:2**

"I beseech Euodias, and beseech Syntyche, that they be of the same mind in the Lord."

Apparently these two people were fighters and were urged to be of the same mind.

- **1 Peter 3:8**

"Finally, be ye all of one mind, having compassion one of another, love as brethren, be pitiful, be courteous:"

4. Live In Peace

The fourth vital need in any local church is for the genuine Christians to live in peace. Some of the meanings of this Greek Word are: *"to make peace, to keep peace, be at peace, be harmonious, be in harmony one to another."*

Verses On Peace

- **Romans 14:19**

"Let us therefore follow after the things which make for peace, and things wherewith one may edify another."

True Christians are to follow peaceful things.

- **1 Corinthians 14:33**

"For God is not *the author* of confusion, but of peace."

God is the Author of peace, not confusion. He wants peace in our churches.

- **Galatians 5:22**

"But the fruit of the Spirit is love, joy, peace, longsuffering, gentleness, goodness, faith,"

God wants genuine Christians to have peace with Him and with fellow Christians.

- **Ephesians 4:3**

"Endeavouring to keep the unity of the Spirit in the bond of peace."

The bond of peace is needed in true local churches.

- **Colossians 3:15**

"And let the peace of God rule in your hearts, to the which also ye are called in one body; and be ye thankful."

The peace of God can rule in the hearts of genuine Christians and in their churches.

- **1 Thessalonians 5:12-13**

"And we beseech you, brethren, to know them which labour among you, and are over you in the Lord, and admonish you; And to esteem them very highly in love for their work's sake. *And* be at peace among yourselves."

Genuine Christians are to be at peace among themselves.

- **Hebrews 12:14**
"Follow peace with all *men*, and holiness, without which no man shall see the Lord:"
Following peace with all men is difficult, but should be tried.
- **1 Peter 3:11**
"Let him eschew evil, and do good; let him seek peace, and ensue it."
Godly people should seek peace, pursue after it.

2 Corinthians 13:12

"Greet one another with an holy kiss."

This word for "kiss" in Greek is PHILEMATI which comes from PHILEMA. It is a two part word: PHIL- and -EMA. The first part, PHIL- means *"love or friendship"* and the second part, -EMA means *"the result of something."*

In the New Testament, the way genuine Christians showed their holy love and friendship was by greeting one another on the cheeks. Today the way true Christians can show their holy love and friendship is by saying hello and shaking hands.

Verses On Kiss

- **Proverbs 27:6**
"Faithful *are* the wounds of a friend; but the kisses of an enemy *are* deceitful."
Enemies, like Judas, give kisses of betrayal and deceit.
- **Luke 7:45**
"Thou gavest me no kiss: but this woman since the time I came in hath not ceased to kiss my feet."
This woman loved the Lord Jesus Christ and humbly kissed His feet.
- **Luke 22:47-48**
"And while he yet spake, behold a multitude, and he that was called Judas, one of the twelve, went before them, and drew near unto Jesus to kiss him. But Jesus said unto him, Judas, betrayest thou the Son of man with a kiss?"
Judas used a phony kiss of love and friendship for a kiss of betrayal.
- **Acts 20:37**
"And they all wept sore, and fell on Paul's neck, and kissed him,"
As Paul was leaving the disciples for foreign cities, they gave him kisses of love and friendship.

- **Romans 16:16**
  "Salute one another with an holy kiss. The churches of Christ salute you."

This is explained in the first part of this chapter.

- **1 Corinthians 16:20**
  "All the brethren greet you. Greet ye one another with an holy kiss."

This is explained in the first part of this chapter.

- **1 Thessalonians 5:26**
  "Greet all the brethren with an holy kiss."

This is explained in the first part of this chapter.

- **1 Peter 5:14**
  "Greet ye one another with a kiss of charity. Peace *be* with you all that are in Christ Jesus. Amen."

This is explained in the first part of this chapter.

2 Corinthians 13:13

"All the saints salute you."

"All the saints" refers to all genuine Christians. Nowhere in the Bible does it ever refer to the "saints" of the Roman Catholic Church or any other church.

- **Acts 26:10**
  "Which thing I also did in Jerusalem: and many of the saints did I shut up in prison, having received authority from the chief priests; and when they were put to death, I gave my voice against *them*."

Before he was saved, Paul shut up many genuine Christians in prison.

- **Romans 1:7**
  "To all that be in Rome, beloved of God, called *to be* saints: Grace to you and peace from God our Father, and the Lord Jesus Christ."

True Christians were being named here as saints.

- **Romans 8:27**
  "And he that searcheth the hearts knoweth what is the mind of the Spirit, because he maketh intercession for the saints according to *the will of* God."

The Lord Jesus Christ is going to make intercession for all genuine Christians according to the will of God.

- **Romans 15:25-26**
  "But now I go unto Jerusalem to minister unto the saints. For it hath pleased them of Macedonia and Achaia <u>to make a certain contribution for the poor saints which are at Jerusalem</u>."

They helped the poor true Christians at Jerusalem.

- **1 Corinthians 1:2**
  "Unto the church of God which is at Corinth, to them that are <u>sanctified in Christ Jesus, called *to be* saints</u>, with all that in every place call upon the name of Jesus Christ our Lord, both theirs and ours:"

These were genuine Christians who were called by God.

- **1 Corinthians 6:2**
  "Do ye not know that <u>the saints shall judge the world</u>? and if the world shall be judged by you, are ye unworthy to judge the smallest matters?"

At the judgement seat of Christ, God will use true Christians with the Lord Jesus Christ to judge Christians. They will also join him at the Great White Throne judging the unbelievers.

- **1 Corinthians 16:1**
  "Now <u>concerning the collection for the saints</u>, as I have given order to the churches of Galatia, even so do ye."

Genuine Christians would receive a collection to help them.

- **Ephesians 1:1**
  "Paul, an apostle of Jesus Christ by the will of God, <u>to the saints which are at Ephesus</u>, and to the faithful in Christ Jesus:"

Paul was writing to the true Christians at Ephesus.

- **Jude 1:3**
  "Beloved, when I gave all diligence to write unto you of the common salvation, it was needful for me to write unto you, and <u>exhort *you* that ye should earnestly contend for the faith which was once delivered unto the saints</u>."

Genuine Christians must earnestly contend for the doctrines of the Christian faith which were once for all delivered to the true Christians. The Biblical faith is being forsaken and denied all over the world today and it must be tirelessly and continuously defended by genuine Christians in these apostate days.

2 Corinthians 13:14

"The grace of the Lord Jesus Christ, and the love of God, and the communion of the Holy Ghost, *be* with you all. Amen."

In this ending of this letter, Paul invoked the whole Trinity, Father, Son and the Holy Spirit. He prayed, "The Lord Jesus and the love of God the Father and the communion of the Holy Spirit be with you. Amen." This is a wish that Paul has. Here are a few **verses on the word 'grace' of Christ, the grace of the Lord Jesu**s Christ. Grace is giving us something we do not deserve.

Verses On Grace

- **Romans 16:20**

"And the God of peace shall bruise Satan under your feet shortly. The grace of our Lord Jesus Christ *be* with you. Amen."

As Paul ends this letter, and many other letters, he reminds the true Christians at Corinth about the Saviour's grace.

- **Romans 16:24**

"The grace of our Lord Jesus Christ *be* with you all. Amen." God's grace is in many of Paul's letters.

- **2 Corinthians 8:9**

"For ye know the grace of our Lord Jesus Christ, that, though he was rich, yet for your sakes he became poor, that ye through his poverty might be rich."

The Lord Jesus Christ left the riches of Heaven, came to this earth enduring the poverty of being Perfect Man, as well as the glory of being Perfect God. For men, He became poor that through his poverty all humans might be made rich if they would truly trust Him as their Saviour. He died on the cross of Calvary to bear the sins of the world so those who receive Him and trust Him might receive everlasting life.

- **Galatians 6:18**

"Brethren, the grace of our Lord Jesus Christ *be* with your spirit. Amen."

God's grace should be with those at Galatia and elsewhere.

- **Philippians 4:23**

"The grace of our Lord Jesus Christ *be* with you all. Amen." God's grace.

- **1 Thessalonians 5:28**
"The grace of our Lord Jesus Christ *be* with you. Amen."
- **2 Thessalonians 3:18**
"The grace of our Lord Jesus Christ *be* with you all. Amen."
- **Philemon 1:25**
"The grace of our Lord Jesus Christ *be* with your spirit. Amen."
- **Revelation 22:21**
"The grace of our Lord Jesus Christ *be* with you all. Amen."

God's grace is giving us something we do not deserve. May every genuine Christian be gracious to fellow-Christians. This is what they must do. The Lord Jesus Christ gave them all these things so they might know His will for their lives.

Index of Words and Phrases

1 John 1:9 . . . . 24-27, 32, 44, 105, 150
356 doctrinal passages 82, 126
absent from the Lord 92
Achaia 1, 169-171, 175, 198, 235, 246, 301
Acknowledgments . . . . ii, iv
Affliction 6-9, 18, 19, 26, 84, 122, 131, 165, 172, 297
Afflictions 7-9, 11, 18, 46, 62, 75, 84, 121-123, 127, 195, 201
    273
Agreement 141
apostle 1, 9, 16, 33, 62, 121, 146, 166, 174, 213, 244, 263, 274
    290, 301
Appearance 98, 99, 227, 228, 289
Approved . . . 41, 121, 129, 131, 163, 198, 201, 236, 237, 274, 288
    292
Ashamed . . . 8, 36, 37, 42, 54, 96, 97, 103, 119, 122, 126, 127, 155
    166, 167, 171, 190, 200, 201, 228, 237, 270, 292, 294
ASV 81
Beguile 85, 240, 241
Belial 139, 140, 143
BFT #4194 i
Bible . . . i-iv, 8, 13, 21, 22, 39, 42, 43, 46, 54, 59, 60, 64, 70, 80
    81, 83, 91, 120, 123-126, 128, 134-137, 139, 146, 155, 161,
    165, 172, 175, 178, 185, 189, 190, 202, 207, 229, 230,
    232, 234-237, 241, 257, 265, 272-275, 279, 280, 284,
    286-288, 290-293, 295, 297, 300, 316, 318, 320, 321,
    323
Bible For Today Baptist Church . . . . i, iii, 316
Blameless 191, 192, 198, 251, 254
Bold 155, 178, 219-221, 253
Boldness 5, 53, 96, 103, 154-157, 201, 221
Bountiful 210
Caring 163, 185
Caring For Others 163
Cast Down . . 6, 73, 75, 78, 157, 158, 165, 177, 223, 225, 278, 296
charis 1
Cheer 205
church of Corinth 1, 20, 26, 29, 31, 208, 270, 278
Church Phone: 856-854-4747 i
cleanse ourselves from all filthiness 149, 223
clothed 89-91, 210
Collingswood, New Jersey 08108 U.S.A. i

Come Out 57, 141, 143, 144, 255
Comfort 2-7, 21, 24, 27-30, 53, 154, 156, 157, 162, 164, 165
    278, 281, 295-297
commendation 41, 236, 237, 274
Communion............................ 24, 135, 138, 302
Condemn 154
confess 25-27, 32, 44, 96, 105, 115, 150, 181
confidence .. 18, 155, 168, 193, 194, 221, 250, 251, 254, 269, 321
Consolation 5, 6, 157, 158, 295, 296
Corinth..... 1, 6, 15, 18-20, 22, 23, 26, 29, 31, 41, 43, 53, 70, 79
    121, 134, 135, 139, 151, 154, 156, 158, 164, 166-170, 174
    177, 178, 184, 185, 187, 194, 195, 198, 207, 208, 213, 219,
    228, 229, 234, 246, 252, 268, 270, 274, 276-279, 282,
    284, 288, 293, 301, 302
Corrupt.. 13, 22, 24, 39, 62, 65, 72, 124, 152, 188, 241, 247, 249
    250, 281, 287, 288
Critical Gnostic Greek text 81
crucified 21, 49, 60, 79, 100, 162, 205, 283, 285
Darby version 81
Darkness . 11, 32, 33, 49, 68-72, 96, 108, 135, 137-139, 143, 145
    182, 248-250, 263
death.... 3, 5, 9, 10, 24, 28, 31, 38, 43, 46, 48, 49, 51, 71, 76, 77
    79-81, 86, 87, 89, 93-96, 103, 107, 111, 119, 129, 131, 141,
    155, 156, 161, 163, 166, 180, 181, 201, 205, 210, 213, 214,
    232, 235, 250, 252, 255, 262, 265, 283, 286, 300
Deceitful........................ 34, 64, 65, 247, 277, 299
Defraud 34, 68, 153, 154
deliver........... 7, 10, 11, 23, 58, 59, 107, 108, 256, 288, 289
Deliverance 10, 11, 59, 107, 249
Destroy................ 30, 35, 65, 78, 93, 141, 204, 284, 294
Destruction 23, 228, 280, 284, 294
devil 9, 35, 46, 67-69, 106, 109, 111, 127, 140, 141, 204, 243
    248, 250, 274, 291
Diligence 178, 179, 188, 189, 194, 203, 206, 301
dishonesty 64
disobedience 227, 243
Distress 9, 18, 73-75, 77, 297
Door 36, 37, 85, 93, 140, 152, 156, 178, 190, 206
Dying 79, 100, 102, 115, 126, 128, 129, 133, 185, 266
Edify........................... 28, 228, 279-281, 294, 298
Enduring 6, 8, 63, 180, 302
ESV... 81, 323
eternal ... 7, 62, 66, 84, 87, 91, 119, 134, 160, 161, 209, 216, 232

233, 243, 273, 294
Evil 3, 20, 25, 28, 30, 39, 54, 69, 73, 76, 108, 127, 128, 130
134, 137, 147, 149, 159, 167, 188, 193, 219, 222, 228, 243,
248, 249, 266, 277, 278, 288-290, 299
Exhort 28, 65, 125, 189, 201-203, 301
Faint 61, 63, 83
Fainting 63, 83
Faith 4, 8, 9, 16, 32, 33, 36, 42, 50, 55, 57, 63, 68, 70, 71, 75
77, 80, 82, 83, 85, 86, 92, 93, 100, 110, 114-116, 122,
124, 125, 127, 128, 132, 133, 139, 140, 155, 160, 161, 165,
171, 173, 177, 178, 181, 182, 189, 194, 200, 202-205, 208,
209, 211, 214, 216, 220, 221, 227, 234, 264, 270, 273,
275, 277, 279, 280, 286-288, 293, 296-298, 301
faithful ... ii, 22, 25, 27, 32, 44, 46, 61, 62, 64, 96, 101, 103, 105
121, 124, 128, 150, 155, 167, 168, 177, 202, 236, 242, 258,
273, 289, 299, 301, 326
Father .. 1, 2, 6, 25, 27, 31, 48, 49, 51, 53, 63, 66, 67, 77, 86, 104
105, 107-110, 112, 113, 115, 129, 132, 135, 137, 147, 151,
153, 154, 161, 165, 167, 177, 181, 200, 202, 203, 210, 212,
213, 230, 233, 237, 242, 243, 262, 265, 266, 279,
288-291, 293, 295, 296, 300, 302
FAX: 856-854-2464 i
Fellowship . 5, 8, 25, 42, 71, 91, 96, 104, 105, 135, 137-140, 142-
144, 146, 147, 150, 173, 175, 197, 286
Fellowship With Christ.............................. 96
Fervent 6, 158, 296
Flesh 8, 23, 31, 34, 43-45, 48, 50, 53, 54, 64, 73, 79, 91, 100
103, 106, 129, 149, 150, 152, 156, 170, 175, 180, 203,
221-223, 229, 239, 244, 248, 249, 251, 254, 259-261,
263, 268, 269, 274, 285, 290
Fool 34, 80, 124, 239, 248-250, 254, 267, 274
Foreword .... iii, iv
Forgive 24-27, 29-32, 44, 96, 105, 150, 162, 276, 295
forsaken 75, 77, 78, 158, 301
Fruit . 5, 39, 55, 106, 125, 151, 165, 172, 173, 192, 208, 220, 224
241, 288, 298
Gamaliel 244, 245
Gentleness 125, 165, 173, 219, 220, 298
Gift .. 12, 50, 82, 175, 189, 191, 192, 197, 215-217, 226, 231, 232
271, 278, 280
Gift Of A Resurrected Body........................... 216
Gift Of Everlasting Life.............................. 215
Gift Of Forgiveness Of Sins 215

Gift Of Never Perishing 216
Gift Of Peace With God 216
Gift Of Redemption 215
Gift Of Salvation 215, 231
Gift Of The Indwelling Holy Spirit 216
Giving 36, 52, 61, 65, 114, 119, 170, 171, 177-179, 183, 200
      204, 206-212, 230, 245, 269, 284, 302, 303
glad 16-18, 21, 29, 66, 76, 102, 159, 160, 167, 190, 202, 293
Glorify 24, 43, 48, 53, 107, 142, 193, 212, 213, 290
glorious 16, 46, 48, 50, 51, 53, 59, 67, 125, 214, 216, 271
glory 4, 5, 7, 16, 38, 44-46, 48-54, 59, 70, 79, 82, 84, 86, 90
    92, 98, 99, 106, 109, 132-134, 149, 150, 156, 166, 173,
    177, 178, 181, 190, 191, 195, 200, 208, 212, 214, 223, 227,
    235, 236, 247, 251, 261, 263, 265, 267, 269, 272-274,
    276, 279, 285, 288, 290, 294, 302
god Of This World 67
God our Father 1, 300
Godhead... 1
Godly Women 239
God's Gift.................................... 215-217, 231
God's Power.......................... 8, 190, 270, 271, 285
good fruit..................................... 39, 288
Gospel..... 4, 8, 25, 36, 59, 61, 65, 67, 91, 97, 102, 110, 112, 113
    119, 120, 122, 126, 127, 144, 146, 166, 169, 171, 173, 178,
    189-191, 200, 201, 212, 220, 232-235, 242-245, 247,
    264, 270, 275, 285, 296, 297, 326
Grace 1, 2, 5, 6, 12, 15, 32, 34, 38, 39, 42, 45, 48, 50, 51, 53
    54, 61, 62, 82, 117, 119, 120, 132, 133, 138, 169, 177-180,
    191, 202, 204, 207, 213-215, 231, 232, 237, 244, 261,
    269, 271, 274, 275, 279, 281, 290, 294, 300, 302, 303
Grace Of God..... 5, 12, 51, 61, 117, 119, 120, 169, 180, 202, 213
    214, 231, 232, 244, 271
grief............................... 15-17, 20-22, 28
Guile............................ 111, 277, 278, 289
Having Many Things 134
Having Very Little................................. 134
He is a merciful God 2
Heart ... 15, 16, 18, 19, 31, 33, 39, 41, 43, 51, 55, 56, 60, 64, 72-
    74, 85, 94, 98, 99, 108, 113, 115, 126, 131, 134, 137, 162,
    164-166, 173-175, 177, 179, 185, 187, 188, 192, 202, 204,
    205, 208, 212, 225-227, 236, 247, 248, 252, 279, 287,
    297, 321, 323
Heaven ... 2, 4, 7, 8, 16, 26, 32, 35, 36, 39, 45, 47-49, 72, 73, 75

    76, 79, 85, 86, 89-95, 103, 108-111, 113, 116, 118, 129, 131, 132, 144, 153, 155, 162, 163, 180-182, 185, 188, 212, 213, 215, 217, 223, 225, 232, 236, 242, 251, 257, 263-265, 267, 274, 285, 286, 288, 297, 302, 326
heaviness 15, 16
Hell 10, 22, 58, 62, 65, 72, 85, 88, 93, 107-110, 141, 161, 162 186, 189, 232, 243, 250, 266, 284, 286, 294
Helping True Christians 175
Holiness 106, 108, 127, 149-151, 223, 285, 299
Holman Study Bible 81
home in the body 92
HOMOLOGEO 25, 26, 44
Honesty 192
hope..... iii-6, 8, 53, 63, 81, 96, 103, 112, 132, 155, 156, 162, 173 201, 214, 220, 234
house which is from heaven 89
Idols 141-143
imprisonment 101, 167
incest....... 1, 15, 23, 28, 151, 159, 198, 219, 228, 246, 274, 277
Index Of Words And Phrases .... iii, iv, 305
Jews Being Blinded 55
Jews Not Understanding 56
Joy .. 5, 17-19, 21, 22, 53, 61, 84, 86, 120, 122, 125, 131, 132, 162, 164-166, 168, 172-174, 220, 236, 278, 292, 297, 298
Judas Iscariot 1, 64, 67, 224, 244
Judging 96, 301
judgment seat of Christ 95, 96
Kiss 64, 224, 299, 300
Knowledge 12, 37, 49, 70, 124, 133, 134, 145, 155, 167, 178 198, 209, 225, 244, 245, 287
Labors 124
labour 8, 88, 95, 103, 117, 118, 172, 199, 200, 214, 253, 254 298
Lake of Fire 22, 67, 69, 93, 95, 107-109, 119, 232, 250, 265 284, 286
Latin Vulgate 81
law of Moses... 12, 46, 48, 50, 51, 53-55, 59, 199, 222, 223, 229 244, 245
liberty 58, 59, 106, 137, 223
Life ... 9, 13, 21, 23, 28, 33, 34, 36, 38, 45, 51, 54, 61, 62, 66, 69 70, 79, 80, 83, 86-88, 91, 93, 96, 100, 102, 103, 106, 117, 118, 120, 125, 131, 134, 138, 151, 155, 160, 161, 172, 179, 181, 184, 188, 193, 199, 201, 203, 204, 214-216, 222,

225, 232, 233, 239, 243, 244, 267, 273, 278, 287, 289, 291, 302, 326
Light . . . 2, 7, 10, 32-34, 49, 67-71, 84, 88, 96, 105, 135, 137-139 145, 150, 182, 194, 212, 232, 236, 248, 249, 251, 265
Live In Peace 295, 298
Lord Jesus Christ . 1, 2, 4-6, 13, 22, 23, 25, 31-38, 41, 48-53, 56-67, 69-73, 75, 76, 78-83, 85-88, 90-97, 100, 103, 105, 108, 110-115, 117-124, 127, 129, 131-134, 137, 138, 140, 144, 146, 150, 151, 154, 155, 160-162, 164-167, 169, 172, 173, 177, 178, 180-187, 189-192, 197-200, 202-205, 209-216, 219, 221, 222, 224-227, 229-233, 235-237, 239-244, 247, 249-251, 253, 256, 258, 260-262, 264-267, 269-273, 276-279, 283-291, 293, 295, 297, 299-303, 326
love 5, 7, 13, 18-20, 29, 34, 35, 38, 62, 68, 69, 75, 77, 85, 86 100, 124-126, 130, 132, 133, 138, 153, 158, 165, 166, 173, 178-180, 182, 186, 191, 195, 199, 209, 219, 220, 223, 230, 246, 260, 277, 278, 281, 289, 291, 292, 295-299, 302
love of Christ 75, 77, 100
Macedonia 37, 73, 156, 169-171, 174, 175, 189, 198, 200, 201 246, 276, 301
Mathias 1
Measuring 41, 230, 231
Meekness 3, 81, 125, 161, 173, 219, 220
Ministering 129, 175, 176, 197
Ministry 8, 34, 41, 46, 61, 62, 75, 110, 118-122, 126, 128, 129 131, 171, 176, 195, 234, 235, 259, 275, 276, 278, 280, 293
Ministry In Regions Beyond 235
mortality 91
Moses 12, 46-48, 50-56, 59, 86, 144, 145, 152, 174, 176, 199 206, 214, 222, 223, 229, 244, 245, 287, 290
NASV 81
Necessities 7, 46, 75, 121, 123, 229, 260, 261, 272, 273
Necessity 175, 190, 204-206
Nestle-Aland Greek editions 82
New Century Version 81
NKJV 81
obedience 30, 93, 156, 167, 195, 209, 225, 227, 276
Obedient 30, 31, 129, 130, 135, 167, 181, 195, 230, 239, 275
Offence 33, 61, 119, 120, 124, 245, 260
Offence And Offending 260
Offering 12, 38, 174, 183, 191, 199, 206, 207, 232

One Mind 213, 295, 297, 298
Orders: 1-800-John 10:9 i
paradise 266, 267
Patience .. 4-7, 46, 75, 84, 121, 122, 125, 149, 156, 192, 204, 271
   273, 274
Patricia Canter....................................... iii
Paul.... 1, 4-6, 8-13, 15-20, 22, 23, 26, 27, 29-31, 34, 36-39, 41-
   43, 45, 46, 50, 53, 56, 59, 61-64, 68-70, 73, 75-80, 84,
   91, 92, 94, 96-101, 103, 109, 112, 117, 120-125, 129, 132,
   134, 135, 139, 146, 149, 151, 152, 154-161, 163-171,
   173-175, 177-179, 181-185, 187-195, 198-202, 204, 205,
   207, 209, 212, 213, 219-221, 224, 228-235, 237, 239,
   244-247, 250-272, 274-286, 288, 289, 293, 294, 296,
   299-302, 326
Paul's Background.................................... 254
Paul's Eight More Difficulties 258
Paul's Further Persecutions........................... 257
Paul's Many Punishments 254
Paul's Nine Other Difficulties 258
peace.... 1, 34, 52, 56, 73, 125, 160, 165, 173, 177, 190, 192, 205
   216, 220, 233, 242, 260, 279, 289, 295, 298-300, 302
Perfect...... 38, 45, 48, 60, 80, 86, 113, 119, 149, 185, 186, 207
   225, 236, 245, 261, 269, 272, 293-295, 302, 320
Perplexed 73
Persecuted 75-77, 158, 198, 244, 254
Persecution 18, 75-77, 235
Persons in the Godhead 1
Poor.... 12, 59, 74, 82, 131-133, 170, 175, 180-183, 186, 189, 191
   192, 200, 201, 207-213, 276, 301, 302
Poverty 82, 133, 172, 180, 184, 209, 273, 302
Poverty And Riches.................................. 180
Power .. 5, 8, 11, 16, 23, 28, 32, 33, 35, 36, 38, 43-45, 49, 53, 63
   68, 70-72, 78, 90, 97, 108, 112, 119, 122, 125-127, 134,
   139, 157, 165, 166, 173, 174, 181, 182, 184, 190, 200, 201,
   221, 226, 231, 233, 235, 243, 245, 249, 261, 269-272,
   275, 280, 285, 286, 288, 294
Preaching ...... 1, iii, 11, 43, 53, 70, 112, 127, 172, 178, 232, 233
   235, 250, 316, 318, 320, 326
Promises.................. 16, 51, 93, 104, 149, 182, 223
Proof......................... 8, 30, 62, 121, 122, 195, 284
punishment 22, 113, 255
Purpose... 4, 5, 18, 19, 95, 113, 117, 118, 125, 173, 202, 204, 257
   279, 280, 296

raise up us also by Jesus 81
Rejoicing 12, 17, 18, 29, 131, 132, 156, 160, 180, 181, 209
Repent 17, 18, 26, 27, 159, 226
Repentance 18, 32, 119, 160, 161, 208, 228
Reproach 15, 69, 225, 253, 272, 273
Reprobate 287
Resurrected Bodies........................... 87, 89-91, 95
Rich..... 62, 72, 82, 131, 133, 134, 180-183, 209, 210, 235, 266
   302
Riches.... 32, 44, 82, 132-134, 172, 180, 182, 184, 209, 210, 215
   235, 271, 296, 302
RSV.. 81
saints .. 1, 12, 61, 133, 142, 151, 170, 175, 176, 184, 189, 191, 192
   197, 199-201, 203, 207, 208, 211-213, 271, 280, 293,
   300, 301
Salvation .. 3, 6, 16, 36, 42, 43, 50, 51, 54, 59, 72, 82, 91, 97, 115
   117-119, 126-128, 160, 161, 166, 172, 189, 190, 197, 200,
   203, 209, 210, 214, 215, 220, 231, 233, 242, 270, 286,
   301, 326
Satan.... 11, 23, 32-35, 67-71, 104, 135, 139-141, 153, 209, 240-
   243, 247-250, 268, 285, 291, 302
Satan And His Followers
   Preach And Follow Another Gospel................. 243
Satan Is Darkness And Evil........................... 249
saved.... 1, 7, 16, 22-24, 35, 36, 38, 43, 50, 51, 55, 57, 61, 65-67
   70, 71, 82, 85, 91, 93, 100, 102-105, 107, 109-112, 114,
   115, 117, 118, 123, 127-130, 152, 154, 161, 168, 204, 214,
   215, 225, 232, 233, 243, 244, 251, 273, 300
Saviour.... 1, 13, 16, 25, 27, 32, 35, 41, 50, 51, 56-58, 61-63, 65-
   67, 69, 73, 75, 82, 85, 93, 95-97, 101, 104, 108-113, 117,
   119-122, 124, 129, 134, 154, 160, 166, 167, 172, 177, 178,
   180, 181, 186, 189, 200, 201, 208, 212, 214-216, 220,
   225, 232, 233, 236, 239, 240, 242, 243, 250-254, 258,
   260, 265-267, 272, 273, 279, 286-288, 302, 326
schoolmaster... 55
Scripture .... iii, 9, 24, 100, 114, 115, 200, 206, 264
Sealing 91
seen.. 45, 49, 71, 84-86, 92, 98, 105, 115, 131, 132, 137, 147, 166
   169, 173, 189, 202, 227, 235, 260, 264, 269, 290
Separate......................... 1, 29, 75, 77, 90, 143-146
Separation 134-136, 138-141, 143, 144, 146, 147
shalom 1
Signs.................... 35, 97, 121, 190, 237, 263, 274, 275

2 Corinthians Preaching Verse-By-Verse

Sincerity 12, 13, 39, 179, 180
Sorrow 15-21, 24, 27, 28, 88, 95, 119, 123, 131, 132, 161-163
    168, 173, 205, 209, 265, 295
sorry 16-20, 27, 29, 159, 160
Sowing 203, 210
Speech. 5, 43, 53, 54, 99, 154, 156, 157, 228, 229, 233, 244
    260, 264, 268, 278, 316
Spirit . . . 5, 8, 23, 33, 35, 37, 43-45, 48, 50, 53, 55, 56, 58, 59, 67
    80, 84, 89, 91, 98, 103, 104, 106, 107, 111, 124-126, 132,
    138, 141, 142, 147, 149, 157, 158, 164, 165, 169, 170,
    172-175, 190, 192, 203, 205, 212, 213, 216, 219-224, 229,
    233, 239, 242, 243, 247, 251, 259, 261, 263, 267, 270,
    271, 275, 278, 285, 290, 291, 295, 297, 298, 300, 302,
    303
Spirit of the living God 43
Stedfast. 8, 9, 117, 199
Strength 7, 9, 17, 37, 38, 45, 46, 63, 74, 77, 78, 83, 88, 168
    229, 261, 269
stripes 56, 80, 114, 123, 124, 254-256
Suffering. 5, 6, 19, 84, 214, 253, 255
tabernacle. 87, 91, 95, 146, 174, 207, 265
Table of Contents iv
tears 10, 18, 19, 95, 210, 265, 323
Temple 43, 74, 107, 141, 142, 216, 245
Terror Of The Lord 97
Thanksgiving 82, 83, 209-211
The Common English Version. 81
things which are seen 84
Throwing Down Strongholds. 224
Timothy 1, 4, 8, 11, 35, 46, 62, 69, 73, 77, 78, 121, 122, 124
    125, 127, 134, 161, 164, 167, 171, 187, 189, 195, 201, 202,
    204, 209, 224, 237, 253, 287, 289, 292, 296, 318
Titus . . . 6, 13, 31, 37, 54, 73, 78, 119, 151, 157, 158, 164-167, 170
    177, 185, 188, 189, 191, 193, 195, 202, 214, 239, 278, 279,
    287, 296
Treasure 39, 72, 188, 209, 271
Tribulation . . . 4, 5, 20, 35, 53, 57, 75, 77, 108, 154, 156, 157, 165
    202, 205, 209, 263, 295
Trinity. 1, 243, 302
Triumph 37
Triune God 1
Troubled 73, 74, 94, 156, 170
Uncleanness. 57, 144, 146, 150, 151, 249, 282

unequally yoked together with unbelievers. 135
Utterance. 36, 178, 209
vail 47, 48, 54-57
Vain 8, 51, 88, 117, 118, 199, 200, 213, 225, 244
Verses On Non-Christians Status. 243
Want. . . 9, 12, 15, 17-20, 29, 41, 45, 53, 54, 56, 61, 78, 90, 92, 98
   100, 103, 116, 129, 144, 171, 176, 183, 184, 188, 191, 192,
   200, 201, 205, 209-212, 223, 228, 230, 231, 234, 237,
   245, 246, 261, 263, 267, 268, 276-278, 281, 286, 289,
   294
Weak. 28, 54, 75, 99, 123, 175, 228, 229, 253, 259-261, 269
   270, 272, 284, 285, 293
Weakness. 38, 45, 90, 229, 260, 261, 269, 270, 285
Weapons Of War. 223, 224
Website: www.BibleForToday.org i
Westcott and Hort 82
what communion hath light with darkness?. 135
willing mind. 183
Willingness 93, 174
Without Blame 191
Witnesses. 64, 112, 270, 283, 284
Witnessing. 97, 220
word of God. . . . 13, 15, 22, 31, 39, 64, 73, 98, 104, 123, 126, 135
   239, 244, 289
Wrong. . . . 17-23, 25, 27, 29, 39, 125, 127, 144, 152, 163, 168, 172
   187, 198, 221, 227, 242, 246, 274, 276, 277, 291
Yokes 136
Zeal. 124, 163, 170, 198, 251, 254
-mail: BFT@BibleForToday.org i

About The Author

The author of this book, Dr. D. A. Waite, received a B.A. (Bachelor of Arts) in classical Greek and Latin from the University of Michigan in 1948, a Th.M. (Master of Theology), with high honors, in New Testament Greek Literature and Exegesis from Dallas Theological Seminary in 1952, an M.A. (Master of Arts) in Speech from Southern Methodist University in 1953, a Th.D. (Doctor of Theology), with honors, in Bible Exposition from Dallas Theological Seminary in 1955, and a Ph.D. in Speech from Purdue University in 1961. He held both New Jersey and Pennsylvania teacher certificates in Greek and Language Arts.

He has been a teacher in the areas of Greek, Hebrew, Bible, Speech, and English for over thirty-five years in ten schools, including one junior high, one senior high, four Bible institutes, two colleges, two universities, and one seminary. He served his country as a Navy Chaplain for five years on active duty; pastored three churches; was Chairman and Director of the Radio and Audio-Film Commission of the American Council of Christian Churches; since 1969, has been Founder, President, and Director of THE BIBLE FOR TODAY; since 1978, has been Founder and President of the DEAN BURGON SOCIETY; has produced over 700 other studies, books, cassettes, VHS's, CD's, or VCR's on various topics; and is heard IN DEFENSE OF TRADITIONAL BIBLE TEXTS and verse-by-verse preaching, by streaming on the Internet at BibleForToday.org, 24/7/365 on the BROWN BOX.

Dr. and Mrs. Waite have been married since 1948; they have four sons, one daughter, and, at present, eight grandchildren, and seventeen great-grandchildren. Since October 4, 1998, he has been the Pastor of the Bible For Today Baptist Church in Collingswood, New Jersey. His sermons are heard, all over the world on the Internet 24 hours a day and 365 days a year over www.BibleForToday.org on the BROWN BOX.

Order Blank (p. 1)

Name:_____
Address:_____
City & State:_____Zip:_____
Credit Card #:_____Expires:_____

Verse by Verse Preaching Books By Dr. D. A. Waite

[ ] Send 2 Corinthians–Preaching Verse By Verse By Dr. D. A. Waite (447 pages ($25.00 + $10.00 S&H) fully indexed.
[ ] Send 1 Corinthians–Preaching Verse By Verse By Dr. D. A. Waite (447 pages ($25.00 + $10.00 S&H) fully indexed.
[ ] Send Titus–Preaching Verse By Verse By Pastor D. A. Waite, (142 pages ($15.00 + $7.00 S&H) fully indexed
[ ] Send James–Preaching Verse By Verse By Pastor D. A. Waite, (218 pages (16.00 + $7.00 S&H) fully indexed.
[ ] Send *1, 2, & 3 John–Preaching Verse By Verse* By Pastor D. A. Waite, 202 pages ($14.00 + $7.00 S&H) fully indexed.
[ ] Send *2 Peter & Jude–Preaching Verse By Verse* By Pastor D. A. Waite, 237 pages ($16.00 +$7.00 S&H) fully indexed.
[ ] Send *1 & 2 Thessalonians–Preaching Verse By Verse* By Pastor D. A. Waite, 360 pages ($20.00 + $8.00 S&H) fully indexed.
[ ] Send *Hebrews–Preaching Verse by Verse*, By Pastor D. A. Waite, 616 pages ($34.00 +$10.00 S&H) fully indexed.
[ ] Send *Revelation–Preaching Verse by Verse*, By Pastor D. A. Waite, 1032 pages ($55.00 + $10.00 S&H) fully indexed.
[ ] Send *1 Timothy--Preaching Verse by Verse*, by Pastor D. A. Waite, 288 pages, hardback ($18+$7 S&H) fully indexed.
[ ] Send *2 Timothy--Preaching Verse by Verse*, by Pastor D. A. Waite, 250 pages, hardback ($16+$7 S&H) fully indexed.

Send or Call Orders to:
THE BIBLE FOR TODAY
900 Park Ave., Collingswood, NJ 08108
Phone: 856-854-4452; FAX:--2464; Orders: 1-800 JOHN 10:9
E-Mail Orders: BFT@BibleForToday.org; Credit Cards OK

Order Blank (p. 2)

Name:_____
Address:_____
City & State:_____Zip:_____
Credit Card #:_____Expires:_____

Other Books By Dr. D. A. Waite

[ ] Send *Romans--Preaching Verse by Verse* by Pastor D. A. Waite 736 pp. Hardback ($35+$8 S&H) fully indexed
[ ] Send *Colossians & Philemon--Preaching Verse by Verse* by Pastor D. A. Waite ($16+$7 S&H) hardback, 240 pages.
[ ] Send *Philippians--Preaching Verse by Verse* by Pastor D A. Waite ($14+$7 S&H) hardback, 176 pages. fully indexed.
[ ] Send *Fundamentalist Deception on Bible Preservation* by Dr. D. A. Waite, ($8+$4 S&H), paperback, fully indexed
[ ] Send *Fundamentalist MIS-INFORMATION on Bible Versions* by Dr. Waite ($7+$4 S&H) perfect bound, 136 pages
[ ] Send *Fundamentalist Distortions on Bible Versions* by Dr. Waite ($6+$3 S&H) A perfect bound book, 80 pages
[ ] Send *Fuzzy Facts From Fundamentalists* by Dr. D. A. Waite ($8.00 + $4.00) printed booklet
[ ] Send *Foes of the King James Bible Refuted* by DAW ($10 +$4 S&H) A perfect bound book, 164 pages in length.
[ ] Send *Central Seminary Refuted on Bible Versions* by Dr. Waite ($10+$4 S&H) A perfect bound book, 184 pages
[ ] Send *The Case for the King James Bible* by DAW ($7 +$3 S&H) A perfect bound book, 112 pages in length.
[ ] Send *Theological Heresies of Westcott and Hort* by Dr. D. A. Waite, ($7+$3 S&H) A printed booklet.
[ ] Send *Westcott's Denial of Resurrection*, Dr. Waite ($4+$3)
[ ] Send *Four Reasons for Defending KJB* by DAW ($3+$3)

Send or Call Orders to:
THE BIBLE FOR TODAY
900 Park Ave., Collingswood, NJ 08108
Phone: 856-854-4352; FAX:--2464; Orders: 1-800 JOHN 10:9
E-Mail Orders: BFT@BibleForToday.org; Credit Cards OK

Order Blank (p. 3)

Name:_____
Address:_____
City & State:_____Zip:_____
Credit Card #:_____Expires:_____

[ ] Send *Galatians--Preaching Verse By Verse* by Pastor D. A. Waite ($15+$7 S&H) hardback, 216 pages. fully indexed.

[ ] Send *1 Peter–Preaching Verse By Verse* by Pastor D. A. Waite ($15.00 + $7.00 S&H) hardback, 176 pages. fully indexed.

[ ] Send *Ephesians--Preaching Verse by Verse* by Pastor D. A. Waite ($15+$7 S&H) hardback, 224 pages. fully indexed.

[ ] Send *BJU's Errors on Bible Preservation* by Dr. D. A. Waite, 110 pages, paperback ($8+$4 S&H) fully indexed

[ ] Send *A Critical Answer to God's Word Preserved* by Pastor D. A. Waite, 192 pp. perfect bound ($11.00+$4.00 S&H)

[ ] Send *Defending the King James Bible* by DAW ($12+$5 S&H) A hardback book, indexed with study questions.

[ ] Send *Holes in the Holman Christian Standard Bible* by Dr. Waite ($3+$2 S&H) A printed booklet, 40 pages

[ ] Send *Contemporary Eng. Version Exposed*, DAW ($3+$2)

[ ] Send *NIV Inclusive Language Exposed* by DAW ($5+$3)

[ ] Send *26 Hours of KJB Seminar* (4 videos) by DAW($50.00)

[ ] Send *Making Marriage Melodious* by Pastor D. A. Waite ($7+$4 S&H), perfect bound, 112 pages.

[ ] Send *Burgon's Warnings on Revision* by DAW ($7+$4 S&H) A perfect bound book, 120 pages in length.

[ ] Send *The Superior Foundation of the KJB* By Dr. D. A. Waite ($10.00 + $7.00 S&H)

[ ] Send *Biblical Separation–1,896 Bible Verses About It* by Dr. D. A. Waite ($14.00 + $7.00 S&H)

Send or Call Orders to:
THE BIBLE FOR TODAY
900 Park Ave., Collingswood, NJ 08108
Phone: 856-854-4452; FAX:--2464; Orders: 1-800 JOHN 10:9
E-Mail Orders: BFT@BibleForToday.org; Credit Cards OK

Order Blank (p. 4)

Name:_____
Address:_____
City & State:_____ Zip:_____
Credit Card #:_____ Expires:_____

Books By Dean John William Burgon

[ ] Send *The Last 12 verses of Mark* by Dean Burgon ($15+$5 S&H) A hardback book 400 pages.
[ ] Send *The Traditional Text* hardback by Burgon ($16+$5
[ ] Send *The Revision Revised* by Dean Burgon ($25 + $5 S&H) A hardback book, 640 pages in length.
[ ] Send *Dean Burgon's Confidence in KJB* by DAW ($3+$3)
[ ] Send *Vindicating Mark 16:9-20* by Dr. Waite ($3+$3S&H)
[ ] Send *Summary of Traditional Text* by Dr. Waite ($3 +$3)
[ ] Send *Summary of Causes of Corruption*, DAW ($3+$3)
[ ] Send *Summary of Inspiration* by Dr. Waite ($3+$3 S&H)

Books By Dr. Jack Moorman

[ ] Send *The Doctrinal Heart of the Bible--Removed from Modern Versions* by Dr. Jack Moorman, VCR, $15 +$4 S&H
[ ] Send *Modern Bibles--The Dark Secret* by Dr. Jack Moorman, $5+$3 S&H
[ ] Send *The Manuscript Digest of the N.T.* (721 pp.) By Dr. Jack Moorman, copy-machine bound ($50+$7 S&H)
[ ] *Early Manuscripts, Church Fathers, & the Authorized Version* by Dr. Jack Moorman, $18+$5 S&H. Hardback
[ ] Send *Forever Settled--Bible Doc*uments *& History Survey* by Dr. Jack Moorman, $20+$5 S&H. Hardback book.
[ ] Send *When the KJB Departs from the So-Called "Majority Text"* by Dr. Jack Moorman, $16+$5 S&H
[ ] Send *Missing in Modern Bibles--Nestle-Aland/NIV Errors* by Dr. Jack Moorman, $8+$4 S&H

Send or Call Orders to:
THE BIBLE FOR TODAY
900 Park Ave., Collingswood, NJ 08108
Phone: 856-854-4452; FAX:--2464; Orders: 1-800 JOHN 10:9
E-Mail Orders: BFT@BibleForToday.org; Credit Cards OK

Order Blank (p. 5)

Name:_____
Address:_____
City & State:_____Zip:_____
Credit Card #:_____Expires:_____

[ ] Send *Westcott & Hort's Greek Text & Theory Refuted by Burgon's Revision Revised--Summarized* by Dr. D. A. Waite ($7.00+$4 S&H), 120 pages, perfect bound.
[ ] Send *Soulwinning's Versions-Perversions* By Dr. D. A. Waite ($6.00 + $5.00 S&H)
[ ] Send *Causes of Corruption* by Burgon ($15+$5 S&H) A hardback book, 360 pages in length.
[ ] Send *Inspiration and Interpretation*, Dean Burgon ($25+$5 S&H) A hardback book, 610 pages in length.

Books By Miscellaneous Authors

[ ] Send *Guide to Textual Criticism* by Edward Miller ($7+$4) Hardback book
[ ] Send *Scrivener's Greek New Testament Underlying the King James Bible*, hardback, ($14+$5 S&H)
[ ] Send *Samuel P. Tregelles--The Man Who Made the Critical Text Acceptable to Bible Believers* by Dr. Moorman ($2+$1)
[ ] Send *8,000 Differences Between TR & CT* by Dr. Jack Moorman [$65 + $7.50 S&H] Over 500-large-pages of data
[ ] Send *356 Doctrinal Errors in the NIV & Other Modern Versions*, 100-large-pages, $10.00+$6 S&H.
[ ] Send *Scrivener's Annotated Greek New Testament*, by Dr. Frederick Scrivener: Hardback--($35+$5 S&H); Genuine Leather--($45+$5 S&H)
[ ] Send *Why Not the King James Bible?--An Answer to James White's KJVO Book* by Dr. K. D. DiVietro, $10+$5 S&H
[ ] Send Brochure #1: "*1000 Titles Defending the KJB/TR*" No Charge

Send or Call Orders to:
THE BIBLE FOR TODAY
900 Park Ave., Collingswood, NJ 08108
Phone: 856-854-4452; FAX:--2464; Orders: 1-800 JOHN 10:9

Order Blank (p. 6)

Name:_____
Address:_____
City & State:_____Zip:_____
Credit Card #:_____Expires:_____

More Books By Miscellaneous Authors

[ ] Send *The LIE That Changed the Modern World* by Dr. H. D. Williams ($16+$5 S&H) Hardback book
[ ] Send *With Tears in My Heart* by Gertrude G. Sanborn. Hardback 414 pp. ($25+$5 S&H) 400 Christian Poems
[ ] Send *Able To Bear It* By Gertrude Sanborn ($14.00 + $7.00 S&H)
[ ] Send *Visitation In Action* By Mr. R. O. Sanborn ($10.00 + $7.00 S&H)
[ ] Send *Daily Bible Blessings From Daily Bible Readings* By Yvonne Sanborn Waite ($30.00 + $10.00 S&H)
[ ] Send *Husband-Loving Lessons* By Yvonne Sanborn Waite ($25.00 + $8.00 S&H)
[ ] Send *Gnosticism–The Doctrinal Foundation of New Bibles* by J. Moser ($20.00 + $8.00 S&H)
[ ] Send *Dean Burgon's Defense of the Authorised Version* By Dr. David Bennett ($14.0 + 8.00 S&H)
[ ] Send *Drift in Baptist Missions, Churches & Schools* by Dr. David Bennett ($12.00 + $8.00 S&H)
[ ] Send *God's Marvelous Book* By Dr. David Bennett ($15.00 + $8.00 S&H)
[ ] Send *CCM Not The Problem–Only A Symptom* By Dr. David Bennett ($12.00 + $7.00 S&H)
[ ] Send *English Standard Bible (ESV) Deficiencies* By several authors ($7.00 + $4.00 S&H)
[ ] Send *Strong's Micro-Print Concordance* By the Sherbornes ($21.00 + $8.00 S&H)

Send or Call Orders to:
THE BIBLE FOR TODAY
900 Park Ave., Collingswood, NJ 08108
Phone: 856-854-4452; FAX:--2464; Orders: 1-800 JOHN 10:9
E-Mail Orders: BFT@BibleForToday.org; Credit Cards OK

The Defined King James Bible
UNCOMMON WORDS DEFINED ACCURATELY

I. Deluxe Genuine Leather

✦Large Print--Black or Burgundy✦
1 for $44.00+$12.00 S&H
✦Case of 12 for✦
$34.00 each+$50.00 S&H
✦Medium Print--Black or Burgundy✦
1 for $39.00+$8.00 S&H
✦Case of 12 for✦
$29.00 each+$40.00 S&H

II. Deluxe Hardback Editions
1 for $22.00+12.00 S&H (Large Print)
✦Case of 12 for✦
$17.00 each+$40.00 S&H (Large Print)
1 for $19.50+$8.00 S&H (Medium Print)
✦Case of 12 for✦
1 For $19.50 +$12.00 S&H (Large Print)
Order Phone: 1-800-JOHN 10:9
CREDIT CARDS WELCOMED

Pastor D. A. Waite, Th.D., Ph.D.

Paul's Victorious Life In Christ

Paul's Wicked Former Life. Paul was a Pharisee who hated Christians. He was in charge of the stoning of Stephen. Those who stoned him laid their clothes at Paul's feet. Before he became a Christian, he was on his way to Damascus to imprison as many Christians as he could find.

Paul's Miraculous Salvation. While on this journey, the Lord Jesus Christ spoke to him from Heaven, asking why he was persecuting Him. Paul asked the Lord what he should do. He trusted the Lord as his Saviour and became a true Christian. He then preached the Gospel of Christ around the world.

Paul's Faithfulness To The Lord Jesus Christ. After his sound conversion to the Lord Jesus Christ, whom he once hated, Paul traveled around the then-known world preaching salvation and everlasting life by genuinely trusting the Lord Jesus Christ as their Saviour.

Paul's Sufferings For Faithfulness To His Saviour. The cost for Paul being such a strong and faithful Christian was great. He was criticized by the Jews, by the Gentiles, and by other Christians who had some false doctrines. He stood firm despite many physical and painful sufferings.

www.BibleForToday.org

BFT 4174   ISBN #978-1-56848-120-3

www.ingramcontent.com/pod-product-compliance
Lightning Source LLC
Chambersburg PA
CBHW050125170426
43197CB00011B/1725

9781568481203